# THE FIRST TRANSCONTINENTAL RAILROAD

# THE FIRST
# TRANSCONTINENTAL
# RAILROAD

## CENTRAL PACIFIC
## UNION PACIFIC

*by* JOHN DEBO GALLOWAY C. E.

DORSET PRESS
New York

This edition published by Dorset Press
a division of Marboro Books Corporation.

1989 Dorset Press

ISBN 0-88029-409-4

Printed in the United States of America
M 9 8 7 6 5 4 3 2 1

# CONTENTS

# ILLUSTRATIONS

## CENTRAL PACIFIC SECTION

Officers of the Central Pacific Railroad Company, *Southern Pacific*

Theodore Dehone Judah Memorial, *J. F. Coleman, Pres., Amer. Soc. of Civil Engineers*

Theodore Dehone Judah, *Carl I. Wheat*

Map drawn by Theodore D. Judah, *National Archives and Southern Pacific*

Central Pacific construction chiefs, *Southern Pacific*, *(Clement) R. M. Clement*

Fill at Heath's Ravine in the Sierra Nevada, *Southern Pacific*

Owl Gap Cut near Blue Canyon, California, *Southern Pacific*

Track-laying operations in Nevada deserts, *Southern Pacific*

Central Pacific construction town of Carlin, Nevada, *Southern Pacific*

Two types of Central Pacific wooden bridges, *Southern Pacific*

First railroad bridge over the American River, *Southern Pacific*

Early Central Pacific bridges, *Southern Pacific*, *(Howe truss) D. L. Joslyn*

Snow protection in the high Sierra, *Southern Pacific*

Two Central Pacific tunnels and a cut, *(Donner Lake) D. L. Joslyn, Southern Pacific*

Scene at Truckee Depot, *Southern Pacific*

Stage coaches met trains at Colfax, California, *Southern Pacific*

Fire-fighting train "Grey Eagle," *W. A. Lucas*

Two commissioners on pilot beam of the "Falcon," *W. A. Lucas*

The locomotive "Hercules" at Cisco, *W. A. Lucas*

Water train pulled by locomotive "El Dorado," *W. A. Lucas*

"C. P. Huntington" as it looks today, *W. A. Lucas*

"C. P. Huntington" during the building of the railroad, *W. A. Lucas*

Engine No. 60, the "Jupiter," lets off steam, *W. A. Lucas*

President Stanford's train on the way to the meeting of the rails, *W. A. Lucas*

Historic scene at Promontory on May 10, 1869, *W. A. Lucas*

Sign marking end of ten-mile section of track laid in one day, *Southern Pacific*

## UNION PACIFIC SECTION

Officers of the Union Pacific Railroad, *Union Pacific*

Leaders in Union Pacific engineering and construction, *Union Pacific*, *(Dey) Iowa Hist. Soc., (Casement) D. M. Casement*

# ILLUSTRATIONS

Railroad supplies being unloaded from a river steamer, *W. A. Lucas*

View of Omaha in the 'sixties, *W. A. Lucas*

General Casement's twelve-car construction train, *Union Pacific*

Union Pacific construction train joins a wagon party, *Union Pacific*

Union Pacific rails parallel Oregon trail in Echo Canyon, *Jackson*

Burning Rock Cut showing rock stratification, *Union Pacific*

Carmichael's Cut at Granite Cayon, Wyoming, *W. A. Lucas*

Granite Canyon located west of Cheyenne, *Union Pacific*

Eastern portals of Union Pacific Tunnel No. 3, *Union Pacific*

Bridges of the Union Pacific, *Union Pacific*

Devil's Gate in Utah's Weber Canyon, *Union Pacific*

Echo City, Utah, a Union Pacific construction town, *Union Pacific*

Engine No. 119 represented Union Pacific power at Promontory, *W. A. Lucas*

"Vice Adm. Farragut" was an early Union Pacific locomotive, *W. A. Lucas*

Locomotive No. 75, a typical passenger engine, *W. A. Lucas*

Engine No. 121 heads east from Ogden, *W. A. Lucas*

Enginer No. 86 at Green River Station, *W. A. Lucas*

Telegraph linemen in Weber Cayon, *W. A. Lucas*

Union Pacific's famous 1,000 Mile Tree, *Jackson*

Officers of the Union Pacific hold a conference, *W. A. Lucas*

Engine No. 119 crosses a Central Pacific trestle near Promontory, *Union Pacific*

Abandoned Central Pacific and Union Pacific grades run parallel, *Union Pacific*

Author at Last Spike Monument at Promontory, *Southern Pacific*

vii

# PREFACE

John Debo Galloway will ever be rated as one of the great engineers who had an important part in the development of Western America. A recital of the list of important engineering projects with which he was associated through more than half a century and the many honors bestowed upon him may not be so interesting to the readers of *The First Transcontinental Railroad* as is a word as to his personality and the interests which led him to write on this subject.

Mr. Galloway, the son of James and Emily (Hoover) Galloway, was born on October 13, 1869, at San Jose, California. His ancestors were residents of Maryland, New Jersey and Pennsylvania prior to the American Revolution. His boyhood experiences, some of which were acquired at Virginia City, Nevada, when that city was the center of the great mining activity incident to the discovery and development of the famous Comstock Lode, made a deep impression upon him, as is evidenced by his *Early Engineering Works Contributory to the Comstock,* published by the University of Nevada. His parents died when he was quite young. At the age of eight he was taken to live with friends in Napa Valley, California. His technical education was gained, not without some financial struggles, at Rose Poyltechnic Institute from which he was graduated in 1889.

After a brief period of employment in railroad work in the Pacific Northwest, Mr. Galloway returned to California and for more than fifty years maintained his headquarters in San Francisco, although his practice often took him far afield. He was an authority on the design of dams, hydroelectric works and structures generally. He took a leading part in the recontruction of San Francisco following the great fire and earthquake of 1906. He served his country in both World Wars.

Mr. Galloway was a life member and past president of the Astronomical Society of the Pacific; a member of the Society of Military Engineers; a member of the Seismological Society of of America; a member of the California Historical Society and a charter member and life member of the Commonwealth Club of California. He was also a member of San Fransico's noted Bohemian Club. He was elected a member of the American Society of Civil Engineers on December 6, 1905, and on October 14, 1940, he was made an Honorary Member, the highest honor which the Society can bestow on one of its members. He passed away March 10, 1943.

"J. D.," as he was affectionately known to his friends and associates, lived a rich life filled with interests far beyond his professional practice. He was a great student. Left to his own resources when quite young, one of his dominant characteristics, self reliance, early came to the fore. With this quality so strongly developed it was very natural that he should admire it in others. This is evident in his analyses of the characters of the great builders who organized and built the first transcontinental railroad. Because of his own great engineering ability, he had a fuller appreciation of the difficulties, which were overcome by the pioneer locators, designers, and builders than would a lay student. He had a passionate fondness for historical research, particularly when it related to the early development of the West. He derived much pleasure in retracing on the ground the scenes of early construction works. Although he had a wide knowledge of the region from his long engineering practice, his historical studies led him over all of the route of the first transcontinental railroad, some parts of it many times in the course of detailed studies. His enthusiasm and his known thoroughness and accuracy gained for him ready access to the early records of the Southern Pacific Railroad (successor to the Central Pacific Railroad) and those of the Union Pacific Railroad. It is fortunate indeed that these studies, begun as one of the author's avocations, should be made available to the general public as well as to those of us of the engineering profession.

Walter L. Huber.
Consulting Civil Engineer, San Francisco.

# THE FIRST TRANSCONTINENTAL RAILROAD

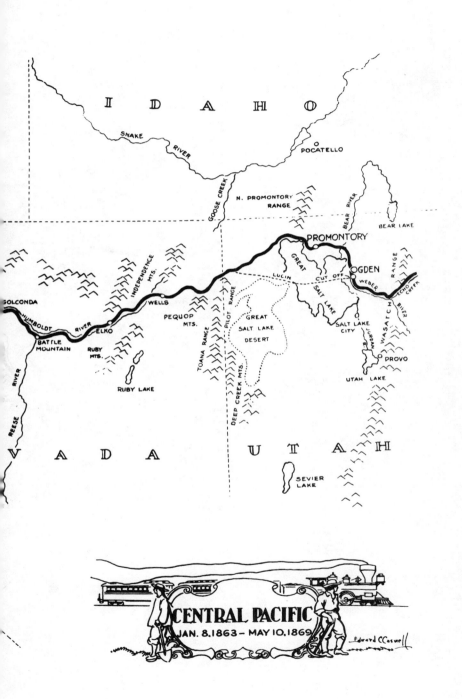

IDAHO

SNAKE RIVER

POCATELLO

GOOSE CREEK

N. PROMONTORY RANGE

BEAR RIVER

BEAR LAKE

PROMONTORY

GREAT

CUT OFF

OGDEN

LUCIN

WEBER RIVER

INDEPENDENCE MTS.

GREAT SALT LAKE

ECHO CREEK

GOLCONDA

HUMBOLDT RIVER

WELLS

PEQUOP MTS.

SALT LAKE CITY

BATTLE MOUNTAIN

ELKO

RUBY MTS.

PILOT RANGE

GREAT SALT LAKE DESERT

PROVO

REESE RIVER

RUBY LAKE

TOANA RANGE

DEEP CREEK MTS.

UTAH LAKE

WASATCH RANGE

JORDAN RIVER

NEVADA

UTAH

SEVIER LAKE

CENTRAL PACIFIC
JAN. 8, 1863 – MAY 10, 1869

Edward C. Caswell

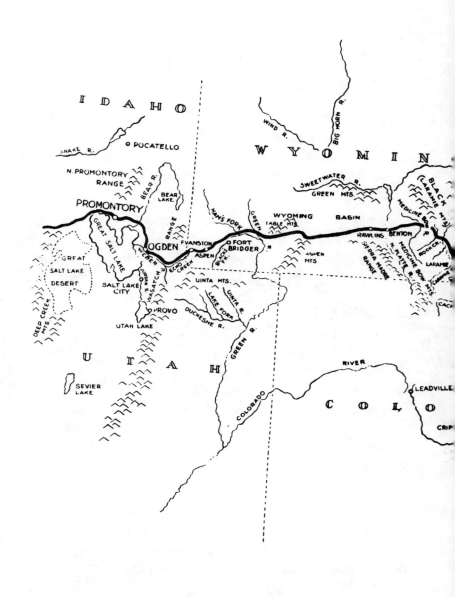

# CHAPTER 1

# The Pacific Railroad

THE TRAVELER speeding west from Omaha on the Overland Route may give but little thought to the smooth roadbed and comfortable train on which he is journeying. He is on one of the world's great travel routes, that of the first transcontinental railroad, which was built in the sixties, linking Omaha on the Missouri with Sacramento in California. The construction of this 1,800-mile railroad across grassy plains and sagebrush deserts and through the passes of the Rockies and the high Sierra was, without doubt, the greatest engineering feat of the nineteenth century.

As he glances through the window of his air-conditioned car, he may observe what appears to be an abandoned road, overgrown with brush. Leaving the track and passing around a rock spur or river bend it returns to the roadbed on which he is riding. Occasionally it parallels the tracks on a higher level; at times it disappears. What the traveler sees is not an abandoned dirt road, but the original roadbed of the railroad on which he is riding.

[3]

## THE FIRST TRANSCONTINENTAL RAILROAD

The nineteenth century witnessed the development of two modes of transportation, one by water and the other by land, which changed entirely the course of human affairs. The steamboat came first, but the railroad worked the greatest change. More progress was made in transportation in fifty years than had been made during the thousands of years that had passed since the human race rose from savagery. George Washington had no better means of travel than had Julius Caesar, or the Pharaohs of ancient Egypt. All this was changed by the invention of the steam-driven locomotive and by the development of the railroad.

The culminating effort in the building of the railroads in the United States was the construction of the Pacific Railroad—the Union Pacific from Omaha to Ogden, Utah, and the Central Pacific from Sacramento to Ogden. Slightly less than a third of a century had passed since the day when the first feeble attempts were made to construct a railroad on the eastern seaboard for commercial use until ground was broken at Sacramento for the Central Pacific. In that short space of time the eastern United States had been threaded with railroad lines that reached out as far west as the Mississippi and Missouri rivers. The great project, however, was to build a line across the plains, the mountains, and the deserts of America to California on the Pacific Ocean. The distances were great, the country unsettled, the prairies filled with warlike Indians, and the mountain ranges the highest in the United States.

The work was done by men of courage, ceaseless determination, skill and ability. Along with the rest of their generation, the railroad builders who overcame the forces of nature and the man-made difficulties have long since passed from the scene. The story of the railroad is rapidly fading into the past and the interests of the American people have turned toward new projects and later events.

When construction of the Central Pacific was started at Sacramento early in 1863 and the building of Union Pacific began at

Omaha in the latter part of the same year, an organization was brought into being that has lasted until the present day and is still capably performing its intended service. The big job was to build the railroad, but of equal importance was the creation of an organization to operate the line after it was built. Since the linking of the roads on May 10, 1869, the Central Pacific, through its successor, the Southern Pacific, has built and added other lines to the original track to Ogden, until it now operates more than 15,000 miles of roadbed and employs 90,000 persons. The Union Pacific now operates 9,751 miles of main line track and employes 50,000 people. The total of the two organizations represents 24,751 miles of railroad and 140,000 employees. Trains of these two great railroad systems pass and repass over a large portion of western America.

Where once roamed wild animals and wilder Indians there has developed a rich empire providing homes and livelihood for millions of people. All this has come into existence since two groups of men in 1863, one on the east bank of the Sacramento and the other on the west bank of the Missouri, performed simple ceremonies and started the work on the railroad that was to open for settlement the vast expanses of the American West.

When the railroad was started, the nation was engulfed in a Civil War that was to last well into 1865. The national government considered it necessary to build the road as a link connecting the East with the Pacific Coast in order to retain the western section of the country within the Union. There is no doubt that even the beginning of construction was an important factor in accomplishing this purpose of Lincoln and his advisors. Land and rights of way were given to the projectors of the railroad, and the national credit was loaned in order to assist in the financing of the project. Much controversy arose out of the financial assistance given by the government, and from these debates a measure of criticism was leveled at the master builders of the railroad.

It cannot today be maintained that the strong and able men

who built the Pacific Railroad were models of the abstract virtues. Such men often have the spirit of enterprise that moves them to override opposition. An impatience with restraint and opposition soon gives rise to the spirit of dominance. Obstacles are brushed aside or overpowered ruthlessly in order to achieve their objectives.

The builders of the railroad were men of restless energy, driven by ambition to attempt and accomplish great things. Engineers like Theodore Judah and Grenville Dodge, businessmen like the Associates of the Central Pacific—Stanford, Huntington, Hopkins and Crocker—or those who comprised the scheming, quarreling group that drove the Union Pacific through to completion are never satisfied to live in quiet security. Without question, the desire for gain actuated these men, for money is power, but beyond the desire for gain lay the driving desire to initiate, build, and control great enterprises.

That explains why Stanford, Huntington, Hopkins, and Crocker, in response to Judah's urgings, were willing to leave their profitable businesses and embark upon the uncertain project of building a railroad across the continent. It explains why Oakes Ames and his brother Oliver, wealthy and leaders in a thriving industry, were willing to come to the rescue of the projectors of the Union Pacific and by utilizing their wealth and example provide the means by which the project was put through. Here indeed was epitomized the restless spirit that in all ages has driven men forward to discover the secrets of the world.

It is regrettable that this great constructive work had to be accompanied by so much distrust, politics, and internal dissention. However, all of the men connected with the work are now dead and their deeds are one with the past. The location and construction of the railroad was a great work, and as such deserves a place in history with other works of its kind.

In the city of Rome there is a stone bridge over an arm of the river Tiber, from the city to the Island of St. Bartholomew.

For two thousand years the bridge of the Commissioner Fabricius has carried the traffic across the yellow river and it still stands as a monument to the practical skill of the Romans. In our own country the railroad which has carried a much greater volume of traffic across mountains and deserts of Western America for more than three-quarters of a century bids fair to last as long as rail transportation continues. This account of the building of the Pacific Railroad seems of sufficient import to warrant a detailed description of what was, in spite of some human failings, one of the greatest engineering and construction feats of all time.

CHAPTER 2

# The Origin and Development
# of Railroads Prior to 1870

THE BUILDING of the Pacific Railroad marked the culmination
of a movement that began in the years close to 1830, when the
first railroad locomotives were brought to America. Not
over a third of a century, hardly half the allotted three score
and ten years of a man's life, elapsed from the opening of the
first short section of the Baltimore and Ohio to the breaking of
ground for the Central Pacific at Sacramento in 1863. In this
brief time more than 30,000 miles of railroad were constructed
in the United States. By 1870, over 52,000 miles of line had
been built and placed in operation. Railroad building was one
of the principal evidences of the rapid expansion of the
American nation.

The first railroad in the world operated for general purposes
was the Stockton and Darlington in northeastern England. Although projected in 1817 for transporting coal from the Wilton

colliery near Darlington to tidewater below Stockton-on-Tees, a distance of about thirty-eight miles, the necessary permission from Parliament was not obtained until 1821. George Stephenson made the surveys for the railroad and it was constructed under his direction. Stephenson strongly advocated the use of locomotives as being superior to animal power, and to convince the owners of the railroad he had them visit the Killingsworth tramway, where he operated his locomotives for their instruction. The Stockton and Darlington Railway was opened for traffic on September 27, 1825. The locomotive, No. 1, "The Locomotion," with Stephenson in control, drew a miscellaneous train of thirty-eight vehicles having a total gross load of ninety tons at a speed of twelve to fifteen miles per hour. The railroad proved a financial and mechanical success from the day of its opening.

The second railroad of importance in England was the Liverpool and Manchester. Projects for a tramway between these cities had been under consideration for years. In May, 1824, George Stephenson was appointed engineer, and after interminable delays in Parliament and other general opposition, the railroad, about thirty miles in length, was opened for traffic on September 15, 1830. The road involved much heavy construction, such as one long tunnel, deep rock cuts, masonry viaducts and bridges. It was laid directly across the country, for Stephenson felt that his rigid framed engines required a more or less straight track. The cost of the road is stated to have been $187,495 per mile, which in terms of modern monetary value would represent probably $500,000 per mile.

The power to be used in operating the line was the subject of much debate. Horses were suggested, but it was proved that they could not possibly handle the traffic. Another suggestion was that stationary engines be used, located a mile and a half apart and drawing cars by cables. This plan had many advocates. Finally a prize of 500 pounds sterling was offered and this brought forth four locomotives that were tested at Rainhall in

October, 1829. After many trials, Stephenson's locomotive, the "Rocket," won the prize. The superiority of the locomotive over all other forms of power was so clearly demonstrated that the subject was considered settled. From that time on, there was a rush to build railroads all over England.

## THE FIRST AMERICAN RAILROADS

News of the success of railroads in England was not long in reaching America and in two cases, and probably others, Americans were sent to that country to investigate and to report upon what they saw. In December, 1824, there was organized the "Pennsylvania Society for the Promotion of Internal Improvements in the Commonwealth," and in 1825 the society sent William Strickland, an architect, to England to collect information on the subject of canals, railways, steam engines, and the industrial arts. In 1827 Horatio Allen, a young engineer, went to England to study railroads, and while there he executed a commission to purchase rolling stock and rails for an American railroad. Several English locomotives were purchased in the earlier years of railroad building.

By the time the first railroads were projected, many men had become aware of the limitations of canals. It was clear that railroads paralleling the Atlantic Ocean were unnecessary. What was required was a means of traffic between the cities on the coast and the great interior beyond the Appalachian Mountains, which was rapidly filling with settlers. To a limited extent, rivers and steamboats supplied an answer, but they could not cross the mountains. Charleston in South Carolina, Baltimore, Philadelphia, New York, and to some extent Boston, required a cheap, quick, dependable transportation link between the two sections of the country. New York had solved the problem in a partial manner by building the Erie Canal to Buffalo, opened in 1825. The canal gave New York a pre-eminence that the city has never lost. The Chesapeake and Ohio Canal, designed to connect tidewater with the Ohio River, never crossed the mountains. Further means of transportation was needed.

### THE BALTIMORE AND OHIO RAILROAD

A number of railroads were projected in 1828, 1829, and 1830, but by general consent the Baltimore and Ohio Railroad is acknowledged as the first to organize and build a line for general traffic. That railroad, long ago grown to be one of the great systems of the country, is the only one to retain the original name and to preserve its corporate existence throughout a history of well over a hundred years. On the evening of February 2, 1827, a number of Baltimore merchants met at the home of one of their members and launched the project. Incorporation followed, and Virginia and Pennsylvania soon confirmed the charter.

To mark the beginning of construction, a cornerstone was laid in Baltimore on the Fourth of July, 1828, the event being signalized by the presence of Charles Carroll of Carrollton, the last survivor of the brave group of men who assembled at Philadelphia and signed the Declaration of American Independence, fifty-two years before.

After the usual difficulties of financing had been overcome, and in spite of the opposition of Congress, which was supporting the canal, and in opposition to the general public, the road was completed to Ellicotts Mills, thirteen miles from Baltimore. It was put in operation in May, 1830, with horses as its motive power. Operation by horses did not last long, however, since the small experimental locomotive, "Tom Thumb," was successfully run to Ellicotts Mills, on August 28, 1830. The road was extended to Point of Rocks on the Potomac River, seventy-two miles from Baltimore, and opened for traffic April 1, 1832. Disputes with the Chesapeake and Ohio Canal were compromised and on December 1, 1834, the road reached Harpers Ferry. A branch to Washington from Baltimore was opened August 25, 1835. Cumberland, on the Potomac, 178 miles from

Baltimore, was reached November 5, 1842, after many difficulties, mostly financial. The extension to the Ohio River at Wheeling was a difficult piece of work, involving eleven tunnels, thirteen bridges, and a switchback across the mountains while a long tunnel was under construction at an elevation of 2,620 feet above sea level. Wheeling was reached January 1, 1853. An extension to Parkersburg on the Ohio was opened May 1, 1857, and by connections with other roads across Ohio, Indiana, and Illinois, St. Louis was reached in the same year. There was then a continuous line west from Baltimore that required only five changes of cars and two short steamboat trips.

### THE SOUTH CAROLINA RAILROAD

At practically the same time that the Baltimore and Ohio was projected, a railroad from Charleston to the Savannah River opposite Augusta, about 136 miles, was chartered by the South Carolina legislature on May 12, 1828. Although chartered under the name South Carolina Canal and Railroad Company, the line was generally known as the Charleston and Hamburg. By January 1, 1830, six miles of the road were in operation. When the railroad was completed to Aiken in 1833, it was the longest railroad in the world. The chief engineer was Horatio Allen, who had worked as an engineer on the Delaware and Hudson Canal, and while in England had examined a number of the coal tramways operated by stationary engines and by locomotives. He had also visited the Stockton and Darlington Railway and had seen the operation of the line by horses and by locomotives. Employed by the Charleston and Hamburg he strongly recommended steam power. A locomotive, the "Best Friend of Charleston," was built in New York and placed in regular service on January 15, 1831. A second locomotive designed by Allen, went into service March 31, 1831. The Charleston and Hamburg Railroad was a financial and mechanical success, and continues today under other names as a part of the Southern Railway System.

[12]

## PROGRESS OF RAILROAD BUILDING UP TO 1880

While the railroad work done in England preceded that in America and had influenced train and track design, it was not long before the Americans had originated and made use of railroading practices more adapted to the new country they were to serve.

The success of the first projects soon opened men's minds to the value of this new means of transportation, which far surpassed canals. Railroads not only could cross mountains and could be operated at all seasons, but they cost less than canals, and traffic was moved at far greater speed on them than on canals. However, the first canals generally moved bulk freight very cheaply and their investments paid a greater rate of interest than did those of the railroads.

The country grew rapidly in population and in area, and railroad building kept pace with the westward movement. The following table illustrates this growth.

| Year | Population | Miles of Railroad | Increase in Decade |
|------|------------|-------------------|--------------------|
| 1830 | 12,866,020 | 23 | |
| 1840 | 17,069,453 | 2,818 | 2,795 |
| 1850 | 23,191,876 | 9,021 | 6,203 |
| 1860 | 31,443,321 | 30,626 | 21,605 |
| 1870 | 38,558,371 | 52,922 | 22,296 |
| 1880 | 50,155,783 | 93,267 | 40,345 |

The growth in mileage in the several decades is interesting when different sections of the country are considered. In 1850 there was no direct line from New York to Boston. Construction was only beginning in the southern states, notwithstanding the fact that one of the first railroads had been built by South Carolina. In the 1850-1860 decade many lines were built in the South connecting the principal centers, and 30 per cent of the railroads were in that section. The largest growth, however, was in the North, especially in Ohio, Indiana, and Illinois. Those three states accounted for one third of the mileage built in that

[13]

decade. In spite of the Civil War, when so many railroads were destroyed in the South, the construction of railroads continued in the 1860-1870 decade, and it was during this period that the Pacific Railroad was built.

In the West, Chicago had become the central point from which railroads radiated. In 1850 that city, which had a population of 23,722, had one short road. By 1860 the city had grown to a population of 109,260, and several lines went out from it. St. Louis was an early competitor of Chicago, but when the time came in 1863 for President Lincoln to designate the terminus of the Pacific Railroad, there was no questioning his wisdom in selecting Omaha and Council Bluffs, because those towns were situated on the direct line from Chicago to the Pacific coast. Of the roads extending westward from Chicago, the Rock Island reached the Mississippi River in 1854, and shortly after it was followed by the Galena and Chicago Union Railroad, afterward the Chicago and North Western. In 1855 the Chicago and Alton, and in 1856 the Chicago, Burlington and Quincy, reached the Mississippi River. Near St. Louis, the Hannibal and St. Joseph reached the Missouri River in 1859.

Up to 1860, railroad building was carried out by numerous scattered companies. When public resistance had been overcome, there was a rush to build railroads everywhere in the country. Short lines were projected between any two points, although many were never built. There was little or no preconceived plan for the numerous lines, and since the financial resources of many of the projectors were limited and their knowledge of costs pitiably inadequate, the results were often receiverships and foreclosures in which the original stockholders lost their money. After the Civil War, in the decade 1870-1880, numbers of independent lines were united to form single systems in the several sections of the country. This process of amalgamation went on in the years that followed. An early example of this was in 1853, when the New York Central was formed by a combination of eleven companies; by 1858 five other lines had been added. Later followed the union of the Hudson River road, the Harlem, the Lake Shore, the Canada Southern, the Michigan Central, and others, thus making a system of 4,000 miles of line.

The variety of systems and independent lines is indicated by one of the major troop movements during the Civil War. It had become necessary to send some 20,000 troops from the Army of the Potomac to General Rosecrans near Chickamauga. After considerable discussion it was decided to move the troops by rail, President Lincoln making the final decision. Estimates of the time required varied from fifteen days to three months. Railroad officials took charge of the movement, the principal one being from the Baltimore and Ohio. The troops entrained in Virginia, passed through Washington and thence by the Baltimore and Ohio to Wheeling, crossed the Ohio River on a ferry, and again entered cars to Bellaire. The route then lay across Ohio and Indiana to Indianapolis, where the troops marched across the city to another railroad, by which they again reached the Ohio River. They crossed the river on a pontoon bridge made of barges and by another railroad reached Chattanooga. The first troops arrived in seven days, and by eleven days the movement of 20,000 men over a distance of 1,000 miles had been completed. Several railroads and two crossings of the Ohio River by ferries or boats were required, and it was only by the close cooperation of the managements of several lines that it was made a success.

## STATE RAILROADS

There were ambitious politicians in that early period, so it was not surprising that seven states went into the business of building railroads: Pennsylvania, Massachusetts, North Carolina, Georgia, Indiana, Michigan, and Illinois. Michigan tried the experiment after the panic of 1837, and after going into debt over $5,000,000, sold out at a loss. The effort of Illinois in that direction was one long series of misdirected endeavors, characterized by political incompetence, mismanagement, and corruption. In the end, all the state roads were sold, bringing a heavy loss to the taxpayers. This result could have been foreseen by investigating the failure of most of the canals that had been built, projects that had earlier nearly bankrupted the states that entered into them.

### EVOLUTION OF RAILROAD DESIGN

At the period when the Pacific Railroad was built, railroad design was still in a state of transition. However, many, if not all, of the essential elements had already been developed—track, bridges, rolling stock, telegraph, construction, and repair shops and terminals. The important executive and operating forces had been brought into being. But, many changes were taking place, and larger and more efficient equipment was being manufactured and used. It can be said, with equal truth, that similar changes are still taking place.

### TRACK

It is a truism that the track of a railroad as a part of the physical plant is the one thing upon which everything else depends. In the early tramroads and on many of the early railroads, the rails were made of timber, often supported on stone blocks embedded in the earth or resting upon wooden ties. The rails were usually of pine, upon which was fastened a strip of hardwood or, in later practice, a strip of flat iron as a running surface. Such rails were not of great strength and were subject to rapid decay and excessive wear. George Stephenson's first locomotive upon the Killingworth coal tramway in 1814 ran on cast-iron rails made in sections three feet long.

When the Camden and Amboy Railroad was started in 1830, Engineer Robert L. Stevens advocated the use of all-iron rails in place of wooden rails with the strap iron surface. Stevens went to England to order rails, and on the way devised the "T" rail in substantially the same form that has been used since that time. In form and proportion, the Stevens rail may be seen on any track today.

Stevens also devised the hook-headed spike for fastening the rail to the wooden ties, a form of fastening that is still employed on American roads. He connected the rails together at the ends by what he called an "iron tongue," which has developed into the fishplate or angle-bar construction of the present day.

It was not long before the costly method of supporting the rails upon stone blocks was abandoned in favor of the wooden tie. The blocks could not keep the gauge true, and what was more important, the blocks gave a support that was too rigid. Therefore the wooden tie, of dimensions similar to those now in use, became standard, for it was found that it provided a track bed over which locomotives and cars rode with greater ease and security.

Early railroads were bedeviled by the different gauges adopted on different lines. In England, Stephenson had adopted a gauge of four feet eight and one half inches, following the practice of the coal tramways, which probably were made the width of the wheels of an ordinary wagon. In America there was a variety of six or more gauges, ranging from three feet up to six feet. Horatio Allen advocated a gauge of five feet and it is to be regretted that his advice was not taken, for the extra width over the now standard gauge of four feet eight and one half inches would have been much better for the heavy rolling stock of modern times. However, the English gauge prevailed, and other American gauges were changed to that standard, with some 12,000 miles altered in the South alone in 1886.

For forty years or more wrought-iron was used for rails, the length gradually increasing from fifteen feet to thirty feet, and the weight up to fifty or sixty pounds per yard. The first iron rails were imported from England, but in October, 1845, iron "T" rails were rolled at the Montour Rolling Mills in Danville, Pennsylvania. When steel rails first came into use, they were imported from England, but the cost was almost prohibitive

[17]

until Bessemer in 1855 introduced his process for manufacturing steel rails. After that the use of steel became general. The first steel rails rolled in America came from the Chicago Rolling Mills in 1865. Steel rails were first used on the Pennsylvania Railroad in 1865, but iron rails were used throughout the entire length of the Pacific Railroad.

LOCOMOTIVES

The development of the modern American locomotive brought on a corresponding development in track. In fact, the increasing weight of locomotives forced the development of a proper track.

Long before locomotives were invented, James Watt had perfected the steam engine, and in 1775 the British firm of Boulton and Watt began the manufacture of engines at their Soho Works near Birmingham. A number of names, French and English, are connected with the early use of steam, and years before Watt was born Newcomen engines were operating pumps at a number of Welsh mines. However, the many improvements made in the steam engine by Watt transformed it from a crude, inefficient, and wasteful machine into the one we know today.

When Stephenson built the "Rocket" that won the prize at Rainhall in 1829, he abandoned all the complex gear of the previous locomotives and placed two cylinders in an inclined position on each side of the boiler, each connected to a single pair of driving wheels. The cross heads of the pistons were connected directly by a rod to the crank on the outside of the wheels. Stephenson also invented the device for directing the exhaust steam from the cylinders up the smoke flue, which greatly increased the draft across the fire. He used a boiler with fire tubes and provided a tender that weighed four and a half tons.

Meanwhile, the subject of locomotives was actively considered in America in connection with the new railroads. When in England in 1828, Horatio Allen purchased one locomotive, the

"American" from Stephenson and Company. It arrived in New York in January, 1829. Allen also bought three locomotives from Foster, Renwick and Company of Stourbridge, England. The first to arrive, the "Stourbridge Lion," reached this country in May, 1829. When Allen gave a trial trip August 8, 1829, on a road with wooden and strap iron rails, the engine operated successfully. However, it was later discarded as being too heavy for the track. The "America" had two pairs of driving wheels that were directly connected to the two cylinders placed in an inclined position, somewhat similar to the "Rocket." The "Stourbridge Lion" was the "grasshopper type," the cylinders being vertical and operating a type of walking beam fixed at one end. Vertical rods fastened to the other end of the walking beam connected to the rear pair of driving wheels.

The cost and delay incident to the importation of locomotives from England eventually led to the building of locomotives in America. The year 1830 is notable for the introduction of two American-built locomotives. On the Baltimore and Ohio, Peter Cooper tried out the "Tom Thumb," which was a success, in spite of failing in a contest with a horse. The boiler of the "Tom Thumb" was vertical and was provided with tubes made of gun barrels, and a blower was used to keep up steam. The other locomotive built that year was the "Best Friend of Charleston," designed by E. L. Miller and C. E. Detmold. Its boiler was vertical but the two cylinders were nearly horizontal and were connected to cranks on the axle of one pair of the two pairs of driving wheels.

From the very beginning, improvements in American locomotive building were rapid. Locomotives increased in weight and power and new devices were constantly being added. Among these may be mentioned the reversing gear, the cab for engine driver and fireman, the steam whistle, the headlight, the bell, the equalizing levers and springs, engine brakes, and a multitude of other accessories. By 1860-1870, locomotives weighing forty to fifty tons, having eight driving wheels and burning

[19]

either wood or coal, were available. In thirty years a new and powerful machine had been brought into existence in response to a pressing need.

## CARS

At the same time that the development of the locomotive was taking place there was a corresponding evolution of railroad cars, both for passenger and freight. The first railroads were projected as carriers of freight, but the demand for passenger transportation rapidly increased and cars were accordingly designed for people who wanted to travel.

On the first railroads, horse-drawn passenger cars were made with a boxlike enclosure resting on four wheels and without springs. Two long seats were provided on each side. When it became necessary to build cars to be drawn by a locomotive, stagecoach bodies, which were available, were used, each coach being mounted upon four wheels. This type persisted in Europe, but American builders soon developed the long car with a center aisle and seats placed at right angles thereto. In 1834, Ross Winans constructed a car, the "Columbus," mounted on four bogie trucks at each end and large enough to accommodate sixty passengers, some seated on top of the car. By 1840 passenger cars measured thirty-five to forty feet in length with a width of eight feet and a height of six feet six inches. The seats were narrow and the ventilation bad, and the heating was provided by a stove at each end. By 1870, when the Pacific Railroad was in operation, passenger cars were of the same pattern, but larger, and it was only in later years that more comfortable coaches were provided.

The greatest improvement in passenger cars was made when George M. Pullman perfected the sleeping car. The increasing length of railroad lines resulted in night travel, and as early as 1836 crude sleeping cars with tiers of bunks were built to accommodate it. Pullman placed his first real sleeping car, the "Pioneer," in operation in 1865. The "Pioneer" was made one foot wider than the ordinary cars and there was a raised portion of the roof arranged with ventilators. George Godfrey Leland, in a letter dated October 31, 1866, describes an early Pullman car in the following excited terms:

"A remarkable subject of interest, which our party examined this morning, was the City of Chicago—not the metropolis itself, but its reflection, as regards splendor and enterprise, in a 'sleeping car' of that name, which runs on the 'Illinois Central.' This car cost twenty thousand dollars, and is said to be cheap at the price. Every comfort which can be placed in such a vehicle is to be found between its wooden walls. The seats, the sides of the car and the ceiling are exquisitely adorned in *marquetrie* or inlaid woods, while the gilded glass frames, in *ormolu,* and the general tone of color, are truly artistic. It is heated by a separate furnace beneath, and its lounges and mirrors, with every other luxury, make it in fact a rolling palace. Not less remarkable is the corresponding seat-car for day passengers which surpasses in splendor, and still more in comfort, any car which I have even seen on an Eastern road. There is yet another car, which cost *thirty thousand dollars,* which I did not see, but which is described as a miracle of its kind. Luxury and enterprise are advancing with rapid steps in the West. It is said that the most costly diamonds, the richest laces, and the finest cashmeres sold in Broadway or Chestnut streets, find their way, for the most part, to these ultra-montane towns. Perhaps in this rapid action of expenditure, as well as acquisition, we may find one of the leading causes of the active growth of every industrial interest in the West."

The Pacific Railroad had passenger cars for the use of poor people that were anything but splendid. They were arranged somewhat like Pullman sleepers. The seats faced each other in pairs and the passengers sat on a frame of wooden slats. At night the slat seat could be drawn out to form a bed. The traveler provided his own straw mattress and blankets, if he had any. In 1885, the author traveled from Sacramento to Ogden in one of those "emigrant" cars attached to a freight train, a trip that took three nights and three days.

The evolution of freight cars went forward at the same time as that of passenger cars. The trucks and supporting frame were and still are substantially the same in both types. The various car bodies, flat, box, or open, were built at an early date to accommodate the several kinds of freight. Brakes on the wheels were operated from the end platforms or the roof of box cars. One important part of a train is the connection between the cars that transmits the pull of the locomotive to the following cars. At first this connection was by a chain, an unsatisfactory device because of the violent jerks and bumps given the train by the locomotive. Chains were replaced later by a draft gear arranged with springs, but for a long time afterward the coupling was made with an iron link and pin. It was not until the decade of the 1880's that the automatic coupler came into use.

### TRAIN OPERATION

In England the railroads were built double-tracked, and operation of the trains by schedule was not difficult. But in America, owing to the long distances traversed by the railroads and the undeveloped state of the country, it was necessary to utilize the single-track line, with passing tracks being provided at stations. In the beginning, train operation was by schedules with designated points where trains should pass; but if one train was delayed, the entire system was thrown into confusion. A number of devices were therefore introduced, some of which depended upon the locomotive driver seeing distant signals. It was not until after the perfection of the telegraph by Samuel F. B. Morse that the problem was solved. In 1851 the telegraph was first used by the Erie Railroad to direct train movements.

### BRIDGES

In the beginning, American railroad engineers patterned their bridges after construction that had been followed for highway traffic through the preceding ages. Stone arches had been used by Roman builders and the remains of their bridges formed the models from which modern stone arches had been built. The Romans had also built timber and pile bridges, types which were in common use long before the advent of railroads. The first iron bridges had been constructed in England at Coalbrookdale, where a cast-iron arch highway bridge was erected in 1776.

The first railroads in England were built on a very expensive plan compared with American railroads. In America, both on highways and on the railroads, it was recognized that inexpensive structures were essential. Therefore wood was used freely in developing various types of timber and metal bridges that answered the purpose and were economical. It was soon seen that it was not necessary to build permanent structures for the first railroads. A wiser plan was to build structures that would serve for a time and then be replaced later. One reason for this point of view was the rapid increase in weight of the locomotives and other rolling stock. Heavier loads required that older structures be replaced long before they wore out.

Before 1847, the art of bridge building was empirical, as no theory of the relation of the stresses in bridge members to the loads imposed by a railroad train had been developed. The work was largely in the hands of intelligent carpenters who fashioned their structures in accordance with their judgment. It was in 1847 that Squire Whipple of Utica, New York, published a work on bridge building in which he set forth the essential principles of bridge design, and from that time on the design of bridges was based on a mathematical treatment of the relation of loads to the stresses and the strength of the materials used.

The names of a number of the early bridge builders are attached to the forms of trusses that they originated. The truss most used in early wooden bridges was that patented in 1840 by William Howe. In the Howe truss the vertical members are of iron or steel, and all the other members, chords and diagonals, are of timber. In any other truss some of the members are subjected to compressive stresses and some to tensile stresses. The chief difficulty lies in connecting the pieces of timber together to take the tensile stresses. Wood is also subject to decay. However, the Howe truss, or its modification, the Burr truss, was for many years the best form of bridge truss in the United States. Up to the time the Pacific Railroad was built, the wooden Howe truss bridge was the standard for railroad bridges.

Iron bridges also were built to a limited extent. One was used on the Philadelphia and Reading Railroad in 1845, and in 1846 some were installed on the Baltimore and Ohio. When that road was extended from Wheeling, the chief engineer, Benjamin Latrobe, installed several Bolman iron bridges. The use of iron bridges slowly made its way, but at the time of the building of the Pacific Railroad they had been used only on some of the older railroads.

When the Mississippi River was reached by the railroads, the engineers were confronted with crossing the largest river in the country. A bridge over the Mississippi was built in 1855 by the Chicago and Rock Island Railroad at Davenport and was the first of a number built on the upper reaches of that great stream. It was not until the seventies that the design and construction of large bridges took on its present character.

Pile trestles were used for many of the crossings of ordinary streams. For crossing deep ravines, trestles were made of framed timber, resting upon piles or sills placed directly on the ground. Each set of piling or of framed trestle, called bents, was built about sixteen feet apart and the space between was spanned by wooden girders upon which the railroad ties were fastened to support the rails.

In the openings where an earth fill was used, the stream, usually of moderate size, was passed through the fill by a culvert. Such culverts were sometimes built of timber, with sufficient clearance to permit the building of a more permanent masonry arched structure at a later date.

## LOCATION

The evolution of railroads quickly brought into being a group of engineers who learned and developed the science of railroad location in the school of experience. Among these pioneer railroad engineers were Benjamin H. Latrobe, John B. Jervis, Horatio Allen, Robert L. Stevens, and George Lowe Reid.

The early general belief that a locomotive could not ascend a grade was quickly dissipated. However, it was understood that the rate of grade was an important factor in fixing the number of cars a locomotive could haul. Grades of 2 per cent, 106 feet per mile, were recognized as a reasonable maximum that was rarely exceeded except on the steepest lines in the mountains.

The straight sections of the lines, called tangents, were joined by circular curves of different radii, but it was soon found that sharp, short-radius curves offered much resistance to the passage of the train. Experience indicated that curves of ten degrees (radius 574 feet), were as sharp as should be used, except in rare cases. Where the topography permitted, curves of larger radius would be used.

Normally, a railroad should be located as close to a straight line as possible and with a level grade. On the open plans of the Mississippi Valley this was often possible. However, the location generally followed the valley of a river or creek, where the stream course was favorable. The location of the Union Pacific from Omaha directly to the west illustrated this principle. The line followed the valley of the Platte River and its tributary, Lodgepole Creek, for nearly 500 miles. By following the stream, the hills or rolling plains, cut by tributary drainage, were avoided.

However, it is not always true that a stream should be followed, particularly in the case of rivers that have their source in high mountains. In the Sierra Nevada, the rivers, rising in the highest part of the range, have a steep descent into canyons they have cut to depths of 3,000 feet or more. A railroad follow-ing such a river would eventually wind up at the bottom of a deep canyon. It is to the eternal credit of Theodore D. Judah that in the location of the Central Pacific Railroad across the Sierra Nevada, with an elevation of over 7,000 feet, he carefully avoided streams and placed the line on a ridge between two rivers. General Dodge followed the same plan when, in climb-ing the Rocky Mountains, he turned from Lodgepole Creek and followed a ridge near Crow Creek past Cheyenne up to the Sherman Summit at Evans Pass in the Black Hills, now called the Laramie Mountains, at an elevation of 8,262 feet.

# CHAPTER 3

# Early Projects and the
# Railroad Surveys

THE BUILDING of the Pacific Railroad was preceded by the usual discussion that accompanies proposals of this kind. Dreamers, writers, politicians, and promoters precede the practical men who finally take up the project and carry it through to completion. The promotional effort was necessary in order to arouse public interest, inasmuch as an undertaking of the magnitude of the Pacific Railroad could be accomplished only by the assistance of some portion of the public, either as investors or as those who influence the representatives of the people in state or national legislatures.

While it is not possible to determine with certainty who first suggested a railroad to the Pacific coast, there is a definite record of such a proposal being made by a writer in the *Emigrant*, a weekly newspaper published by Judge S. W. Dexter at Ann Arbor, Michigan. The editorial was probably written by Judge Dexter in the issue of February 6, 1832. After remarking on the probability that the public would consider the idea a visionary one, the writer outlines the project for a railroad in the following terms:

> The distance between New York and the Oregon is about three thousand miles. From New York we could pursue the most convenient route to the vicinity of Lake Erie, thence along the south shore of this lake and of Lake Michigan, cross the Mississippi between forty-one and forty-two of north latitude, cross the Missouri about the mouth of the Platte, and thence to the Rocky Mountains, near the source of the last named river, thence to the Oregon, by the valley of the south branch of that stream, called the southern branch of Lewis' River.

The writer suggested that the United States should build the road, or that a company be permitted to do so.

This article in the *Emigrant* is remarkable for two reasons. First it appeared at a time when just two railroads were getting started in the country, the Charleston and Hamburg in South Carolina, and the Baltimore and Ohio, and when there were probably less than 200 miles of track in operation. However, news of English railroads was available to the American public. The other remarkable feature was the editorial writer's location of the line, which was followed in later years by the railroads west from Chicago and specifically by the Union Pacific across the plains and over the Rocky Mountains by way of the Snake River and the Columbia River on to Oregon.

In Bancroft's *History of California,* it is stated that Hartwell Carver of Rochester, New York, published articles in the *New York Courier and Enquirer* advocating a transcontinental railroad to the Columbia River, and outlining a scheme for constructing the line. It would seem that Carver was one of those who followed the articles in the *Emigrant.* Carver later tried to obtain a charter for a railroad from Lake Michigan to California by way of the South Pass, but his schemes came to naught. Carver's ideas were elaborated in 1847 when he stated that he wanted 8,000,000 acres of public land to be selected from a strip of land sixty miles wide along the line. An alternate idea was to secure a tract of land twenty miles wide on each side of the track. The gauge of the track was to be eight or ten feet, the rails to be laid on felt to lessen the vibration of the cars. He visualized cars 100 feet long, with sleeping berths, a kitchen, and a dining room. For climbing grades, the engines would be provided with cog wheels engaging holes in the rails. His memorial to Congress stated that the enterprise would "bring about a kind of earthly millenium, and be the means of uniting the whole world in one great church, a part of whose worship will be to praise God and bless the Oregon Railroad."

A railroad along the proposed route was built long ago, but the great church foundation seems to have been deferred. However, such spiritual adjuncts to a promoter's scheme were popular in those days.

In 1833 or 1834, a fairly complete scheme for a Pacific Railroad was outlined by Dr. Samuel Bancroft Barlow, a physician of Granville, Massachusetts. He wrote an article for the *Intelligencer,* a weekly journal published in Westfield, Massachusetts. This article is given in full in Eugene V. Smalley's *History of the Northern Pacific Railroad.* Dr. Barlow states that he had read the article in the *Emigrant.* He assumes a railroad of a length of 3,000 miles, and reaches the conclusion that while the cost per mile in the settled sections of the country might be $10,000, that for the regions beyond would be greater. If the average cost was $10,000 per mile, 3,000 miles would cost $30,000,000, which was a cost that the United States could stand, since the annual service of the national debt was then from twelve to thirteen million dollars. The plan called for three years to be devoted to surveys, estimates, and other preliminaries, during which period the then existing national debt would be liquidated. When work on the railroad was undertaken, expenditures would range from six to fifteen million dollars a year, a sum that the country could bear without effort. The writer then goes into rhapsodies over the results to follow from the building of the road in integrating the country. The gorgeous West would be brought to our doors and "riches and glory will ultimately be conferred upon a great and magnanimous people." There is no record that anything came of the proposal.

About the same time that Barlow was writing about his project, the Reverend Samuel Parker, a missionary who was associated with Dr. Marcus Whitman in his labors to convert the Indians of the Far West, wrote a book of his travels. This was in 1835. His book, *The Tour Beyond the Rocky Mountains*, was published in 1838, and in it he said:

"There would be no difficulty in the way of constructing a railroad from the Atlantic to the Pacific Ocean. There is no greater difficulty in the whole distance than has not already been overcome in passing the Green Mountains between Boston and Albany, and probably the time may not be far distant when tours will be made across the continent as they have been made to the Niagara Falls to see Nature's wonders."

Another claimant for the honor of having first proposed a railroad to the Pacific was Willis Gaylord Clark, who wrote an article for the *Knickerbocker Magazine* in June, 1838, outlining a project. Apparently he claimed that he was the one who first proposed the road. Clark reviewed the book of the missionary, Parker, and described in glowing terms the transformation that would take place in the West when the railroad was built. It is of interest to read some of his description, of which the following is a part:

> The work will yet be accomplished! Let the prediction be marked. This great chain of communication will yet be made, with links of iron. The treasures of the earth in that wide region are not destined to be lost. The mountains of coal, the vast meadow seas, the fields of salt, the mighty forests, with their trees two hundred and fifty feet in height, the stores of magnesia, the crystallized lakes of valuable salts—these were not formed to be unemployed and wasted. The reader is now living who will make a railroad trip across this vast continent. The granite mountain will melt before the hand of enterprise; valleys will be raised, and

the unwearying fire-steed will spout his hot, white breath where silence has reigned since the morning hymn of young creation was pealed over mountain, flood, and field. The mammoth's bone and the bison's horn, buried for centuries, and long since turned to stone, will be bared to the day by the laborers of the 'Atlantic and Pacific Railroad Company;' rocks which stand now as on the night when Noah's deluge first dried will heave beneath the action of 'villainous saltpetre;' and where the prairie stretches away, 'like the round ocean girdled with the sky,' with its wood-fringed streams, its flower-enameled turf, and its herds of startled buffaloes, will sweep the long hissing train of cars crowded with passengers for the Pacific Seaboard. The very realms of chaos and old night will be invaded; while in the place of the roar of wild beasts, or howl of wilder Indians, will be heard the lowing of herds, the bleating of flocks; the plough will cleave the sods of many a rich valley and fruitful hill, while, from many a dark bosom shall go up the pure prayer to the Great Spirit.'

Another of the early advocates of the Pacific Railroad was a civil engineer who had had considerable experience in railroad work as it was then understood. John Plumbe, who lived in Dubuque, Iowa, published a pamphlet in 1836 advocating a railroad from Lake Michigan to Oregon, and on March 31, 1838, he called a convention in Dubuque to discuss the subject. Resolutions were passed and sent to Congress asking for an appropriation for surveys, and a small sum was granted. In 1839-1840, Plumbe secured a memorial from the Wisconsin legislature addressed to Congress, asking that the surveys be continued west of the Mississippi. He took the memorial to Washington and spent considerable time on the subject, but nothing tangible resulted from his labors. His plan proposed a company capitalized at $100,000,000, to which would be given a land grant of alternate sections along the line of the railroad. Plumbe was the first to appreciate the magnitude of the task of building the railroad and to outline a practical method for accomplishment of the work.

Others, at later dates, claimed to have advocated the railroad at about the same time. One of these was Lilburn W. Boggs, one-time governor of Missouri, whose son claims that his father wrote an article for the *St. Louis Republican* in 1843 advocating the railroad and estimating the cost. The article was not published. Another claimant was Robert Mills, who addressed a memorial to Congress advocating a road and stated that in 1819 he had projected a railway to connect the Atlantic with the Pacific. His claims seem to have been for a road and not for a railway.

Enough evidence has been cited to show that some men were alive to the possibilities of the railroad in the decade 1830-1840, but that there was little to justify action on their plans. Railroads were too new and untried, and practically nothing was known of the western country and the difficulties that would be encountered, both from Nature and from the Indians. All of the projects were for a road to the Columbia River, and even the ownership of that region was disputed by Great Britain. More than that, most of the West and Southwest was then in the possession of the Republic of Mexico.

### THE PROJECTS OF ASA WHITNEY

The second stage in the agitation for the Pacific Railroad began with the work of Asa Whitney in the decade 1840-1850. The indefinite projects of the earlier writers gave place to a feasible plan that was advocated by an educated promoter with tireless energy and undying persistence.

Asa Whitney was a merchant from New York City, who, in the course of business, had visited England and had made a trip over the Liverpool and Manchester Railroad. He had undoubtedly read the literature that has been mentioned in preceding pages. In 1842 he visited China and spent two years there before returning home. He was impressed with the extent of Oriental trade and with the possibility of diverting a large part of that trade across the United States. From the time when he returned to this country until his death, he devoted his entire fortune and efforts to promoting the project of a Pacific Railroad.

[32]

In 1845 he made a 1,500-mile trip up the Mississippi, but before starting he presented to Congress a memorial that was introduced in the Senate and the House, in which he outlined his project of a railroad to the Pacific coast. His first plan was for a railroad from Lake Michigan to the mouth of the Columbia River, in Oregon. The cost was estimated at $50,000,000, and incidental expenses would increase the amount to $65,000,-000. The cost was to be defrayed by the sale of public lands to colonists who would build the railroad and afterwards settle on the land. A strip of land sixty miles wide would be granted to the settler and the railroad and the land would be his property but the control would rest with the national government. Excess profits would be devoted to education and other public purposes.

However, despite the merits of the plan, no action was taken by Congress on the memorial. From that time on, Whitney visited all parts of the country, explaining his project and obtaining resolutions from legislatures and public bodies in favor of the scheme. In general, he and his idea were favorably received and the public was interested. It was difficult at times to secure the approval of representatives and public men, as at Philadelphia, where it took some time to arrange a public meeting. At the meeting of December 23, 1846, the Mayor presided and Whitney and other speakers explained the project, with the result that a favorable resolution addressed to Congress was passed. At a meeting in New York on the Fourth of July, 1847, the public permitted a group of radicals to take possession of the Mayor and others on the platform, including Whitney, and force them to leave the hall. The mob denounced the project as a swindle and as an attempt to seize lands that properly belonged to the people.

Whitney's second memorial to Congress was presented in 1846 and was favorably reported by the Senate Committee on Public Lands on July 31, but after some debate nothing was done. A third memorial presented to Congress in January,

1848, was referred to the Committee on Public Lands, but instead of reporting on the memorial, the committee, in June, reported a resolution for survey and exploration of one or more routes for a railroad from the Mississippi below the Falls of St. Anthony to the Pacific Ocean. As the committee would not report Whitney's bill, another introduced by Senator Niles favored the grant of land to Whitney. Referred to a select committee, it was reported on favorably, but was lost by a vote in the Senate, largely owing to the opposition of Senator Benton of Missouri. In January, 1849, the bill was re-introduced but dissension prevented action and the bill died. The Thirty-first Congress referred all memorials and projects for a railroad to the Committee on Roads and Canals, with the result that an exhaustive report was made favoring the grant of lands to Whitney. Nothing came of it except that the discussion informed the country of the merits of the project. A final bill was presented to the Thirty-second Congress on April 1, 1852, permitting the sale of public lands to Whitney to enable him to build a railroad from the Mississippi River, to commence south of Memphis and proceed by way of the Rio Grande to San Francisco. Sectionalism defeated the bill and this action terminated Whitney's efforts. His fortune had been dissipated and he lived in comparative poverty until he died.

In his efforts to arouse the people of the country, Whitney had published a pamphlet in 1849 that summarized all the information he had gathered on his projects. The plans varied as time went on and the country changed, owing to the accession of California and the discovery of gold. While there were a number of impractical features in all of Whitney's projects, they contained the germ of the plan on which the road was built at a later date—the location, the grant of public lands, and the construction by private parties assisted by the government. Some of the reasons for Whitney's failure were described in the *American Railroad Journal* of April 5, 1851:

We freely admit that Mr. Whitney possesses some qualities which eminently fit him to head a great enterprise. He is enthusiastic and possessed to a remarkable degree with the capacity for inspiring others with his own views. He is deterred by no obstacle and discouraged by no defeats. But here his qualifications for conducting to a successful issue a work of such magnitude as that of a railroad from the Atlantic to the Pacific end. He is self-confident without experience or training, arrogant in his opinions, and overbearing toward all who differ from him. He has a hearty contempt for the whole engineering profession and loses his temper the moment one of that class talks about tunneling, bridging, excavation, etc., which are certainly great annoyances in railroad construction and which have made others beside Mr. Whitney lose their temper. He can never tolerate the introduction of such disagreeable topics as these, but is never tired of poring over maps and enlarging upon the grandeur of his scheme. So long as his mission was confined to the matter of arousing the attention of our people to the importance of the proposed work, his success was remarkable. The moment he came to the question of construction his plans failed to receive respectful attention . . . We are sorry for his disappointments and heartily wish he would adapt his scheme to the practical ideas of the present day of which he appears to have not the least appreciation.

The writer of the above probably came close to a correct estimate of the man. The rising tide of sectionalism that finally culminated in the Civil War was already apparent when Whitney was endeavoring to put his scheme into effect and this could be cited as another reason for his failure. The most practical of men could hardly have accomplished much when that subject engrossed the attention of the country. In spite of his shortcomings Whitney deserves great credit for finally placing the subject of a Pacific Railroad on a fairly firm basis and for arousing the population to the need of such a work.

### THE ERA OF POLITICIANS

There comes a time in the history of all great enterprises when the politicians of the country find it to be to their interests to adopt the ideas of other men and to ride to public favor on them. This is just what happened when Whitney pounded the idea of a Pacific Railroad into the reluctant heads of the men in Congress. When that body began to consider the subject, numerous members of both houses became experts with the certain knowledge that the railroad should commence in their district. Other promoters also appeared with their schemes and each one had his adherents. It is not necessary to follow these schemes in detail.

One plan was proposed by P. P. Degrand, whose railroad was to extend from St. Louis to San Francisco. Stock was to be sold to raise $2,000,000 and the government was to loan $98,000,000 and to give a ten-mile strip of land.

Another man whose name is connected with the Pacific Railroad projects was Josiah Perham of Boston, who had promoted railroad excursions to Boston to see a painted panorama of Niagara Falls, in which activity he made considerable money. His plan, which he called the "People's Pacific Railroad," was for the general public to subscribe $100 each, and with 1,000,000 subscribers he would build the railroad.

Senator Benton of Missouri helped defeat Whitney's plan, but he had his own ideas on the subject. The Senator's first plan was for a national highway similar to the Cumberland Road that extended from Washington to St. Louis, but he waxed eloquent about a "plain old English road." Later he referred in equally glowing terms to the railroad and proposed a statue of Columbus, "hewn from the granite mass of a peak of the Rocky Mountains." Many other senators were equally eloquent and each one was certain that his route was the best. Senator Seward favored the northern route from Chicago; Benton favored a route across what he called the Buffalo Trail through Colorado on a route explored by Frémont; while the southern men wanted the railroad built from the East by way of El Paso to San Diego. A promoter named George Wilkes advocated a line due west from Chicago to the South Pass and thence to Oregon, and his schemes were favored by many northern senators.

Finally, on October 16, 1849, a railroad convention was held in St. Louis, at which Stephen A. Douglas presided. Benton clashed with a lawyer named Loughborough as to the best route, and an adjourned meeting was held in Philadelphia in April, 1850, at which representatives from fourteen states were present, two of the states being southern ones. Another convention was held at Memphis in July, 1849, and at all these meetings there was much talk and little action. On one point and on one only was there fairly general agreement: the route should terminate at San Francisco, since that city was the center of the most populous region on the Pacific.

## THE PACIFIC RAILROAD SURVEYS

The inability of Congress to reach a decision finally forced the men there to resort to the only sensible procedure, which was to have surveys made over a number of routes to determine the best possible railroad location. Senator Gwin of California finally moved an amendment to the Army Appropriation Bill, approved by President Fillmore March 1, 1853, which read as follows: "And be it further enacted, that the Secretary of War be, and he is hereby authorized, under the direction of the President of the United States, to employ such portion of the Corps of Topographical Engineers and such other persons as he may deem advisable, to ascertain the most practicable and economical route for a railroad from the Mississippi River to the Pacific Ocean, and that the sum of $150,000 or so much as may be necessary, be, and the same is hereby appropriated out of any money in the treasury not otherwise appropriated, to defray the expense of such explorations and surveys.

"That the engineers and other persons employed in said explorations and surveys shall be organized in as many district corps as there are routes to be surveyed, and their several reports shall be laid before Congress on or before the first Monday in February, 1854."

[37]

Congress must have been very optimistic as to the ability of the engineers to examine and report on such a vast subject in nine months. The fact seems rather to emphasize a pronounced lack of senatorial comprehension of the great size of the country and of the engineering problems involved in the surveying project.

After the railroad surveys had been in progress for some months it became apparent that they could not be completed by the date set. They were therefore continued and an additional appropriation of $40,000 was approved May 31, 1854. This sum was not sufficient, and still another appropriation of $150,000 was approved August 5, 1854, making the total appropriations $340,000.

It was not until February 27, 1855, that Secretary of War Jefferson Davis was able to submit a somewhat incomplete report. His annual report of December, 1855, contained a summary of progress, and it was not until his annual report of December, 1856, that the project was completed. It had taken nearly three years to make the surveys and to formulate the report. Much work was done both in the field and in the office, and judging by the extent of the surveys and the difficulties encountered, the time consumed was well spent.

The selection of the routes to be examined apparently was left up to Secretary Davis, and he undoubtedly had the advice of many men who favored different routes, but his final selection showed his sincere desire to determine the merits of many possible routes and to balance one against the other. While the Army bill required that the routes should start at the Mississippi River, it was not necessary in most cases to commence the surveys there, because by that time several railroad lines had already been built or were in the process of building westward beyond the Mississippi. In general, the western borders of Iowa, Missouri, and Arkansas were made the starting points of all but the northern route, that being the only route that actually commenced at the Mississippi River. The routes selected may be described as follows taking them in their geographical order from north to south:

*Route No. 1.* Near the forty-seventh and forty-ninth parallels of north latitude. The route commenced at St. Paul and followed across the plains near the Missouri River to the Rocky Mountains. It crossed those mountains into eastern Washington and followed thence southward and along the Columbia River and then northward to Seattle on Puget Sound. A cross-country line over the Cascade Mountains to Seattle was also explored. The general route was that followed later by the Northern Pacific and the Great Northern railroads.

*Route No. 2.* Near the forty-first and forty-second parallels of north latitude. This route commenced at either Council Bluffs on the Missouri River, about 267 miles west of the Mississippi River, or at Fort Leavenworth on the same stream, 245 miles west of the Mississippi River. It followed up the Platte River, taking the north fork along the Emigrant Trail, crossed the South Pass and the Green River, and followed over the Wasatch Mountains to Salt Lake City. Westward the route passed south of Great Salt Lake, and over the deserts and mountains to the Humboldt River, which stream was followed to the vicinity of Winnemucca, Nevada. Leaving the Humboldt, the route crossed the deserts and mountains into northern California, and following down the Pit River, reached the Sacramento River. From that point the Sacramento Valley was to be followed to San Francisco. The greater portion of the route is near the one followed by the Union and Central Pacific railroads from Omaha to San Francisco, except that the long detour into northern California was not followed.

*Route No. 3.* Near the thirty-eight and thirty-ninth parallels of latitude. The route commenced at the junction of the Kansas Mountains south of the Arkansas River. It crossed the mountains of Colorado and Utah somewhat along the line of the Denver and Rio Grande Western Railroad, but the line led across the Wasatch Mountains to the neighborhood of Sevier

Lake. The survey party was massacred by Indians at that point and the survey was not continued, although it was later thought possible to cross central Nevada and the Sierra Nevada at the headwaters of the Carson River.

*Route No. 4.* Near the thirty-fifth parallel of north latitude. This route commenced at Fort Smith on the Arkansas River, about 270 miles west of the Mississippi River. It crossed the plains of Oklahoma and the northern part of the Texas Panhandle, and followed around the southern end of the Rocky Mountains in the vicinity of Santa Fe and Albuquerque. The route across the high plateaus of central New Mexico and Arizona is practically the same now followed by the Atchison, Topeka and Santa Fe Railroad into California at Needles on the Colorado River. A line was indicated across the Mohave Desert and through the Cajon Pass to Los Angeles, or through the Tay-ee-chay-pah (Tehachapi) Pass into the Tulares (San Joaquin) Valley to San Francisco.

*Route No. 5.* Near the thirty-second parallel of north latitude. This, the most southern route, commenced at Fulton on the Red River and crossed the intervening plains and deserts, the Llano Estacado to the Pecos and thence to the Rio Grande at El Paso. From that point the route followed across the mountains and deserts of southern New Mexico and Arizona to the border of California at Fort Yuma, at the junction of the Gila and Colorado rivers. A line westward was projected to San Diego but the main line was to follow across the desert and through the San Gorgonio Pass to Los Angeles. From that point several routes were examined, one across the mountains to the San Joaquin Valley and thence by several alternate routes to San Francisco. This route is the one followed in later years by the Texas and Pacific and the Southern Pacific railroads, especially from El Paso westward.

A number of survey parties were assigned to each route, sometimes working independently over different sections of the route, but in one case, that of Route No. 1, the entire survey

[40]

was under the direction of one man, Governor Isaac I. Stevens of Washington Territory, a civil engineer. The work was in charge of officers of the army, generally of the Topographical Corps, but sometimes it was handled by the Engineer Corps. Instructions for the conduct of the surveys were issued in detail, which Secretary Davis summarized as follows:

> They were directed to observe and note all the objects and phenomena which have an immediate or remote bearing upon the railway, or which might seem to develop the resources, peculiarities, and climate of the country; to determine geographical positions, obtain the topography, observe the meteorology including the data for barometric profiles, and two of the parties were to determine the direction and intensity of the magnetic force. They were to make a geological survey of the lines; to collect information upon and specimens of the botany and zoology of the country; and to obtain statistics of the Indian Tribes which are found in the regions traversed. Thus would be obtained all the information for the general consideration of the question, as well as the data upon which the cost of construction and working of a railroad depend.
>
> If the results of the explorations made under these instructions do not furnish the data required to solve every question satisfactorily they at least give a large amount of valuable information and place the question in a tolerably clear light. We see now, with some precision, the nature and extent of the difficulties to be encountered, and at the same time, the means of surmounting them.

Under the instructions given, a great mass of information was obtained. In difficult regions, actual surveys with transit and level were made, grades determined, and sufficient information taken to determine quantities and costs. As detailed estimates of the entire line could not be made, nor were they then necessary, comparison was made with existing railroads. Note was made of stone for culverts and walls and of the presence or absence of timber for bridges, ties, and fuel. Explorations were made for coal and the development of water supplies for the railroad were carefully considered. In each case of the two southern routes across the arid plains of Texas and New Mexico, wells were drilled for this purpose. Meteorological observations were made and all available information collected regarding snow, rainfall, and general weather conditions. The geology of the country traversed was carefully examined and information obtained regarding the amount of arable land, the occurrence of minerals, the nature of soils, etc. The natural history of the regions was studied, especially that relating to animals, birds, insects, and similar data, together with the plant life encountered.

When the data came in, it was arranged and edited by an officer of the army. Maps were made of the entire western part of the country, the first correct ones ever prepared. The reports from different engineering parties, with lithographs of drawings of important scenery, detail maps of each line, cost estimates, data regarding railroads, and everything that could pertain to the subject, were printed in eleven quarto volumes that remain today models of the way such information should be presented. Owing to the nature of the problem and to the fact that many men were engaged on the work, the individual studies are of unequal value. One criticism of the work might be that the surveys were entrusted to army officers, whose knowledge of railroad work was necessarily limited. A board of consulting railroad engineers would have systematized the work and established standards under which the several cost estimates would have been more easily comparable than they were. It is but just to the army officers to say that within the limitations mentioned, their work was of excellent character, and their conclusions generally sound.

The work on Route No. 1 seems to have been the best organized and the most complete from one end of the line to the other. Governor Stevens had the entire survey under his direction and thus was able to present a complete report. In the crossing of the Rocky Mountains, especially the eastern ranges, nine passes were examined and surveyed. The passage of the Cascade Mountains, either by way of the gorge of the Columbia River or across the mountains directly to Seattle, was well studied. While later surveys of railroads as they were being built indicated some variation from his route, in general the line was wisely located.

In the case of the central route, No. 2, a number of surveys and reports were included, made by different men and at different times. Some dependence was placed on the explorations of John C. Frémont, and the line from the Missouri River to the Green River followed largely the old traveled route of the Overland Trail. Reference should be made to the explorations and surveys of Captain Howard Stansbury of the Corps of Topographical Engineers. In 1849, at the time of the gold rush to California, Stansbury was sent with a party to survey Great Salt Lake. He traveled by the Overland Trail to Salt Lake City, organized his party, and made the first survey of the lake. He also investigated the possibilities of a road westward around the southern end of the lake, and on his return trip in 1850 investigated the route for a railroad or road from Salt Lake up the Timpanogas (Provo) River as a crossing of the Wasatch Mountains and thence to Fort Bridger on a tributary of the Green River. Instead of following the route homeward by the South Pass and the North Fork of the Platte, he crossed the Wyoming Basin directly eastward along the base of the mountains that border the basin on the south.

Jim Bridger was Stansbury's guide and perhaps credit should be given that old mountain man for first indicating the route that was afterward taken by the Union Pacific. Jim Bridger came into the mountains in 1822 and worked in the fur trade, first as one of General Ashley's men and later as one of a company. In 1843 he built his fort or trading post on Black's Fork of the Green River. When in 1850 he was asked to guide the Stansbury party westward, he led them across the open lands of the Wyoming Basin by way of Bridger Pass and crossed the

Black Hills (Laramie Mountains) near the Cheyenne Pass. They were proceeding eastward down Lodgepole Creek when Stansbury was severely injured and forced to return by way of Fort Laramie. Stansbury in his report dwelt upon the advantages of the route for a railroad and showed it to be sixty-one miles shorter than the route by South Pass. In the Pacific Railroad Report his route was rejected, but it was substantially the one over which the Union Pacific was finally built.

From Fort Bridger west, the route was surveyed by Lieutenant E. G. Beckwith. He indicated two crossings of the Wasatch Range, either by way of the Provo River or by way of the Weber River, the latter being followed when the railroad was built. His line lay south of Great Salt Lake and across the salt deserts of Nevada. He reached the Humboldt River but followed it only as far as where it bends southwestward toward the Sink. From there Beckwith, for reasons he does not give, left the Humboldt, and crossing mountains and deserts reached northern California and followed westward across the Madeline Plains and down the Upper Sacramento (Pit) River to the north end of the Sacramento Valley, from which point the way to San Francisco was clear. This route seems almost absurd, even in the light of such knowledge as was then available. To have continued down the Humboldt along the Emigrant Trail and across the Sierra Nevada by well-known passes would have seemed the route to be followed. This writer has been on the Pit River over almost its entire length and can vouch that it is no location for a railroad. The distance by the Beckwith route from Winnemucca to Sacramento is approximately 150 miles longer than that of the Central Pacific route.

When the railroad was built, the general course of Route No. 2 was followed along the valley of the Platte River to the junction of the North and South forks, and a short section down the Weber River and along the Humboldt River. The route was over 200 miles longer than the road and in many cases it was in more difficult territory, as on the North Fork of the

[44]

Platte River and in northern California. Next to No. 3, No. 2 was the poorest of the five proposed routes.

Route No. 3 was the least adapted to a railroad of the five courses selected. As in all the other routes, the crossing of the Great Plains by No. 3 presented no difficulty, but the line over the high mountains of central and western Colorado and into Utah was difficult and beyond the capacity of the builders of the time. While the surveys were terminated by the death of Captain Gunnison, a suggestion was made that Nevada could be crossed and the Sierra Nevada surmounted at the headwaters of the Carson River. The estimates from Sevier Lake westward were made on the basis of the travels of Frémont by way of Tehachapi Pass into the San Joaquin Valley, and also by the western route from Sevier Lake via the Humboldt River and the line followed by Route No. 2 into California by way of the Madeline Plains and Pit River. This information is of a fragmentary order. The route was dismissed from consideration as impracticable. However, the estimates of cost are included in the summary, both by way of the Tehachapi Pass and by way of northern California and the Pit River. As has been noted, the Denver and Rio Grande Western Railroad followed part of the route surveyed, and the Gunnison River and Canyon perpetuate the name of the able army officer who, like many others, lost his life in the discharge of his duty.

The two southern routes, No. 4 and No. 5, were well located, and this is borne out by the fact that they were followed in later years by the Atchison, Topeka and Santa Fe, and by the Southern Pacific.

The several routes were compared by means of cost estimates, and it is in this respect that the study is least reliable. On account of the length of the lines, it was not possible to make detailed estimates, nor was it necessary. On the other hand, the several men on the surveys used their judgment and obtained their cost figures by comparison with costs on railroads built in the eastern states. They tried to adapt such costs to conditions as they found them in the unsettled regions of the West, with the result that the estimates are approximations only. Captain A. A. Humphreys, the officer who edited the reports, comments on the fact that over similar territory the estimates varied from $35,000 per mile to $50,000 per mile. In the case of Route No. 1, the editor increases the estimates of Governor Stevens by 60 per cent, thus adding from $30,690,000 to $41,440,000 to the several estimates. In another instance, on Route No. 4, from Fort Smith to San Pedro, a distance of 1,892 miles, the preliminary estimate was $169,210,265, while the revised estimate for a distance of 1,760 miles was $86,130,000—a reduction of $83,080,265, or nearly 50 per cent. Similarly, the preliminary estimate from Fort Smith to San Francisco was reduced by $81,157,265, or nearly 50 per cent.

A summary of the several estimates was given in a table from which the following is abstracted. On all the routes the horizontal distance is increased by adding a length determined by formula to account for the elevations to be overcome, which differed in each project. The latter is not of much importance but it does furnish one means of making a correct comparison.

*See table which follows on pages 48-49.*

# ESTIMATE OF
## DISTANCES AND COSTS
### OF
## DIFFERENT ROUTES

| | Distance by air line—miles | Distance by proposed railroad route—miles | Sum of ascents and descents—feet |
|---|---|---|---|
| No. 1. Route near 47th and 49th parallels—St. Paul to Seattle | 1,410 | 2,025 | 18,654 |
| No. 1. Same—St. Paul to Vancouver | 1,455 | 1,864 | 17,654 |
| No. 2. Route near 41st and 42nd parallels—Council Bluffs to Benicia via South Pass | 1,410 | 2,032 | 29,120 |
| No. 3. Route near 38th and 39th parallels—Westport to San Francisco via Coo-che-to-pa and Tah-ee-chay-pah passes | 1,740 | 2,080 | 49,985 |
| No. 3. Route near 38th and 39th parallels—Westport to Benicia via Coo-che-to-pa and Madeline passes | 1,740 | 2,290 | 56,514 |
| No. 4. Route near 35th parallel from Ft. Smith to San Francisco | 1,550 | 2,096 | 48,521 |
| No. 4. Route near 35th parallel from Ft. Smith to San Pedro | 1,360 | 1,820 | 48,862 |
| No. 5. Route near 32nd parallel from Fulton to San Francisco via Coast Route | 1,630 | 2,024 | 38,200 |
| No. 5. Route near 32nd parallel from Fulton to San Pedro | 1,400 | 1,598 | 30,181 |
| No. 5. Route near 32nd parallel from Fulton to San Diego | 1,360 | 1,533 | 33,454 |

The cost estimates of two cases of No. 1 are those of the office, those of Governor Stevens having been brought to the same standard of increased cost with the other routes, and his equipment reduced to that of the other routes. His estimates were $117,121,000 and

| Length, level route, equal working expense—miles | Comparative cost of different routes | Altitude above sea, highest point of route—feet | |
|---|---|---|---|
| 2,378 | $140,871,000 | 6,044 | Tunnel at elevation 5,219 ft. |
| 2,198 | $130,781,000 | 6,044 | Same |
| 2,583 | $116,095,000 | 8,373 | |
| 3,026 | Impracticable | 10,032 | Tunnel at elevation 9,540 ft. |
| 3,360 | Impracticable | 10,032 | Tunnel at elevation 9,540 ft. |
| 3,015 | $106,000,000 | 7,550 | |
| 2,745 | $ 92,000,000 | 7,550 | Tunnel at elevation 4,179 ft. |
| 2,747 | $ 90,000,000 | 5,717 | |
| 2,169 | $ 68,000,000 | 5,717 | |
| 2,167 | $ 68,000,000 | 5,717 | |

$110,091,000.

For No. 5, Fulton to San Francisco, Lieut. Park's estimate was $84,837,750, and for No. 5, Fulton to San Diego, his estimate was $59,005,500.

The summary tends to favor the most southern route, No. 5, Fulton to San Francisco via El Paso. There is no question that Secretary Davis favored the southern route for many reasons not connected with the physical situation. However, it could never be said that he desired to alter the reports or to influence those who compiled the data. One point not sufficiently developed at the time was the fact that the best route for a railroad would be the route that best served the needs of the country. There was no doubt that San Francisco and the central part of California should be the western terminal; but when it came to the eastern end of the road, every city, town, and hamlet put forth claims to be made the starting point. The important and deciding factor was that the free industrial North was rapidly outdistancing the slave-holding South, as shown by the extensive railroad construction in the northern part of the country. The decision as to just where the Pacific road should be located was reached at a later date and for other reasons.

The most important point developed by the Pacific Railroad surveys was that railroads could be built across the country in as many places as traffic conditions warranted. In the years that followed, the fact that railroads were built along practically all of the five routes examined emphasizes the excellent character of the work done in the location and surveys by the men who did the job.

### LATER DEVELOPMENTS

While the Pacific Railroad surveys were in progress, the agitation in Congress continued. There was some change in the nature of the proposals. In the beginning, the idea had been for the national government to build and operate the road. By 1855 the plan for a corporation building the road with government assistance had been discussed. By this time the disastrous experience of the states in building railroads was well understood. Benton of Missouri changed his views, and his influence in favor of private enterprise was effective. However, sectionalism always succeeded in defeating the many bills that were introduced. Ignorance of the project was in evidence everywhere, at least as far as the real needs of the country were concerned.

In 1856, the national convention of the Democratic party wrote a plank into its platform recognizing the importance of "safe and speedy communication by military and postal roads through our own territory between the Atlantic and Pacific Coasts of this Union." The new Republican party in the same year stated in its platform "that a railroad to the Pacific Ocean by the most central and practicable route, is imperatively demanded by the interests of the whole country, and that the Federal Government ought to render immediate and efficient aid in its construction." The new President, James Buchanan, expressed himself in favor of a road but did not commit himself to any one route, although it was well known that his sympathies lay with the southern route.

From that time on, there were various proposals in the form of bills before Congress, but like most of the measures of that time the issues were debated from the standpoint of the southern states versus the northern states. A possible breakup of the Union was openly discussed, and that subject overshadowed all others. Attempts at a compromise on the location of the railroad failed every time, and so the situation went from bad to worse. In 1860, as four years earlier, the platform of the Republican party stated "that a railroad to the Pacific Ocean is imperatively demanded by the interests of the whole country." The wing of the Democratic party that met at Charleston repeated the sentiment in other words. The election resulted in a victory for the Republicans and Abraham Lincoln was the new President. By the time a special session of Congress was called in July, 1861, the southern states had seceded and that element of sectionalism was absent.

As a result of the Civil War, the South was ruined financially and its industries and railroads largely destroyed. The location problem of the Pacific Railroad was therefore well on the way to a solution.

[51]

# CHAPTER 4

# The Builders of the Central Pacific Railroad

IN A HISTORY of the building of the Pacific Railroad, some mention must be made of the personalities of the men who originated and carried to completion a work that was the outstanding achievement of their time, notwithstanding the fact that the railroad itself is the most important element in the story. Interests will always center around the men who performed the work, and therefore we give here some account of their origin, their character, the incidents of their career, and the life they lived.

## THEODORE DEHONE JUDAH

On the green lawn in front of the station building of the Southern Pacific Railroad in the city of Sacramento, the capital of California, stands one of the few monuments erected in America to the memory of an engineer. Fittingly, the monument is made of massive granite boulders from the high Sierra Nevada, the snowy summits of which can be seen from the capital city on a clear day. It bears in bronze a medallion of the engineer, together with a brief statement of his services in organizing and locating the Central Pacific Railroad, now a part of the Southern Pacific System. The monument was erected to preserve the memory of one of the most gifted engineers of the nineteenth century, Theodore Dehone Judah. Only two other railroad engineers have been honored in this way, Samuel B. Reed of the Union Pacific, whose granite monument stands at Joliet, and John F. Stevens, whose statue was erected on the Marias Pass where the Great Northern Railroad crosses the Rocky Mountains.

The Judah monument at Sacramento, which was started and completed by W. H. Kirkbride, chief engineer of the Southern Pacific Company, was dedicated at a meeting of the American Society of Civil Engineers on April 26, 1930, and the completed monument was unveiled in February, 1931. It bears this inscription:

THAT THE WEST
MAY REMEMBER
THEODORE DEHONE JUDAH
PIONEER, CIVIL ENGINEER AND TIRELESS ADVOCATE
OF A GREAT TRANSCONTINENTAL RAILROAD
— AMERICA'S FIRST —
THIS MONUMENT WAS ERECTED BY THE MEN AND WOMEN OF THE
SOUTHERN PACIFIC COMPANY, WHO IN 1930 WERE CARRYING ON
THE WORK HE BEGAN IN 1860. HE CONVINCED FOUR SACRA-
MENTO MERCHANTS THAT HIS PLAN WAS PRACTICABLE
AND ENLISTED THEIR HELP. GROUND WAS BROKEN
FOR THE RAILROAD JANUARY 8, 1863, AT THE
FOOT OF K STREET NEARBY.
JUDAH DIED NOVEMBER 2, 1863.
THE ROAD WAS BUILT PAST THE SITE OF THIS MONUMENT,
OVER THE LOFTY SIERRA—ALONG THE LINE OF JUDAH'S
SURVEY—TO A JUNCTION WITH THE UNION PACIFIC
AT PROMONTORY, UTAH, WHERE ON MAY 10,
1869, THE "LAST SPIKE" WAS DRIVEN.

[53]

More than two thirds of a century had passed after Judah left the scene of his labors in the mountains of California before his name was perpetuated by the memorial. The history of the Central Pacific Railroad begins with Judah, and in the years before his early death that history was largely involved with his efforts in business and legislative matters as well as with the expected engineering problems.

Theodore Dehone Judah was born in Bridgeport, Connecticut, on March 4, 1826, and he died in New York, November 2, 1863, at thirty-seven years of age. His father was an Episcopal clergyman who moved his family to Troy, New York, when the son was still a baby. Besides Theodore, there were two other sons, Henry M. Judah, who rose to the rank of brigadier general in the Civil War, and Charles D. Judah, who went to California in 1849 and became a member of the firm of Hackett and Judah. As a young man, Theodore D. Judah was destined for the Navy, but he turned to engineering and was graduated from the Rensselaer Polytechnic Institute at Troy.

Judah's first work was with the early Schenectady and Troy Railroad under W. S. Hall, chief engineer. This was the era of railroad building and Judah found work on several of the short railroads of that period, notably with the New York, New Haven and Hartford Railroad, and the Connecticut River Railroad. For a time he was employed on a section of the Erie Canal and also helped erect a large bridge at Vergennes, Vermont. The Niagara Gorge Railroad from Niagara to Lewiston, at that time considered a remarkable feat of engineering, was built under his charge. While in Greenfield, Massachusetts, on his railroad work, he met Anna Ferona Pierce, daughter of a local merchant, and they were married May 10, 1847, twenty-two years to the day before the completion of the Pacific Railroad on which Judah expended the greatest years of his career. The young wife was to follow her husband over land and sea before his death, as did many another engineer's wife in those days. Judah was in Buffalo in charge of construction on the

Buffalo and New York Railroad, now a part of the Erie System, when he was called to California to take charge of the Sacramento Valley Railroad.

The Sacramento Valley Railroad was built from Sacramento along the sloping plain eastward to the town of Folsom. The route lay south of the American River. There were no difficulties in the construction and only one small creek had to be bridged. At that time, 1854, Folsom, situated close to the foothills of the Sierra Nevada, was a starting point to the gold placers on the American River. It was only twenty-two miles to Coloma on the South Fork, where gold was discovered in 1848. When the placer mines were exhausted, Folsom declined in importance, and the railroad lost its principal source of revenue. After Judah had left the road, it was extended northward along the base of the mountains as far as Lincoln. Ultimately the road was purchased by the Central Pacific, the portion to Lincoln was removed, and from Folsom it was extended to Placerville.

The Sacramento Valley Railroad was organized by California men in 1853 with Col. Charles L. Wilson as president. In 1854 Colonel Wilson was in New York purchasing supplies for the road and met Judah, who had been recommended by Governor Horatio Seymour and his brother Colonel Silas Seymour, both of whom had known the young man. Judah was promptly engaged and after hurried preparations he and his wife sailed for California in April, 1854. He told his wife that he was going to California to be the pioneer railroad engineer on the Pacific coast, and this turned out to be true. Even at this early date he was considering the subject of the transcontinental railroad and would say, "It will be built, and I am going to have something to do with it."

For the new railroad, Judah's surveys extended to Mormon Island, a few miles upstream from Folsom, but the line was never built to that point. Judah made a report, "The Report of the Chief Engineer on the Preliminary Surveys and Future

Business of the Sacramento Valley Railroad," dated May 30, 1854, in which he described the line and the favorable conditions surrounding it. In November a contract was given to an eastern firm of railroad builders, Robinson, Seymour and Company, who were paid $1,800,000, of which $800,000 was paid in capital stock and $700,000 in 10 per cent, twenty year bonds. This type of contract, in which the contractor finances the work, nearly always breeds trouble, because the contractor invariably feels that he may do as he pleases with the work. It is probable that Judah locked horns with Robinson about the character of the work, because they became enemies and in later years Robinson tried to place obstacles in the way of Judah and the work with which he was connected. The railroad was completed to Folsom early in February, 1856, at which time Judah left its service.

For the next three years Judah was engaged on several other projects, one of which was with the San Francisco and Sacramento Railroad as chief engineer. The line was projected to run from Sacramento to Benicia. Judah reported on the cost in a report dated February, 1856, which he set at $3,000,000, or $51,707 per mile, and he estimated the possible revenue. The road was to connect at Sacramento with the Sacramento Valley Railroad, and Judah also stated that it would connect with the "Great Pacific Railroad." It was evident that he kept his big project in mind when engaged in other work. The San Francisco and Sacramento line, like several others projected at that time and with which Judah was connected, was never built. One line that he was said to have surveyed led from San Francisco to San Jose, a road that was afterward built and later purchased by the Central Pacific Railroad Company. He also made some explorations of the Sierra Nevada, possibly for the Sacramento Valley Railroad Company.

In addition to his work in California in this period, Judah attended three sessions of Congress in behalf of the Pacific Railroad Project, and Carl I. Wheat says, "The general subject of a Pacific Railroad developed during this period almost to an obsession." When the results of the government surveys became known the agitation for the Pacific Railroad grew in strength. These reports, while complete, could not of themselves produce a railroad. Congress could not agree upon a route and the country was rapidly drifting toward the Civil War. On January 1, 1857, Judah published a pamphlet in Washington entitled, "A Practical Plan for Building the Pacific Railroad, by T. D. Judah, Civil Engineer, San Francisco," in which he outlined the substance of a railroad project to be built by private enterprise without government aid. He said, "The General Government . . . is a house divided against itself; it cannot be done until the route is defined, and if defined, the opposing interest is powerful enough to defeat it." His estimate of the general situation was correct. He maintained that what was required was a definite survey on a selected route and not several general reconnaissance surveys on several routes upon which differences of opinion would certainly arise. He stated in his pamphlet that about $200,000 was required for surveys and that the project for the 2,000 miles of road would average in cost about $75,000 per mile or a total of $150,000,000. There was much additional argument in the pamphlet, but of course Congress did nothing.

Judah returned from Washington convinced that the subject of a Pacific Railroad must be agitated from the West. Probably under the inspiration of Judah, the California State Legislature on April 5, 1859, passed a resolution calling for a convention to consider the subject. The convention, numbering over a hundred members, met in San Francisco on September 20, 1859, with Judah as a representative from Sacramento. Debate, as usual, centered on the route to be adopted and a resolution was passed expressing preference for the central railroad route. There were a number of ideas discussed by the convention, and in all of the actions taken Judah played a prominent part. In the end, on October 11, 1859, the Executive Committee formally appointed Judah as the accredited agent of the convention to convey its memorial to Washington. He sailed for the East on October 20.

On the steamer he met Mr. J. C. Burch, a newly elected congressman from California, and General Lane, senator from Oregon. One result of this acquaintance was that bills were put in shape and introduced in Congress by Burch, and a compromise measure was brought to the Senate by Senator Gwin of California. However, under the press of other more important business, the bills never reached a vote, although Judah established an office in the capitol and filled it with maps and other data for the enlightenment of members of Congress. His work, though, laid the foundation for the later bills that were passed in 1862.

During the time Judah spent in the East, he visited many places, going as far west as Chicago, and he took pains to acumulate information regarding the latest data on railroads, such as grades, especially of lines that cross the Appalachian Mountains, notably the Baltimore and Ohio, which were examples of what could and should be done. Judah returned to California convinced that nothing could be accomplished in Congress until an actual project was outlined, with proper surveys, estimates, and organization.

In 1860, Judah was in the mountains, making a reconnaissance of several routes, using a barometer to determine elevations. He examined a route through Eldorado County, California, by way of Georgetown, another by way of Henness Pass at the headwaters of the North Yuba, and third by the Dutch Flat Route over Donner Pass. Judah's attention to the latter route, which was the one over which the railroad was built, came at the suggestion of Dr. Daniel W. Strong, a druggist of Dutch Flat. Dr. Strong had heard of Judah's explorations and invited him to come to Dutch Flat to examine the Donner Pass route. The route was one traveled by some of the early emigrants who came up the Truckee River and crossed the divide, usually over the Emigrant Pass, some two miles south of the Donner Pass. It was not a much used route, as more favorable wagon roads lay over the Henness Pass to the north, and to the south by the South Fork of the American River over either Carson or Johnson Passes. At that time, the tide of emigration had moved east to the mines of Nevada at Virginia City and Gold Hill, and Dr. Strong, with others, was interested in a possible wagon route through Dutch Flat and over the Donner Pass in order to divert some of the eastbound traffic through his home town. Strong was not acquainted with Judah at that time, but when Judah reached Dutch Flat, a friendship was formed that lasted until the engineer died.

It is not necessary to discuss to whom belongs the credit for determining the route of the railroad over the Sierra Nevada. Dr. Strong undoubtedly is entitled to the credit for the suggestion of the route that had been known as the Emigrant Trail. However, it needed the trained eye of a practical engineer to determine in a preliminary way the merits of the location that was afterward adopted. The two men went over the route across the mountains in the fall of 1860, and on their return, Judah prepared the engineering data at Dr. Strong's store in Dutch Flat. It was agreed that a corporation should be formed and articles were written with that end in view. Dr. Strong secured a number of stock subscriptions and Judah prepared a pamphlet entitled "Central Pacific Railroad to California," which was published in San Francisco on November 10, 1860. In this pamphlet he said:

"Confident of the existence of a practical route across the Sierra Nevada Mountains, nearer and more direct than the proposed line via Madeline Pass and the headwaters of the Sacramento, I have devoted the past few months to an exploration of several routes and passes through Central California, resulting in the discovery of a practicable route from the city of Sacramento upon the divide between Bear River and the North Fork of the American, via Illinoistown, Dutch Flat, and Summit Valley to the Truckee River; which gives nearly a direct line to

[59]

Washoe with maximum grades of one hundred feet per mile.
. . . The elevation of the Pass is 6,690 feet."

Judah made the point that this route was shorter by perhaps
150 miles than the route in the government reports. He also
dwelt on the possibilities of the Nevada mine trade, estimating
the resulting revenue therefrom for both a railroad and a wagon
road. Government aid was contemplated.

Dr. Strong obtained subscriptions amounting to $46,500, and
Judah went to San Francisco to obtain the remainder, some
$70,000. Although he was well received at first, when the time
came for subscriptions no one was willing to enter his name.
Judah, who was called an enthusiastic lunatic, returned to Sacramento disgusted with San Francisco. A meeting in Sacramento,
the first of several, was well attended. At later meetings Judah
met for the first time the men who were to carry out the project
—Leland Stanford, Collis P. Huntington, Mark Hopkins, and
Charles Crocker. Others present were Dr. Strong, Lucius A.
Booth, James Bailey, a jeweler, Cornelius Cole, later congressman and senator from California, and B. F. Leete, one of
Judah's surveyors. Huntington was cautious and agreed only
to share the cost of the surveys; after those were made he would
consider the subject further.

The result was that an organization meeting of stockholders
was held April 30, 1861, and on the 28th of June the Central
Pacific Railroad was incorporated. The company gave Judah
the necessary money for surveys, and field parties were soon
organized. A barometric reconnaissance was made of two other
routes, at that time deemed possible. One was up the Yuba
River via Downieville, and across the North Fork of the Yuba
Pass; the other was by way of Oroville, the Middle Fork of the
Feather River, and across Sierra Valley to Beckwourth's Pass.
Like the other routes formerly examined, they were judged to
be markedly inferior to the selected route via Donner Pass and
the Truckee River. The results of the survey and the other examinations were embodied in a report by Judah dated at Sacra-

mento October 1, 1861, to the president and directors of the Central Pacific Railroad, in which the merits of the route were discussed and the benefits from government assistance set forth. Cost estimates of $12,380,000 were made from Sacramento to the state line, and to several other more distant points as far as Salt Lake City, the total for 733 miles being $41,415,000. Of this, the estimate for 451 miles from Lassens Meadow on the Humboldt River to Salt Lake City was that made by Lieutenant Beckwith of the government surveys in the previous decade. There was a saving of distance of 184 miles over the government route. Following the report, the directors passed this resolution:

> October 9, 1861: "Resolved, that Mr. T. D. Judah, the Chief Engineer of this Company, proceed to Washington on the steamer on the 11th Oct. inst. as the accredited agent of the Central Pacific Railroad Company of California, for purpose of procuring appropriations of land and U. S. Bonds from the Government, to aid in the construction of this road."

On his arrival in Washington, Judah began an active campaign for the bill for a Pacific Railroad. Senator A. A. Sargent of California, whom Judah had met on the steamer, led in arousing the Senate, so that a subcommittee of the Pacific Railroad Committee was appointed to draft a bill. Judah had obtained an appointment as Secretary of the Senate Committee and was also made clerk of a subcommittee in the House. Others were also working for the bill, which finally became a law, signed by President Lincoln July 1, 1862. Lands, rights of way, and aids in the form of first-mortgage government bonds were the essential elements of the bill, which also provided for the organization of the Union Pacific Railroad Company. Bonds were to be issued when forty miles of railroad had been constructed.

After preliminary matters had been adjusted, Judah went to New York to order supplies. Formal acceptance of the contract between the government and the Central Pacific Railroad Company was signed November 1, 1862. Judah sailed for California on July 21, his long struggle for the railroad having been completed.

On his return to Sacramento, Judah filed his second report with the company, dated October 22, 1862. He enumerated the advantages of the arrangement with the government, the value of the land grants, the amount of lumber available, and the anticipated revenue, which was to be largely from local traffic and from traffic with Washoe, as the Virginia City-Gold Hill mining developments were then known. An agent at Strawberry on the American River made an actual count of freight and passenger traffic on the American River route, and upon this Judah's estimates were based. The estimates may have been overly optimistic, but they showed that a good business existed. The Act of 1862 permitted the California company to build eastward until it met the Union Pacific Railroad, and Judah urged the company promptly to extend its surveys as far as Salt Lake City. The road was rapidly taking on the character of a transcontinental line, with the greater cost and larger outlook.

Construction started on January 8, 1863, when ground was broken at Sacramento. In the later months of 1862, surveys had been pushed by several parties in the mountains. In December, Charles Crocker was given a contract for grading the first thirty-miles to Newcastle, subcontractors taking short sections of the line.

In a report to the directors, dated June 1, 1863, Judah, as chief engineer, describes in detail the surveys made up to that date and refers especially to the preliminary location surveys on the adopted route over the mountains. In addition, he again describes the barometrical reconnaissances of other routes and weighs the advantages and disadvantages of these locations. There had been a number of reconnaissances made with the idea of passing by way of Virginia City, all of which showed that no practical route could be found. A possible route was examined that led south from the Truckee River through the Truckee Meadows and to the Carson River in Eagle Valley:

thence down the Carson River to the desert, but this route was obviously longer and no better than the selected route down the Truckee River to the big bend of that stream.

In July, Judah made what was his last report to the directors. In addition to the account of the surveys, there was an estimate of the cost of the first fifty miles. He also gave reasons why the Sacramento Valley Railroad was not adapted to the railroad they were building. The existing road was not in the proper location, being eight miles longer to Auburn. The government bill applied only to a new road. The older road was heavily bonded and since the government bonds would not be available, the worn rails of English make would have to be replaced with American iron and much repair work was necessary. Finally the road did not command the possible traffic from the northern region of the state. The decision was correct, but much criticism was voiced against Judah by the owners of the older road, who wanted to sell out.

During the period of active work and the prosecution of surveys, differences of opinion had developed between Judah and the men who were directing the affairs of the company—Stanford, Huntington, Hopkins, and Crocker. Most of the other directors had dropped out. Judah became impatient and expressed himself in a letter to his friend Strong, dated May 13, 1863:

"I cannot tell you in the brief space of a letter all that is going on, or of all that has taken place; suffice to say that I have had a pretty hard row to hoe.

"I had a blow-out about two weeks ago and freed my mind, so much so that I looked for instant decapitation. I called things by their right name and invited war; but councils of peace prevailed and my head is still on; but my hands are tied, however. We have no meeting of the board nowadays, except the regular monthly meeting, which, however, was not held this month; but there have been any quantity of private conferences to which I have not been invited."

Judah maintained that his stock subscription had been paid for by his previous services, but Hopkins ruled otherwise. Huntington returned from the East and evidently was an influence that Judah resented. He objected to exclusive contracts being given to Crocker and in a letter declared that he had prevented a certain gentleman, probably meaning Crocker, from being a contractor on the road. The Associates had themselves organized the Dutch Flat and Donner Lake wagon road, which was intended to bring to the railroad much needed revenue from Washoe mines. However, it was not a railroad wagon road but one belonging to the Associates, and the revenues, if any, from the wagon road belonged to them and not to the railroad. This was but one of many sources of differences between Judah and his friends on one hand, and the four Associates on the other. Judah was an engineer and wanted to get on with building the road. The Associates had before them the problem of financing the railroad and of meeting the continuous attacks made on their enterprise by antagonistic interests. For them, there was no use going on with the construction unless they could control the venture and assure themselves of a substantial profit. The nature of the men involved in the controversy was an element that made for discord. Judah was a strong, persistent, emphatic character. The railroad project was his own, one that he had developed, and brought to realization. To have others take charge was a thing he could not comprehend. On the other hand, he was dealing with four men equally strong-minded who intended to dominate the enterprise if it was carried out. A clash was inevitable, and while the details are lacking, it is clear that the subject came to a head in the summer of 1863.

The result was that Judah was bought out for the sum of $100,000, but at the same time he was given an option to buy out the Associates for an equal amount each. They evidently were in doubt as to the possibilities for profit and were willing to get out for the sum named. They were all merchants and not railroad builders, and at that time the government help, from the nature of the law, was of little or no benefit. Judah arranged to go East and he left in September. When leaving, he wrote Dr. Strong about the situation and intimated what he intended to do.

> "I have a feeling of relief in being away from the scenes of contention and strife which has been my lot to experience for the past year, and to know that the responsibility of events, so far as regards the Pacific Railroad, do not rest on my shoulders. If the parties that now manage hold to the same opinion three months hence that they do now, there will be a radical change in the management of the Pacific Railroad, and it will pass into the hands of men of experience and capital. If they do not, they may hold the reins for awhile, but they will rue the day that they ever embarked in the Pacific Railroad.
>
> "If they treat me well they may expect similar treatment at my hands. If not, I am able to play my hand.
>
> "If I succeed in inducing the parties I expect to see to return with me to California, I shall likely return the latter part of December."

There is evidence that Judah had arranged to meet certain men in New York, and Mrs. Judah later stated that it was the Vanderbilt group, then in control of the New York Central Railroad, whom Judah expected to see. He sailed from San Francisco on the steamer *St. Louis* early in October, 1863, but contracted Panama fever at the Isthmus. He reached New York on the 28th, and died a few days later. He was buried at Greenfield, Massachusetts, the girlhood home of his wife. He lacked four months of being thirty-eight years of age.

Thus ended the remarkable career of a man to whom must be given the credit for originating a workable plan for the Pacific Railroad in California, of organizing a company to prosecute the work, of determining the location and of commencing construction. On Judah's death, enemies of the railroad endeavored to smirch his character, and none was more ready than one of the former promoters of the Sacramento Valley Railroad

[65]

and of a paper project for a railroad by way of Placerville to the Virginia City mines. Pamphlets were written and distributed, and the officials of the Central Pacific answered. They are of interest now, not as regards the railroad as built, but as an indication of the type of men who would stop at nothing in their efforts to injure the reputation of a man who could not reply, thus hoping to injure the project for which he had given his life.

There has been much criticism of the men of the railroad company for consigning the memory of Judah to oblivion. Therefore facts bearing on this subject are of interest. The board of directors passed a resolution expressing sorrow for the death of their associate and chief engineer, extended their sympathies to Mrs. Judah, and resolved: "That the death of Mr. Judah, in the prime of his manhood and the full career of his usefulness, will be felt far beyond the immediate circle of his acquaintance. His ability as an engineer, his untiring energy of character, and the success with which he followed his profession, place him among those whose lives are a benefit to the State, and in whose death the public experiences an undoubted calamity."

The resolution was signed by Leland Stanford as president and E. H. Miller as secretary. The *Sacramento Union,* headed an article in November: "Death of a Distinguished Engineer." In answer to some of the slanders, Stanford declared that Judah remained the chief engineer up to the time of his death. It is worthy of note in this connection that when the bill of 1862 was passed by Congress, James H. Campbell, Chairman of the Select Committee on the Pacific Railroad, and A. A. Sargent, of the subcommittee of the House, signed a testimonial to Judah reciting his services in assisting the passage of a bill through Congress and especially for the accurate and detailed information he had supplied. This testimonial was signed by thirty-five members of the House and by seventeen Senators. It was a most unusual proceeding. It was only natural that Mrs. Judah should see only the part that her dead husband played in the founding of the Central Pacific and voice some feeling against the men

[66]

of the railroad company. In justice to them, however, it must be said that there was not much they could do. Naming a station or an engine after the dead engineer would hardly have been adequate. It is inevitable that the memory of even exceptional men should pass away, for the living are but little concerned with the dead.

For over seventy years since the completion of the railroad on the lines projected by Judah, the traffic of central California and the West has been carried over the Central Pacific. In spite of the fact that eight other transcontinental railroads have been built, the central route retains its pre-eminence. The railroad was built on the route selected by Judah, and that is his monument. None better could be devised for any man.

### THE ASSOCIATES

After Judah had formulated plans for the Central Pacific project, it was necessary to enlist men of means who could finance and carry on the building of the railroad. It was natural, therefore, for Judah to turn to the friends who had assisted him in his first work, but it was not until the services of the four men who finally took hold of the enterprise had been obtained, that the project became a reality. Those four men were Leland Stanford, Collis P. Huntington, Mark Hopkins, and Charles Crocker. They were all merchants having their headquarters in Sacramento, and prior to the time of starting the railroad had never been conneced with a project of that sort.

The four men, known as "The Associates" and in the popular mind as "The Big Four," formed a group that was unique in American industrial history. They were men of diverse character but all were in the prime of life and each found a place in the work of building the railroad to which he was best suited. Stanford, with a flair for politics and the management of the railroad, became the president. Huntington, who developed into the most able of the group, became vice president and purchaser of supplies in New York, and what was of greater importance, the seller of the railroad securities to meet the construction costs. At the same time he attended to legislation in Washington. Crocker became the head and director of the construction forces and, as such, believed that he built the railroad; while Hopkins, an older man, directed the accounts and harmonized the diverse opinions of his three colleagues. These were the four men who carried the railroad to completion. Not being troubled to any great extent by the government at Washington, and without any material dissension, they worked well together, each in his own place.

### LELAND STANFORD

The man whose activities form a part of the history of California for more than three decades and whose name is perpetuated in the great university that he founded and endowed, was born March 9, 1824, the fourth son of a family of seven sons and one daughter. His parents were then living in the township of Watervliet, not far from Albany, New York, but they were both of families resident in New England since the middle of the seventeenth century.

As a boy, Stanford lived on a farm and was required to help in the work of the farm and in cutting wood for market. He attended public schools, and to complete his education spent a period, 1844-45, at Cazenovia Seminary near Syracuse. He studied law in an office in Albany and was admitted to practice in 1848 when twenty-four years of age. He then moved west to Port Washington, an inspiring town in Wisconsin, where he practiced law for four years until fire consumed part of the town, together with Stanford's law library, papers, and other belongings. He then returned to his home in Albany and on September 30, 1850, married Jane E. Lathrop, who was for forty-three years his good and faithful wife.

Stanford's elder brother, Josiah, had gone to California in 1851 and three other brothers had joined him. Thus it was that Leland Stanford, leaving his wife with her parents, also went to

California, reaching San Francisco July 12, 1852. The brothers engaged in supplying miners in the gold regions, and later Stanford conducted a business alone at Michigan Bluff, on a mountain 2,000 feet above the American River. After operating the business for over two years, Stanford, on hearing of the death of his wife's father, sold his business and returned to Albany for his wife. They made the return trip to Sacramento in the fall of 1855, when Stanford renewed his business alone, although the firm's name was Stanford Brothers. He next entered a mining venture, which, unlike most investments of that nature, was profitable. By the time the railroad project was brought to his attention, Stanford was a man of considerable wealth, and his grocery and mining supply business was making a good deal of money.

Stanford had been a Whig in politics, but at that time the party was dissolving over the slavery question. Having strong views on that subject, he assisted in forming the Republican party in California in 1857, and it was there that he met his future associates, Hopkins, Huntington, and Crocker. Stanford became the nominee of the embryo party for state treasurer in 1857 and for governor in 1859, but was defeated in both elections. However, in the critical election of 1861, Stanford was elected governor and served for the years 1862 and 1863, his influence being an important factor in keeping California in the Union.

Stanford became president of the Central Pacific about the time he was inaugurated governor, and soon afterward sold his grocery business to Booth and Company. From then on, especially after his term expired in 1863, he devoted his full efforts to the railroad.

When the Southern Pacific Company was organized in 1885 and the Central Pacific was leased to the new organization, Stanford became president of the Southern Pacific, which position he held until 1890, when he was ousted by Huntington, his former friend. Stanford, however, remained president of the

Central Pacific Railroad until his death in 1893.

In his later years, Stanford's interest in other things besides railroads became evident. With his wife, and later with his son, he traveled widely in Europe, and his absence from California, and from the railroad specifically, was one of the reasons for Huntington's displeasure. Stanford also engaged extensively in farming, having a 55,000-acre ranch at Vina on the Sacramento River, where the largest vineyard in California was planted and where the making of fine wines was studied. He also held a 19,000-acre ranch near Gridley for the growing of wheat. His principal interest, however, was centered in his 9,000-acre ranch near Palo Alto, where he maintained a large establishment for breeding race horses.

After many years of married life a son was born to Stanford and his wife on May 14, 1868. The boy was trained with the intent of succeeding his father in business, but he died in Florence, Italy, in 1884. He was not quite sixteen years of age, and his death was a stunning blow to the father. It was then that Stanford conceived the idea of founding a university as a memorial to his lost son, and in the succeeding years the project took shape. The enabling act for the Leland Stanford Junior University was passed, and on November 11, 1885, the founding grant was made by Stanford and his wife. The endowment was represented as being about $20,000,000. Construction of the university was started in March, the corner stone was laid May 14, 1887, and the university opened October 1, 1891. Herbert Hoover was a member of its first class.

In 1885, Stanford again entered politics when the state legislature elected him United States Senator from California. This election brought about a final break with Huntington, who claimed that the railroad influence should have been given to A. A. Sargent. Stanford served without distinction during his first term, and made a trip to Europe in 1890. He was then elected to a second term as senator in 1891, took his final trip to Europe in the summer of 1892, and died at his home in Palo

Alto, June 20, 1893. He was close to the allotted life span of three score years and ten, and had achieved success as success is usually measured, greater than most men of his time.

### COLLIS POTTER HUNTINGTON

The second in order of precedence of the four Associates was born in the village of Harwinton, Connecticut, on October 28, 1821, and died at his camp on Raquette Lake, New York, August 13, 1900. In Collis Huntington's seventy-nine years of unremitting work, he raised himself from a poor country boy to a position of being one of the most able builders and operators in the history of American transportation. Huntington's life was one of the best examples of what a man born with the ability and the desire to achieve great things can do in this land of opportunity.

His father and mother, William and Elizabeth (Vincent) Huntington, were of New England ancestry, their forebears having come from England at a nearly date. There were nine children in the family, of which Collis P. was the fifth.

William Huntington was a farmer and the only education his boy received was from the local school that he attended four months out of the twelve, the other months being spent at work. At the age of fourteen the boy left home and hired himself out to other farmers. At sixteen he was in New York City, from which place he engaged in various kinds of trading throughout the country, especially in the southern states. In doing so he accumulated sufficient funds to become, at twenty-one, a business partner with his older brother, Solon, at Oneonta, New York.

In 1848, after the news of the discovery of gold in California had been verified, the firm shipped a consignment of goods to California by way of Cape Horn, and in March, 1949, Huntington started for California with $1,200 in his pockets. Delayed on the Isthmus for three months, he took advantage of the stopover to deal in transportation and in the sale of goods, which

[71]

enterprise netted him an additional $4,000. By the time he reached California he was ready to set up business in Sacramento. In 1854, after accumulating considerable wealth, he formed a partnership with Mark Hopkins, whose store adjoined his on K Street. At that time steamers from San Francisco docked at Sacramento, which was a town of some 12,000 and the center of trade for mines of the Sierra Nevada.

The partnership with Mark Hopkins was ideal, since Huntington dictated the policy of the firm and was the outside man, while Hopkins attended to the bookkeeping and office details. The greatest confidence existed between the two men and their association of twenty-two years was terminated only by Hopkins' death in 1878.

When the Central Pacific was started, Huntington, after becoming vice president of the company, went to Washington with Judah to forward the Act of 1862. Thereafter most of his time was spent in the East, where he was active in Washington until the Act of 1864 was passed, which made financing of the railroads possible. After that, Huntington represented the railroad in New York. There he worked at raising funds by selling railroad securities and the government bonds allotted to the road, purchasing supplies, and chartering ships for freighting the equipment around the Horn or across the Isthmus of Panama. Finally, Huntington continued meeting men in Congress and in the departments where the issuance of bonds was attended to, where patents for the granted lands were made out, and where similar subjects were arranged. It was in these activities that Huntington's experience as a trader came into play to the great advantage of the railroad enterprise.

After the completion of the Central Pacific, Huntington carried on the work of building branch roads, of which the road to Portland, Oregon, was an example, and of extending the Southern Pacific Railroad through California, Arizona, and New Mexico to a junction with Tom Scott's Texas Pacific at El Paso, Texas, in 1883. By the purchase of some Texas roads and the construction of others, the Southern Pacific eventually reached New Orleans. There was a steamer line to New York, but Huntington wanted to extend the rail lines east of New Orleans. The other two Associates refused to go farther. Huntington went on by himself and in later years completed the Chesapeake and Ohio, and by finishing the work on the Louisville and Texas Railroad from Memphis to New Orleans, he became head of a system reaching from the Pacific to the Atlantic coasts. In 1884, the Southern Pacific Company of Kentucky was formed, as a holding company that united by purchase or lease all its railroads west of the Mississippi in addition to its two steamship lines on the Pacific Ocean.

In all of these later ventures, Huntington was the moving spirit. Hopkins was dead, and Crocker, who was not well, was not adapted to that kind of work. Stanford, who retained the presidency of the road up to 1890, was busy with political affairs, his university, and travel in Europe. Huntington, who seldom did anything else but work, complained that his associates placed the burden upon his shoulders, but this was obviously due to the fact that he had long since become the strong man of the Big Four and as such carried the heavy load of responsibility better than did his associates. Finally, in 1890, Huntington ousted Stanford from the presidency of the Southern Pacific and assumed the position himself.

It was well that he did so, for the panic of 1893 came soon after, with the result that many of the railroads of the country went into the hands of receivers. For many years, Huntington had been recognized as one of the great dominating personalities in American railroad and commercial life. Thus by his standing in the financial world he was able to save his road from insolvency. He continued at the head of the railroad system for seven more years, until death finally caught up with the old man in 1900.

Huntington's activities extended into fields other than railroading. The most noted of these was the formation of the

Newport News Shipbuilding and Drydock Company, served by the Chesapeake and Ohio Railroad.

Huntington was twice married. His first wife was Elizabeth S. Stoddard of Litchfield, Connecticut, whom he married on September 18, 1844, and who died in 1884. Later that same year he married Mrs. A. D. Worsham of New York and Alabama. There were no children, but Huntington had adopted his first wife's niece, Clara Prentice, when she was less than a year old, and the child was raised as Clara Huntington. Mrs. Worsham had a son, Archer, who also took the name of Huntington. Huntington, who often regretted the lack of a son such as Stanford or Crocker had, placed his confidence in his nephew, Henry Edwards Huntington, the son of his brother Solon, and to Henry Huntington was left a large share of his uncle's estate. After the death of the elder Huntington, the nephew married his uncle's widow, thus keeping the Huntington fortune intact. H. E. Huntington proved to be a man of ability and was active in the affairs of the railroad. He was also interested in real estate in southern California and in electric power development. He accumulated a large library of rare books and also a gallery of celebrated paintings, largely from Europe. On his death, provision was made for the world famous Huntington Library and Art Galley at San Marino. It was in this manner that the wealth of Collis P. Huntington finally came into the use of the public.

In his later years Collis Huntington indulged a taste for a few interests other than work. He had town houses in New York and San Francisco, a country place at Throggs Neck on Long Island Sound, and a summer camp at Raquette Lake in the Adirondacks, where he died. Andrew Carnegie once said that any man who died rich, died disgraced; and if that statement is correct, Huntington died disgraced. His wealth consisted of ownership of stock in many railroads and other enterprises, so it could be said that in this manner he used his fortune for the benefit of those who worked or rode on his railroads. He was said to have given sparingly to charity, but one who knew him said: "He was

[74]

not a petty person. In his later years, each visit to San Francisco was the occasion for liberal donations to charities, public projects and various enterprises, with none of which he was familiar. One of his associates would prepare the list, it would be given a brief glance and approved." His principle charities were extended to the Negroes, whom he met in his early travels in the South. He was one of the chief supporters of the Hampton (Virginia) Normal and Industrial School for Negroes and Indians, and he also gave liberally to Tuskegee Institute, his idea being that Negroes should receive manual training in the simple arts such as woodworking, blacksmithing, etc. As Huntington detested publicity, it is possible that his charities were more extended than his critics gave him credit for.

A man who knew him said of Huntington:

"My personal contacts with Collis P. Huntington began about 1890. Undoubtedly he was a man of great personal force, and knew what he wanted, when he wanted it. In the nineties he was approachable, and while he never could be classed as genial, he certainly was affable. If his instructions were inadvertently overlooked or neglected, there was no storming on his part, but the offending party sought another job.

"He brooked no opposition, whether from associates or employees, on policies which had to be determined. This may be firmness rather than obstinacy, for he was not only willing to take advice, but welcomed the counsel of those whom he had learned to trust completely. This observation as to his character was well known to his secretary, George Miles, whose counsel was always heeded.

"On the other hand, he ignored his associates in San Francisco in the selection of officers for important posts with the railroad company. A general manager, a general coast representative, a chief counsel, and a director of purchases were appointed without consultation, and no formal action was ever taken by the Board of Directors. In other words, from his New York office he made selections, and notified the directors afterwards, using the appointee as his own messenger. The results were undoubtedly satisfactory

[75]

as the appointments were excellent, and it is probable that the old gentleman would have been surprised if it were suggested that the directors liked to help direct."

The yellow journalists of the country made Huntington the target of some of their worst attacks, but nothing came of their tirades except that the general public even to this day have the impression, if any thought is given to the subject, that the builders of the Central Pacific were a set of unmitigated scoundrels who robbed the government and the people who lived where the railroad was built. A fairer judgment of men like Huntington will be obtained if it is considered that it is often men of his type who project and carry out great enterprises, which in the end benefit everyone. Personalities are forgotten but the great work that men like Huntington did endures. In this light, with all his faults, Collis P. Huntington should be remembered as one of the great builders of the America that the present generation has inherited.

### CHARLES CROCKER

It is noteworthy that none of the four men who built the Central Pacific had any experience in railroad construction or management. However, Stanford, Huntington, and Hopkins all found positions in the enterprise doing work with which they were familiar to a certain degree. Crocker, on the other hand, in his role of chief of construction, undertook a job for which he had no training along similar lines. That he ably filled the position and became a master of construction and handled thousands of men under him in extremely difficult conditions is a tribute to his native ability.

Charles Crocker was the son of Isaac and Eliza (Wright) Crocker, with a New England ancestry dating back to the seventeenth century. Isaac Crocker was a merchant of Troy, New York, and his wife was the daughter of a Massachusetts farmer. There in Troy, Charles Crocker was born on September 16, 1822, and he died at Monterey, California, August 14, 1888, at sixty-six years of age.

In 1836 the family moved to Marshall County, Indiana, where the boy worked as a farm hand, as sawyer, and as an apprentice in an iron forge. In 1845, when twenty-three years old, he discovered a deposit of iron ore and so, characteristically, he opened a forge under the firm name of Charles Crocker and Company. However, as with many of the thousands of young men of that time, the discovery of gold in California called to Crocker. He sold his iron works and with two younger brothers crossed the plains in 1849-1850 to the land of gold. He worked a while in the gold diggings, but in 1852 he had a store in Sacramento. In October of that year he returned to Indiana to marry Mary A. Deming, a union that was rewarded with three sons and one daughter.

By 1854, Crocker had prospered in his store to the extent that he was accounted a wealthy man. In 1855, he was named a member of the City Council, and in 1860, a member of the state legislature. Crocker, along with the other Associates, assisted in the organization of the Republican party and in the election of Lincoln, as they recognized the necessity of keeping California in the Union.

Crocker was one of the group that formed the Central Pacific Railroad Company, but when he took the first contract for building the line out of Sacramento he resigned from the directorate. When the plan of awarding contracts to a number of small contractors, as advocated by Judah, was found unworkable through the lack of laborers, Crocker himself took over and finished the work as far as Newcastle, California. From there to the state line, Crocker took the contract under the name of Charles Crocker and Company, but there is no doubt that the other three associates were silent partners. From the California state line to the junction with the Union Pacific in Utah, the work was done by the Contract and Finance Company, of which Crocker was president.

Worn out by his activity in building the railroad, Crocker in 1870 proposed to his associates that they buy him out. After a good deal of discussion, an agreement was reached in 1871, whereupon Crocker took his family to Europe on a long trip. He had retained his stock interest in the railroad and had taken the notes of his Associates for the money due him. On his return from Europe in 1873, payment could not be made, for the panic was on, so Crocker came back into the organization. It may be assumed that he had recovered his health and, tired of travel and inaction, like many another American, wanted to get back to work.

From that time on, Crocker was active in construction work on the lines that later became the Southern Pacific. When the California and Oregon line was under way, an incident took place that showed his personality and influence on the men who worked with him. Strobridge, the superintendent of construction on the Central Pacific, had retired from active work and was living on his farm near Hayward in a pleasant California valley. Crocker went to see him and told him he had to come back to work. Strobridge resisted, but in vain, and soon the two men were together again building railroad as they had done over many years in the past.

Crocker's fortunes, like those of the other associates, grew with the income from the railroad. They all moved to San Francisco and built their palatial homes on Nob Hill, where Crocker was supposed to have spent $1,500,000 on his. He also had a house in New York. In the years that followed, Crocker was active in other developments, mainly real estate and irrigation projects. The Crocker-Huffman Company built the large irrigation system that in later years, long after Crocker's death, formed the basis of the Merced Irrigation District, one of the largest in California. He also established his sons in industry and in banking. When the railroad company built the Del Monte Hotel at Monterey, Crocker had charge of the work, spending much of his time there. In 1886, while on a visit to New York, he was thrown from his carriage and severely injured, but on his return to California he continued active. Increasing age and sickness overcame him at last, and in 1888 he died at the hotel in Monterey.

Charles Crocker's forte was his ability to organize the construction forces of the railroad to produce the best results. At one time he had over 15,000 men under his command, spread over the mountains and working under harsh conditions of distance, snow blockades, granite cliffs, and, later, the heat and difficulties of the deserts. Crocker, who was always on the job and rarely saw his home in Sacramento, was a large, able man of cheerful disposition. There are many stories told of his violent temper and brutal treatment of his men, but they were usually exaggerated newspaper yarns. William Hood, who as a young man on the engineering force of the Central Pacific worked with Crocker, often spoke of Crocker's qualities:

> I have never heard of Mr. Crocker reproving or speaking to anyone except in encouragement and in a manner to increase the man's self-respect and instill a desire to continue in his good opinion. He was able to convince those working under his direction that he believed they were doing their best, and they did it. Crocker, going among a large force of men, so enthused them with his spirit that, when he went away, instead of work slackening, it went on faster than ever.

However, Crocker left a record that indicated that he was very much a driver of men. Even so, there was little trouble, probably because of the employment of Chinese. One who worked under him referred to the absence of labor trouble in these words:

"Wherever Charlie Crocker was engaged, labor and capital were just like this," illustrated by locking both hands together, "and it was some fist."

The fact remains that in the construction of the Central Pacific Crocker accomplished one of the greatest feats in the annals of construction. In a century noted for great works Charles Crocker was a great builder, and as such he should be remembered.

[79]

# THE FIRST TRANSCONTINENTAL RAILROAD

## MARK HOPKINS

The fourth of the Associates was a quiet, retiring man, older than the others by eight to eleven years, whose life was neither spectacular nor positive. However, he was one of the adventurous throng who came to California in the Gold Rush and prospered there. He was forty-nine years of age when the Central Pacific was organized.

Mark Hopkins was born September 1, 1813, at Henderson, New York, the son of Mark and Anastasia Lukins (Kellogg) Hopkins of Puritan stock. His father was a merchant. The family moved to St. Claire, Michigan, and on the death of his father in 1828, the son left school to work as a clerk for several years. He also studied law in 1837 with his brother, Henry. His leaning, however was toward a commercial life, with the result that he formed several business partnerships. At Lockport, New York, he became the leading partner in the firm of Hopkins and Hughes. Later he became bookkeeper for the firm of James Rowland and Company, and in time, manager of the firm. When the Gold Rush started in 1849, Hopkins formed a company of twenty-six men, each of whom subscribed $500. Called the New England Trading and Mining Company, the company shipped a consignment of goods to California by way of Cape Horn. Hopkins accompanied the shipment and arrived in San Fransico on August 5, 1849.

Hopkins settled in Sacramento after trying a store at Placerville, and in 1850 he formed a partnership with a friend, E. H. Miller, Jr., who afterwards became secretary of the Central Pacific, the firm doing a wholesale grocery business. The busi-proved profitable, but in 1855 Hopkins entered a partnership with Collis P. Huntington in the hardware and iron business, a partnership that was terminated only by Hopkins' death in March, 1878. In the year 1882, this writer, as a telegraph boy, clad in a bright blue uniform with brass buttons, delivered messages to the firm of Huntington, Hopkins and Co.

When the Central Pacific Company was formed in 1861,

Hopkins became treasurer, continuing in that position until his death. In 1854 he married his cousin, Mary Frances Sherwood, but there were no children from the marriage. A nephew, E. W. Hopkins, was of some assistance to his uncle, but Hopkins relied more upon a young man, Timothy Nolan, the son an an emigrant family whose father was dead. Timothy became known as Timothy Hopkins, and after Hopkins' death was adopted as a son by the widow. He also succeeded to the position of treasurer of the railroad company, and in later years was a member of the successor group that managed the railroad.

One side of Hopkins' character is shown by the trust that the other three associates reposed in him. Older than the others, to whom he became "Uncle Mark," his judgment was respected, and at times he could be firm in carrying out his ideas. Huntington trusted him in everything, which is a trust that the vice president did not repose in many others. "I never thought anything finished until Hopkins looked at it," was his statement to Bancroft, the historian who referred to Hopkins as the "balance-wheel of the Associates and one of the truest and best men that ever lived."

Hopkins, always frugal and disliking display, finally yielded to his wife's entreaties and built an ornate mansion on Nob Hill in San Francisco, where Crocker and Stanford were building. However, his health was failing, and while on a trip to Arizona to recuperate, he died. There was no will and a long series of lawsuits followed his death. His wife after many years married a young man, and with the exception of a partition with Timothy Hopkins, the estate, valued at $20,000,000, was no longer of great influence in railroad affairs.

### THE ENGINEERS

#### SAMUEL S. MONTAGUE

The sudden death of Theodore Judah left the Central Pacific without a chief engineer until the time when his place was taken by one of the men who had worked under him on the surveys that he made. Evidently the choice was a good one, for Samuel Montague continued in that position during the construction of the line and for a number of years thereafter, first as acting chief engineer, and later as chief engineer.

Samuel Skerry Montague, the son of Richard and Content Montague, was born at Keene, New Hampshire, July 6, 1830. In 1836 the family, including another son, John, moved to Rockford, Illinois, where, like thousands of other families of that time, they engaged in farming the new land. He attended public school during the winter months and the Rockford Classical School.

Montague's first engineering employment came in 1852 when he was twenty-two years of age, on the Rock Island and Rockford Railroad. Later he was with the Peoria and Bureau Valley Railroad, then with the Rock Island and Peoria, and finally with the Burlington and Missouri River Railroad. It was on these lines that he gained such engineering education as he possessed when he went to work for the Central Pacific.

In 1859, Montague with three companions joined the rush to the Colorado gold mines, commonly called the "Pikes Peak or Bust" rush. They probably did not find any gold, for the party continued on to California, arriving in the fall of the year. At that time the railroad from Folsom to Marysville was under construction and Montague secured a position with that line, which was a continuation of the road from Sacramento to Folsom, built by Judah.

Apparently Montague became acquainted with Judah, for on February 12, 1862, he went to work for the Central Pacific, probably on the location surveys that Judah was making for the line over the Sierra Nevada. It is also evident that he gained the confidence of the men who were building the road, because when Judah died, Montague was made acting chief engineer, a position he filled with such success that on March 31, 1868, he was made chief engineer, the position he held until his death.

[82]

Evidence of the confidence he inspired may be seen in the cordial approval given the relocation of a part of the line by George Gray, the consulting engineer. Strobridge, the superintendent of construction, who took a slightly dim view of engineers generally, simply said that Montague "was a smart man but had not had much experience when he commenced on the Central Pacific."

Montague directed the extensive surveys across Nevada and Utah as far east as Green River, Wyoming, and had charge of all engineering until the line was completed to Promontory in May, 1869. He continued as chief engineer of the Central Pacific during construction of numerous lines in California up to his death in 1883.

Montague was married in San Francisco on February 13, 1868 to Louisa Adams Redington, a sister of Charles H. Redington, long an official of the Southern Pacific Company. There were four children. The family home was in Oakland, California and when Samuel Montague died on September 24, 1883, it was there that he was buried.

### LEWIS M. CLEMENT

In most big organizations there is an assistant upon whom the chief relies to carry out plans. Such a man was Lewis Clement, practically assistant chief engineer during the location and construction of the Central Pacific.

Lewis M. Clement was born at Niagara in the province of Ontario, Canada, in August, 1837, and after a long and useful life, died at Hayward, California, October 29, 1914. He had married Charlotte Crysler on February 1, 1858, and she followed the wandering engineer, as many another wife did in those days.

Clement was educated at Jesuit College in Montreal, and at the age of twenty he was employed by the Montreal Waterworks. Additional engineering experience was gained on the Welland Canal and also on the Port Dover and Hamilton Railroad. At the outbreak of the Civil War, he was a telegraph operator at St. Louis, from which place he crossed the plains to California on a trip of 149 days, arriving in the fall of 1861.

In 1862, he joined the Central Pacific under Judah and was soon placed in charge of location of the road, on which he worked until its completion. When Judah died and Samuel S. Montague succeeded him, Clement continued as assistant chief engineer, his work then being on location up the western slope of the Sierra Nevada and down the eastern side to the Truckee River. One notable feature of his work was his location of the line around a steep mountain cliff called Cape Horn, some three miles from Colfax. Here the road is 1,200 feet above the American River.

It should be mentioned that the final location of a railroad is made only after a number of preliminary lines have been run and information obtained upon which trial locations are made, cost estimates prepared, and a final decision reached as to where the road is to be built. Such surveys had been made up the mountains by Judah, and the general route determined. After his death more complete examinations were made by additional surveys, and in some important cases material changes were made. Such work was done by Clement, working under Montague, and the line was located where the road was built as it exists today. The revised location was examined by Mr. Gray, who had been appointed consulting engineer for the railroad, and Gray speaks in very complimentary terms of the location, which covered the road from Dutch Flat to the summit of the mountains, a distance of some forty miles of extremely difficult construction.

Clement continued on the location across Nevada and Utah, and in several letters Stanford, working from Salt Lake, mentions the work done by "Clem" over the Promontory Mountains. He was active in operation and devised the system by which the road was patrolled through thirty-seven miles of snow sheds from Blue Canyon to Truckee. He also designed the emigrant sleeping cars that were built at the Sacramento shops. Looking back on those cars, from personal experience this writer cannot regard them as perfection; however, they served the purpose.

Clement remained with the railroad for many years. His position as assistant chief engineer is shown by a circular letter sent by Montague to engineers in charge and assistant engineers, dated August 18, 1869, which reads: "Hereafter and until further instructions, communications to the Chief Engineer's office will be addressed to Mr. L. M. Clement who is authorized to issue instructions and transact business of the engineer department in my absence."

In 1879 Clement's name appeared as superintendent of track, but in 1881 he left the Southern Pacific organization and for two years acted as engineer on the California Division of the Atlantic and Pacific Railroad of the Santa Fe System. Returning to San Francisco, Clement spent several years building street-car systems operated by cable and also helped build two electric street-car systems in San Francisco and Oakland.

In his later years he was frequently consulted by railroad people and was of special assistance to Stanford in erecting the buildings for the new university. Mr. Clement was a man of wide culture, and in addition to being a Mason he was a member of numerous learned societies both in this country and abroad.

### JAMES HARVEY STROBRIDGE

Strobridge, or "Stro," as he was called, was the kind of a man whose ability to command other men brings them to the front in any situation where initiative, willingness to take responsibility, and determination to press forward under adverse conditions are demanded. Strobridge was superintendent of construction during the building of the Central Pacific and, under Crocker, his was the driving force that put the road through.

Of American ancestry, Strobridge was born on a farm in Vermont, April 21, 1827, and he died at his home near Hayward, California. Early in life he engaged in railroad construction, but catching the gold fever, he came to California by way of Cape Horn, landing in San Francisco in July, 1849. He tried gold mining for a time with a partner, E. M. Pitcher, engaged in teaming to the mines, tried farming, and then conducted a hotel. Like many other men, Strobridge drifted from one venture to another and it was while employed as foreman of an hydraulic mine that he came to the notice of Charles Crocker, who employed him in the early construction work on the Central Pacific. For five years he had charge of construction, in which time Crocker came to rely upon him in everything. Strobridge, who lived with his wife in a box car along the line, but was everywhere on the road, gained the reputation of being a hard-driving taskmaster, ruthless in his treatment of men, especially of the Chinese. He was opposed to their employment at first, but soon recognized their many valuable traits and at one time had as many as 15,000 under his charge. Many stories have been told about his character and, as is usual, they have lost nothing in the telling.

Mr. W. B. Storey, who for many years engaged in railroad work in California and was a long-time president of the Santa Fe Railroad, gave the author of this book his impressions of Strobridge.

> In accordance with your request I am giving you my recollections of J. H. Strobridge, Superintendent of Construction during the building of the Central Pacific and later of the Southern Pacific and other subsidiaries of the Central.
>
> I first became acquainted with Mr. Strobridge about 1883 when work was begun on the extension into Oregon, north of Redding. . . . Mr. Strobridge was in complete charge of all grading and track-laying forces. Incidentally, I might mention that Mr. Arthur Brown was in charge of all timber and bridge work and his duty was done so as not to cause delay to the grading and track laying.
>
> The outfit that began working at Redding had just finished building the line from Mohave to Needles, and previous to that had completed the Southern Pacific to a

LELAND STANFORD

MARK HOPKINS

COLLIS P. HUNTINGTON

CHARLES CROCKER

OFFICERS OF THE CENTRAL PACIFIC RAILROAD COMPANY

Theodore Dehone Judah memorial in Sacramento, California, dedicated April 26, 1930, by the American Society of Civil Engineers, unveiled February 25, 1931.

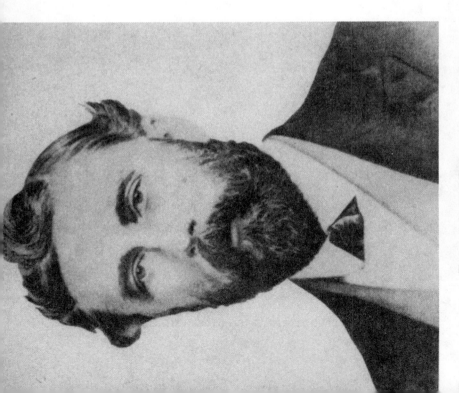

THEODORE DEHONE JUDAH founder of the Central Pacific Railroad and the company's first chief engineer.

**SAMUEL S. MONTAGUE**
Chief Engineer after Judah's resignation.

**LEWIS M. CLEMENT**
Assistant Chief Engineer.

**JAMES H. STROBRIDGE**
Superintendent of Construction.

CENTRAL PACIFIC CONSTRUCTION CHIEFS

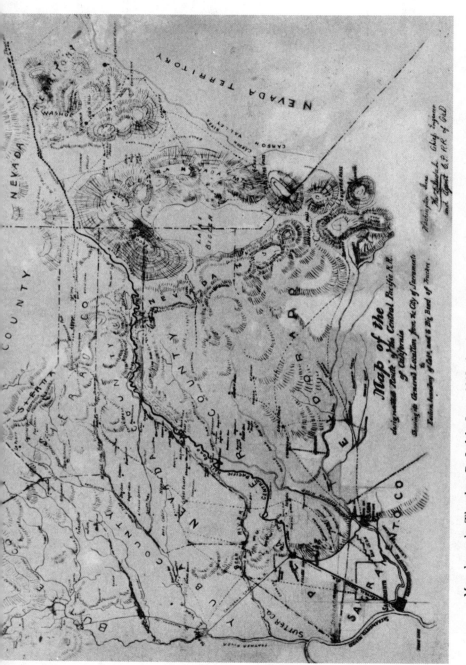

Map drawn by Theodore D. Judah, June, 1862, showing "Designated Route" of the Central Pacific Railroad through the Sierra Nevada. Judah's signature appears in the lower right-hand corner.

All earth material for this fill at Heath's Ravine in the Sierra Nevada was hauled either by wheel barrow or by one-horse dump carts such as can be seen on the level roadbed above. This picture was taken in 1865.

Central Pacific cuts were dug on more than one level to provide working room for as many laborers as possible. This is Owl Gap Cut near Blue Canyon, California, in 1866, in the heart of the Sierra Nevada.

Central Pacific track-laying operations progressed rapidly across the Nevada deserts during 1868. Lightweight rail in use at that time can be seen in the picture below. Heavier rail was laid not long after the road was completed.

Carlin, Nevada, located on the upper reaches of the Humboldt River was a typical Central Pacific construction town.

Two types of wooden bridges erected by the Central Pacific. The 1100-foot Secrettown bridge and trestle in the Sierra Nevada.

The first railroad bridge over the American River at Sacramento.

EARLY CENTRAL PACIFIC BRIDGES.
*Top*: The original span across the Truckee River. *Center*: Framework being erected for the Newcastle trestle. This crossing was filled in after the road was completed. *Below*: This Howe truss bridge at Lower Cascade was the model for the bridge shown on the Judah memorial.

## SNOW PROTECTION IN THE HIGH SIERRA

*Top*: Snowshed construction at Cisco near Emigrant Gap. *Center*: Snow drifts in mountain passes were invariably higher than the stacks of the early locomotives. *Bottom*: Snowsheds were sturdily built with braced peaked roofs supported by heavy timbers.

TWO TUNNELS AND A CUT.
*Top*: Portal of tunnel above Donner
Lake showing grading before tracks
were laid. *Center*: The ubiquitous one-
horse dump cart hauled excavated rock
from tunnel's interior. *Bottom*: A construction train enters famous Bloomer
Cut located between Auburn and Newcastle, California.

A Central Pacific freight train ready to depart from Truckee's barn-like depot while three wood burners with steam up await duty on a siding.

Central Pacific passengers were met at Colfax, California, by stagecoaches bound for mining towns in the mountains.

The fire-fighting train "Grey Eagle" tries out its hose at Blue Canyon, California.

Two commissioners settle themselves for an inspection trip on the pilot beam of the Central Pacific engine "Falcon."

The locomotive "Hercules" pulls out of Cisco with a load of baled hay and assorted freight.

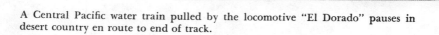

A Central Pacific water train pulled by the locomotive "El Dorado" pauses in desert country en route to end of track.

"C. P. Huntington," one of the Central Pacific's first locomotives, as it looks today.

"C. P. Huntington" as it looked while in service during the building of the railroad.

Close-up view of Engine No. 60, the "Jupiter," as it lets off steam.

President Stanford's train, powered by the "Jupiter," on its way to the meeting of the rails ceremony passes covered wagons going west.

May 10, 1869. The historic scene at Promontory, Utah, on the day that the rails of the Central Pacific joined those of the Union Pacific to complete America's first transcontinental railroad.

Picture taken in 1927 showing sign marking east end of the ten-mile section of track laid in one day by Superintendent Strobridge's laborers.

connection with the Galveston, Harrisburg, and San Antonio in Texas, this connection giving the Southern Pacific access to Galveston.

We of the Central Pacific engineers had heard of the forcefulness of Strobridge and the arbitrariness of his methods, neither he nor his men taking any orders from the engineers, and the only function of the latter being to give grades and centers and to cross section. I found, however, upon coming in contact with Strobridge, that he was an able organizer and a most competent executive.

The following which I learned of his record with the Central Pacific may be of interest. Shortly after work was started, Mr. Crocker, the member of the Big Four who was given charge of construction, in conversation with a friend of his who was engaged in hydraulic mining in the mountains, mentioned the fact that he needed a superintendent to handle the work and asked if the friend knew anyone who was competent to handle that job. The friend said he had a foreman in his employ that he felt sure would fill the bill and named Strobridge, who was employed and soon showed his ability as a driving force in the very difficult construction over the mountains, including heavy cuts and fills, tunnels, granite rock, snow of great depths, labor, keeping supplies going to the front, building wagon roads to reach the heavy work ahead, and the innumerable things necessary in this task which was of unprecedented magnitude. He has told me of problems he met and how they were solved. He was particularly proud of the way in which the Union Pacific was circumvented in its plan to reach the eastern base of the Sierras. That company did not get started building from Omaha until months after the Central started at Sacramento, but hoped to cover all the relatively easy country while the Central was getting over the mountains. A representative was sent to California to size up the situation. He inspected the work already done, saw all the difficulties and decided that the summit tunnel alone would take three years to complete. As soon as he was gone, Strobridge transferred forces to the east side, graded down the Truckee Canyon, hauled rail, cars, and a locomotive over the divide and laid forty miles of track, sank a shaft on the tunnel so as to work from four faces, finished the tunnel in one year instead of three, and was ready to rush the construction across Nevada, thus enabling the Central to get its share of the easy work.

Another thing in which he took satisfaction was the laying of ten miles of rail in one day. The rival railroad gangs had made successively larger records until the Union Pacific made an unusually large one and that record was apparently to be allowed to stand. Mr. Crocker asked Strobridge if he was beaten. The latter answered that while he felt he could exceed what was done he was willing to let the Union Pacific record stand, as he could see no good to be gained and the cost would be heavy. Mr. Crocker expressed the wish to have the attempt made. Accordingly Strobridge made his arrangements and actually laid ten and a quarter miles of rail in one day and ran a locomotive over the track. This was done, however, when the ends of the track were so close together that the other side had no opportunity even to attempt to do better. That record stands, so far as I know, the best that has ever been made. The rail was fifty-four pounds and one set of men handled the entire amount laid that day. Mr. Strobridge told me that he had provided a second gang to relieve the first at noon, but when the relief gang came, the first refused to quit and carried on for the entire day.

The roads were connected in May, 1869, and Mr. Strobridge then settled on a farm near Hayward, California. Subsequent construction for a number of years was carried on by the subsidiary construction company with some small extensions handled by contract. The main piece of work was the building of the Southern Pacific over the Tehachapi Mountain to Los Angeles and its extension to the Colorado River at Yuma, which was reached, if memory serves me, about 1877. Mr. Crocker then sent for Strobridge, said he was not satisfied with the way the work was being handled and asked him again to take charge of construction and name his own terms. Mr. Strobridge consented, but stipulated that he would not live on the work, as he had on the Central Pacific, that he would organize the work and visit it as often as he felt necessary and named what he considered a high salary in those days. He pushed the Southern Pacific through to a connection with the G. H. &

S. A. near Devil River, Texas, then built the Mohave-Needles line, and began, in 1883, the line up the Sacramento Canyon, where I first met him.

His organization consisted of a superintendent who represented him in everything when he was not on the line, several assistant superintendents called Riding Bosses, a wagon master who had charge of all teams and the forwarding of all supplies, a track-laying foreman, a work train outfit, and a clerk. The grading forces were entirely Chinese in gangs of about fifty-five with a white foreman, generally Irish.

He worked on the Oregon line for about a year and completed the track to a station called Delta. We were then transferred to construction work in Lang Canyon near Los Angeles. Mr. Strobridge had charge of this and of all construction for a number of years, up to, I should say, about 1889. He then continued to live on his farm and after 1889 took no active part in construction matters.

Mr. Strobridge was extremely energetic, forceful, very profane, and had a biting tongue. Nearly all who worked for him were afraid of him, but I always believed that the violent temper he sometimes showed and his bitter remarks at such times were assumed for the effect on his hearers. I know that his neighbors at Hayward always considered him a mild man and expressed surprise when told what a wild man he was counted to be on the railroad work. He was particularly hostile to saloons and liquor-selling near the work. I am told that on the construction of the Southern Pacific through Arizona, New Mexico, and Texas he usually had a United States marshal on the payroll, and if a saloon tried to open near the front the keeper would be arrested because his license was not ready, taken to some court a long distance away, and his stock of liquor would be destroyed by parties unknown.

I called upon him about 1897 and found him well and hearty, although nearly blind. He had lost one eye in his early construction work by going into a cut before all the blast charges had gone off and a delayed explosion destroyed an eye. He lived many years after my visit, but that was the last time I saw him.

Mr. Strobridge was a wonderful specimen of a man and

I admired him greatly. I counted myself fortunate in knowing him and always regarded him as a friend.

The letter from Mr. Storey has been quoted in full, as it gives a good picture of the type of man, who, in command of a large organization, drove the pioneer railroad across mountains and deserts to a connection with the Union Pacific.

### ARTHUR BROWN

Owing to the special nature of railroad bridges, and to a certain extent railroad buildings of various kinds, it is customary to place one man in charge of these structures. To him is delegated the preparation of plans and also the supervision of construction in the field. On the Central Pacific, Arthur Brown occupied that position during the building of the major portion of the line, so that when the unusual problem of the snow sheds in the higher reaches of the Sierra Nevada was encountered, it was he, as superintendent of bridges and buildings, who designed and superintended the work.

Arthur Brown was born at the village of Kentore near Aberdeen in Scotland, in 1830. Like many another of that wandering race, he was brought to Canada as a child by his widowed mother. There he lived at Ottawa with his family, securing such primary education as was then available.

When a young man, he was engaged with an uncle, Alexander Christie, in railroad construction of bridges and culverts. Coming west with his uncle to the Fraser River country, young Brown took a contract for a pier at Victoria, British Columbia. Then in 1864 he journeyed south to California, and in 1865 obtained work on the Central Pacific under Strobridge, with whom he remained one month. He was then placed in charge of bridges and buildings, continuing in that position until the road was completed. One of his most noteworthy achievements was his rebuilding of the bridge over the American River forty hours after it was burned.

Brown remained with the railroad and its successor organiza-

[90]

tions until the early 1890's, during which time a large portion of the Southern Pacific System was built. In addition to being responsible for buildings and bridges, he was called upon to construct the elaborate mansions of Stanford and Crocker on Nob Hill in San Francisco, as well as the original Del Monte Hotel at Monterey.

Arthur Brown was married to Victoria Runyon in 1870. He died on March 7, 1917, at the age of eighty-seven years, having long outlived most of the men with whom he was associated in the building of the Central Pacific Railroad.

### GEORGE EDWARD GRAY

It often happens in engineering construction that outside advice is sought by those in charge of the work. Such advice is usually of great assistance, not only to the owners, but also to the engineers in charge. It was the need for service of this kind that led to the employment of George E. Gray on the Central Pacific.

Gray was born at Verona, New York, on September 12, 1818, and after years of retirement, died at the advanced age of ninety-four in Berkeley, California, on January 1, 1913. He studied civil engineering under Pelatiah Rawson, a pioneer in the profession in this country. He was employed as resident engineer on the Black River Canal, New York, at two different periods, and once on the Erie Canal. He was also employed as assistant engineer on the New York and Harlem Railroad, was appointed chief engineer of the Utica and Schenectady and the Mohawk Valley Railroads in 1852, and in 1853 was made chief engineer when those roads were consolidated into the New York Central System. In that capacity he built the first wrought-iron bridge, and from 1860 to 1865 he acted as chief engineer of the Hudson River Bridge at Albany.

It was in a letter of July 10, 1865, that Stanford requested Gray to "make a thorough and careful examination and inspection of work already completed and the line as located." This referred to the changed line from Dutch Flat as located by Montague. Gray's comment was fair and approved the changes proposed. From that time on, Gray retained the position of consulting engineer on the Central Pacific to its completion. He also held the post of chief engineer of the Southern Pacific after the consolidation of October 12, 1870, for fourteen years, until he retired in 1885. It was under his direction that a large portion of the Southern Pacific System was built. After retiring from the railroad, he engaged in consulting service.

The preceding pages have given sketches of the men who directed the construction of the Central Pacific. Immediately behind them were a number of men who occupied responsible positions and to whom were delegated certain powers, the exercise of which was an important factor in forwarding the work.

In the executive branch of the firm, there appeared the name of E. H. Miller, Jr., one-time partner of Mark Hopkins in Sacramento, who was made secretary of the company in 1864, following James Bailey. Miller held that position during the construction period and for many years afterward. Mr. Edwin B. Crocker, brother of Charles Crocker and for many years attorney for the company, was also designated as general agent, positions which he held up to the time of his death. A. P. Stanford, brother of Leland Stanford, appears among the list of directors during the years of construction. The operating force of the railroad was built up slowly, since most of the traffic over the completed portion of the line came from material being sent to the end of the track. Out of the men who were employed, there grew an organization for the operation of the railroad after it was completed.

The engineering forces formed a notable group, as they were in the forefront of the preliminary surveys as well as in charge of work during construction. B. F. Leete was a friend and associate of Judah in the earlier work. Montague had three men, Ives, Eppler, and Buck, in charge of the preliminary surveys made through Nevada and into Utah and Wyoming.

[92]

Among the names of assistant engineers on construction are found those of Guppy, Phelps, Bates, Finley, Eaton, and Root. Charles Cadwallader acted as chief engineer for the Contract and Finance Company, and J. M. Graham was his principal assistant from Cisco to Promontory. William Hood, later chief engineer of the Southern Pacific Company, was employed as a young man on the survey parties. When the road was completed, most of these names disappeared from the rolls of the Central Pacific.

# CHAPTER 5

# The Central Pacific Railroad Company

THE CENTRAL PACIFIC RAILROAD of California was incorporated
June 28, 1861, with James Bailey, Lucius A. Booth, Charles
Crocker, Collis P. Huntington, Mark Hopkins, Theodore D.
Judah, Charles Marsh, Leland Stanford, and D. W. Strong
named as directors. The officers were Leland Stanford, president; C. P. Huntington, vice president; Mark Hopkins, treasurer; James Bailey, secretary; and Theodore Judah, chief engineer. All the directors were residents of Sacramento except
Marsh, who lived in Nevada City, and Dr. Strong, who came
from Dutch Flat. The directorate remained substantially the
same throughout the building of the road.

The entire organization from start to finish was dominated by
Stanford, Huntington, Hopkins, and Crocker. The other men
were of small means compared to the Associates, and they were
financially unable to undergo the stress of meeting the early

demands for money. The situation might have been different had Judah lived, but his early death left the Big Four in complete possession of the company.

The Central Pacific Railroad Company was a corporation organized under the laws of California. Unlike the Union Pacific, which was created by acts of Congress, the Central Pacific was not troubled by government directors or by national politicians.

Although the Central Pacific was a California corporation, it came into contact with the government at Washington through the Laws of 1862 and 1864, which defined the land grants and the terms of the subsidy bonds to be given the road. One item in the Law of 1862 about which there has been much misinformation was the limitation on the length of the Central Pacific's line. The clause of the law covering the matter reads as follows:

"The Central Pacific Railroad Company of California, a corporation existing under the laws of the State of California, is hereby authorized to construct a railroad and telegraph line from the Pacific Coast, at or near San Francisco, or the navigable waters of the Sacramento River to the eastern boundary of California, upon the same terms and conditions, in all respects, as are contained in this act for the construction of said railroad and telegraph line first mentioned (Union Pacific) and to meet and connect with the first mentioned railroad and telegraph line on the eastern border of California . . . and the Central Pacific Railroad Company of California, after completing its road across said state, is authorized to continue the construction of said railroad and telegraph through the territories of the United States to the Missouri River, including the branch roads specified in this act, upon the routes hereinbefore and hereinafter indicated, on the terms and conditions provided in this act in relation to the said Union Pacific Railroad Company, until said roads shall meet and connect, and the whole line of said railroad and branches and telegraph is completed."

It should be borne in mind that the Central Pacific had been organized over a year before the Act of 1862, and that the Union

Pacific was organized by the Act itself. The Central Pacific was permitted to build to the Missouri River simply because the company created by the Act, the Union Pacific, was not then in existence.

The influence of the Union Pacific was exerted in Washington in the Act of 1864 to curtail the rights of the Central Pacific, and therefore that Act limited the Central Pacific to a point 150 miles east of the eastern border of California. Huntington merely remarked that when the time came, that obstacle would be removed. An Act of July 3, 1866, did indeed amend the Act of 1864 to permit the Central Pacific to build eastward until it met the Union Pacific. The failure to control the meeting place of the two roads led the companies to expend possibly $2,000,000 in useless grading on parallel and near-by locations, half of which had to be torn up.

The Pacific Railroad Act of 1862 was approved July 1, and on November 1 of that year the acceptance contract, as required by the Act, was signed. Construction started in a few days, and two months later, on January 8, 1863, the opening ceremonies were held on the levee at Sacramento. This work progressed slowly on account of lack of funds. No government aid was available until forty miles of road had been completed. The projectors had to depend mostly on their own resources for money, and on the proceeds of the city and county bonds that were voted. The most important issue was in San Francisco, funds from which did not become available until a time when the amount was no longer of great importance.

It soon became evident that the provisions of the Act of 1862 were such that no money could be obtained and work would have to stop, which is just about what happened at Newcastle, thirty-one miles from Sacramento. Thereupon both railroads united in pressing for more liberal terms, and these were granted by the amended Act of 1864, after which, and with the ending of the Civil War in the early months of 1865, funds at last became available and construction moved ahead.

Another obstacle that the company had to surmount was the unyielding opposition of large sections of the general public and what was of greater importance, the active opposition of certain interests that felt they were being injured by the building of the road. The builders of the Sacramento Valley Railroad, which was then financially on the down grade, spread reports that the Central Pacific could not be built. Freighting companies, seeing their business threatened by the cheaper transportation of the railroad, joined the wolf pack, as did the existing telegraph company, for the reasons that a rival telegraph line was to be constructed along the railroad line. Steamship companies, seeing their business to the eastern states threatened, were also in action in an effort to defeat the railroad.

The best example of the attacks is found in the pamphlet entitled, "The Dutch Flat Swindle," to which the author purposefully neglected to sign his name. It would be difficult to think of any derogatory statement that the author of the pamphlet failed to include in his work. The railroad was to end at Dutch Flat and was being built merely to serve the wagon road from that town over the mountains. Reputable engineers had stated that no railroad could ever be built over the lofty mountains because no such road ever had been built. Affidavits were presented stating that during the voting in San Francisco for a bond issue in aid of the railroad, Governor Stanford's brother had gone from ward to ward scattering $5 and $20 gold pieces and urging the voters to vote for the railroad. In passing, it might be said that there was probably a modicum of truth in the latter statement, because it was often expedient thus to persuade the intelligent and free electorate to vote right. Such methods were not confined to California nor to that period.

The great obstacle to the building of the railroad was the doubt in the minds of financial men generally regarding the possible success of the enterprise. The desert character of the 1,000 miles of country from western Nevada to central Nebraska was well known. There was little or no traffic in sight and there was a possibility that even with government aid the cost of the road would be so great that funds would not be available to complete the project. It would take years to complete the line and meanwhile only the Nevada mines offered a prospect of revenue, and mines were, at best, uncertain. Again, the Comstock mining boom was on and money commanded high rates of interest. At first the deterring effects of the Civil War also caused doubts, but in time that was removed and the nation was prepared to go ahead in rebuilding.

At the beginning, it was necessary for the Associates to raise money on their personal credit. All were men of moderate wealth, but their resources were often strained to the breaking point. To illustrate, testimony of bankers prominent in California affairs may be cited. Lloyd Tevis, a banker of San Francisco and president of Wells Fargo and Company, who was invited to take a share in the Contract and Finance Company, in answer to the question, "What was your view of the situation of the Central Pacific Railroad Company and the Contract and Finance Company at the time?" replied: "I looked at it as a business question. I thought it was liable to great embarrassment and I very much doubted their ability to carry out their contracts. I was apprehensive it would involve me."

He also stated: "I am aware of the fact that the capital of those gentlemen was very limited—I refer to their individual means—because they were borrowing money in the market all the time, and of anybody that would loan it to them. They applied to me, I might say, hundreds of times. I occasionally loaned them money, and assisted them in procuring money from others. I know the fact to be that they were exceedingly hard run at times, and I was apprehensive they would fail to procure money in time to meet their obligations."

Tevis also testified that interest rates in San Francisco ran from 2 per cent to $3\frac{1}{2}$ per cent a month. Banks loaned at $1\frac{1}{2}$ per cent or more a month.

Mr. D. O. Mills, for many years a banker in Sacramento and

also president of the Bank of California in San Francisco, in answer to questions similar to those asked Tevis, stated that he had declined to come into the railroad, and gave his reasons:

"In the first place, doubtfulness of its success and the ability of the parties to carry it out, and in the second place, the giving up of an important business that it would involve if I went into the railroads.

"My understanding was that their wants were always pretty great during the construction of the road; that is, their wants for money.

"The difficulties were very great, and rendered their credit very poor. It was a constant struggle, and the sense of the community as well as my own, was against their being able to carry out the enterprise."

In connection with the need for money and the efforts to satisfy the demands of the construction, it may seem inconsistent with the known fact that after the passage of the Law of 1864 the first-mortgage bonds of the company and the subsidy bonds of the railroad were salable. The explanation, which has never appeared in any discussion of the subject known to the writer, is found in the nature of the country passed through and the resulting cost of construction.

On the Union Pacific, the easy part of the construction came first. For over 500 miles up the wide, flat valley of the Platte River and thence up Lodgepole Creek, the construction was the easiest on the line. The opposite was true on the Central Pacific. For about twenty-two miles eastward from Sacramento the route lay over a flat rolling plain and then met the Sierra Nevada, foothills at first but growing steeper and more difficult as the road led to the summit.

The maximum rate per mile of the subsidy bonds was $48,000, for which the company received in cash about 75 per cent, as the bonds were merely currency bonds with interest payable in paper money. Actually the company received about $36,000 in gold for the subsidy bonds and the company bonds brought in about the same amount. There was thus available $72,000 per mile to pay the costs of railroad construction, where the cost was running from $100,000 to $150,000 per mile. It was this situation that caused the financial problem that the four builders had to solve. Bank loans and the sale of city and county bonds were the source of revenue that supplemented funds from government and company bonds, which in the end enabled the builders to complete the road across the mountains. Stanford testified before the 1887 Commission that when they finished the road over the mountains the company was $5,000,000 in debt, a statement that does not seem exaggerated in light of the fact that construction costs were so much greater than the money obtained from the sale of bonds. Once the mountains were passed, the government subsidy of $32,000 per mile, discounted to $24,000 per mile in gold, together with the company bonds, enabled the work to proceed without further financial complications.

From the difference in the rate of the subsidy bonds between the $16,000 per mile over the valley lands and the $48,000 per mile for the 150 miles of mountain construction, a situation arose that at that time and later caused a large amount of undeserved criticism of the builders.

The acts of Congress that granted the subsidy bonds left it to the President of the United States to determine the eastern base of the Rocky Mountains, toward which the Union Pacific was building, as well as the western base of the Sierra Nevada, where the Central Pacific started to climb. In the latter case that point could have been anywhere from twenty to twenty-five miles from Sacramento. One of the granite outcrops of the Sierra Nevada was found at Rocklin, and this point was considered the base of the mountains as far as construction was concerned. That point was twenty-two miles east of Sacramento. However, it was to the interest of the Central Pacific builders to have the base of the mountains placed as near Sacramento as possible, as there the subsidy per mile changed from $16,000 to $48,000.

[100]

They therefore fixed on the crossing at Arcade Creek, a small stream seven miles from Sacramento, and a number of geologists of good repute were found who testified that the alluvial valley changed to a mountain formation at that point. J. W. Whitney, the state geologist, E. F. Beale, United States surveyor general for California, and J. F. Houghton, state surveyor general, wrote letters, the first and last locating the base of the mountains at Arcade Creek and the second, approximately midway between Sacramento and Folsom.

With that evidence in front of him, the harassed Abraham Lincoln signed a paper fixing Arcade Creek as the beginning of the mountains. Geographically, this may have been true. From a construction standpoint it was incorrect, since there was no difference in the rolling plain for at least fifteen miles farther. The result was that the builders were able to obtain $450,000 face value additional subsidy bonds, but as the mileage of subsidy bonds at that rate was limited by the law to 150 miles, it merely moved the 150-mile section fifteen miles closer to Sacramento. Actually, it only increased the length of the desert section fifteen miles, and increased the sum obtained from the government $240,000, which in the end netted the builders less than $200,000. The money obtained by this method came at a time when the builders were in desparate need of cash and helped in pushing the road up the mountains. Out of this subterfuge has grown the legend of the deceitfulness of the builders, a legend that is still going the rounds.

### THE CONSTRUCTION CONTRACTS

In 1863, California was a long distance from the eastern states. The Gold Rush of 1849 and the years that followed had spent itself, but California was still a mining state, with labor scarce and mostly undependable. The first decade of the great mining development on the Comstock at Virginia City and Gold Hill in Nevada was at its height, so that prospectors were searching the mountains of Nevada for more gold and silver mines. Some

[101]

of the early California miners had gone back to farming, and for these reasons there was no labor group as it is now understood. This writer experienced the same difficulties in obtaining men for construction when mining excitement is in the air. Men would come to the construction camp dead broke and looking for work. Three weeks' work would provide them with a grub stake and away they would go, searching for that Eldorado that ever lures the prospector. Again it may be noted that the few short railroads that had been built in California before 1863 had not brought into being organized contracting firms, which later become a fixture of railroads in the West.

The first Central Pacific contract was given on December 26, 1862 to Charles Crocker, who had resigned from the directorate of the company two days before. The contract was for eighteen miles of road and included the bridge over the American River. The contract was said to have been based on unit prices for various items. The work took from February, 1863, to October, 1864, to complete, and the payment was $50,000 in stock, $100,000 in bonds of the company, and the balance $250,000 in cash, total of $400,000.

Following the first Crocker contract, the plan of using small contractors was tried. Cyrus Collins and Brother were given the contract for sections 19 and 20, a section being substantially a mile in length. Following this, sections 21 to 24 were given to Truxton, Knox, and Ryan; sections 25 to 27 to C. D. Bates; sections 28 and 29 to S. B. Smith; and sections 30 and 31 to Charles Crocker. It was probably on the insistence of Judah at an earlier date that this method was tried. It resulted in the failure of Collins and Brother to complete their work, which Charles Crocker was forced to finish. Those contracts cost $183,155. Crocker received $11,600 in stock and $65,537.42 in cash.

The delay caused by the segregation of contracts showed that this method could not be followed, since beyond section 31, near Newcastle, the work grew heavier. It was followed by a third contract to Charles Crocker and Company for sections 32 to 43 that was extended, with or without a contract, to section 138, the California state line. The total payments included $8,227,980.53 cash and $14,657,696.68 in stock of the company, a total of $22,885,677.21. The rolling stock, railroad iron, and other equipment for the Crocker contracts was supplied directly by the company.

The final contract was awarded to the Contract and Finance Company in October, 1867, and under it the road was completed to Promontory, Utah. The Contract and Finance Company was made up of the four Associates. Under the contract was included not only the construction but the full equipment of the road. The company was to complete the road, build all depots, station houses, turntables, and roundhouses, and furnish all the equipment, such as cars, locomotives, machine shops, freight shops, machinery in the shops—in fact, everything necessary to the running of the road. The purchase and installation of rail, ties, and fittings were included. For this work the contracting company was paid $23,746,000 in cash and an equal amount in stock, for a total of $47,472,000. It was claimed by Secretary Miller that the reason for forming the Contract and Finance Company was to invite persons with capital to put their money into the work in order to make certain the completion of the road.

In addition to awarding the contracts mentioned, Stanford went to Salt Lake City when the race with the Union Pacific was well on and contracted with Brigham Young for work by the Mormons on an extension from Promontory eastward, with the expectation of keeping the rival road out of the Salt Lake Valley. There he expended $751,964 on rights of way and construction, much of which was wasted. The Union Pacific had spent an even larger sum on grading work west of Promontory as far as Humboldt Wells. All of this was squandered, since it resulted in two parallel graded roads across 200 miles of desert, only one road of which was used.

After the junction of the roads, an arrangement was made by which the Central Pacific bought from the Union Pacific forty-seven and one half miles of its completed road eastward from Promontory to within five miles of Ogden, paying $1,502,000 in Central Pacific first-mortgage bonds and $1,338,000 in United States subsidy bonds, a total of $2,840,000 par value of bonds. On a discount basis of 75 per cent, the cash value of the bonds was $2,130,000, make the rate $45,000 per mile of railroad.

### THE WESTERN PACIFIC RAILROAD

While this history is concerned with the building of the original Central Pacific Railroad from Sacramento to Ogden, the affairs of the Central Pacific Company were involved with other railroads that formed the first rail connection with San Francisco, a logical deep-water terminus of a transcontinental railroad. That connection was made by means of the Western Pacific Railroad, which should not be confused with the existing road of that name, and also by the San Francisco and San Jose Railroad.

To understand why this circuitous route was adopted, one must visualize the topography of the region between Sacramento and San Francisco. The modern road follows a very direct course, but in the decade of the sixties the physical obstacles were great. The river had to be crossed at Sacramento, where it was wide and deep, and subject to heavy floods that inundate the region as much as ten miles westward. When Benicia was reached, it would have been necessary to find a way to cross Carquinez Strait. This strait, a mile in width, carries the combined water of the Sacramento and San Joaquin Rivers from the Valley of California, as well as the ebb and flow of the tidal estuary. In later years the railroad trains were transported across the strait by huge ferry boats, and it was not until 1930 that a bridge was built to take their place. When the Central Pacific was building, another crossing would have had to be made from Oakland, on the eastern shore of San Francisco Bay, to reach San Francisco. Therefore all of these difficulties were avoided by building south from Sacramento to Stockton and thence southwesterly over a low range of the coast mountains to San Jose, from which town the San Francisco and San Jose Railroad led north to San Francisco.

The San Francisco and San Jose Railroad, following the line of the early Spanish development of the country, was projected in the fifties, but it was not completed to San Jose, a distance of some fifty miles, until 1864. At a still later date is was continued southward. By 1868 the Central Pacific group became interested in the San Francisco and San Jose Railroad, which had been built by San Francisco capitalists, and in 1870 it became a part of the Central Pacific System. The location was mainly through a valley and no difficulties other than financial were encountered.

The Western Pacific Railroad, from Sacramento to San Jose, was a more ambitious project, initiated by the same San Francisco interests that controlled the San Francisco and San Jose. The original grant to the Central Pacific contemplated that the road would be built to a point on San Francisco Bay, but the Central Pacific transferred whatever right it had in the grant to the projectors of the Western Pacific. These rights included land grants and government subsidy. The Western Pacific was organized in 1862, and after an estimate of cost of $5,400,000 was made, the work was placed under contract. The road was located along fertile level valley lands except where it crossed the low mountains between the San Joaquin and the Santa Clara Valleys, in which San Jose is located. The contractors proceeded with their work until 1867, when they found themselves unable to complete the road. After negotiations, the road became the property of the Contract and Finance Company, which completed the construction. The road was 123 miles in length, and together with the San Francisco and San Jose Railroad represented a distance of about 173 miles between Sacramento and San Francisco. From a point five miles west of Ogden,

Utah, to San Jose, California, the distance was 861 miles.

It was obvious even at that time that such a route was too circuitous to gain much traffic, so in September, 1868, the San Francisco Bay Railroad was organized by the Associates and built by the Contract and Finance Company, It was twenty-six and one half miles in length, running from Oakland to Niles, on the Western Pacific. Entrance into San Francisco was obtained by ferries operated by two short railroad lines connecting with the ferries from the towns of Oakland and Alameda. All of these line were consolidated with the Central Pacific in 1870.

These lines are mentioned because the statistics of the Central Pacific were given in the testimony before the 1887 Commission, together with those of the Western Pacific. When the line from Oakland to Niles was completed, the distance from Sacramento to San Francisco was reduced from 173 miles by way of San Jose, to 139 miles, which included the ferry distance across the Bay of San Francisco. Entrance into Sacramento was made over the tracks of the Sacramento Valley Railroad, making the length of the two railroads at that time 149½ miles. The roads are still operated as one system, a part of the Southern Pacific Company.

### COSTS

No official company information is still available that would show the costs of the Central Pacific to the contractors, who at one and the same time were officers of the railroad. The books of Charles Crocker and Company and those of the Contract and Finance Company were undoubtedly destroyed to remove all record of the contractors' costs. The investigation by the Congressional Commission in 1887 failed to disclose any data upon which the costs as thus defined could be determined.

The cost to the railroad company, however, is found in the testimony of Senator Stanford and in that of other officers of the company, especially in that of the secretary, Edward H. Miller, Jr. The statements carry practically to the end of 1869, although some of the funds included in this record was for work done in the succeeding year.

The final cost statement of Mr. Miller is as follows:

| | |
|---|---:|
| Sections 1 to 18, cash $250,000 and 100 bonds of $1,000 each at 75 cents on the dollar ........ | $325,000.00 |
| Sections 19 to 31 ......................... | 183,155.05 |
| Sections 32 to 690......................... | 31,963,980.53 |
| Expended by Governor Stanford at Salt Lake.... | 751,963.78 |
| Paid to the U. P. Railroad Co. for road from Promontory to five miles west of Ogden, U. S. and C. P. bonds at 75 cents on the dollar.......... | 2,130,000.00 |
| Expended for track-laying, equipment, buildings, etc. from sections 1 to 138 .................. | 2,502,600.00 |
| Construction of Western Pacific Railroad from San Jose to Sacramento, U. S. bonds and first-mortgage bonds of the company, $3,940,000 at 75 cents (at rate bonds are estimated in Gov. Stanford's statment) amounting to .......... | 2,955,420.00 |
| County bonds issued in aid of the Western Pacific Railroad which had been expended on construction before it came under the control of Stanford, Huntington, Hopkins, and Crocker, net proceeds as per Gov. Stanford's statement.. | 400,000.00 |
| Expended for engineering, machinery in shops, legal and general expenses, shops and shop materials, wood sheds, snow plows, tanks, wharves at Sacramento, real estate, snow sheds, etc..... | 6,971,688.00 |
| For interest, general account, on first-mortgage and convertible-mortgage bonds, chargeable to construction account ..................... | 1,669,332.42 |
| Cash assets .............................. | 491,600.00 |
| Leaving a balance of ..................... | 1,689,340.22 |
| Total ......................... | $52,034,080.00 |

The balance was used to add to the American River bridge, building retaining walls in the Sierra Nevada, strengthening the north levee at Sacramento where the railroad was built, replacing trestles by filling, and similar work.

| | |
|---|---:|
| If the balance on hand January 1, 1870, of...... | $1,689,340.00 |
| be deducted to obtain the direct cost up to that date, the remainder is ................... | 50,344,740.00 |
| Gov. Stanford testified that the cost was more than | 48,000,000.00 |

The above figures are given for what they are worth as indicating about what the construction costs were to the railroad company. It will be noted from the above table that many payments were made from bonds rated at seventy-five cents on the dollar, which apparently was pretty close to the discount at which the bonds were sold.

The Commission of 1887 employed an engineer to estimate what the Central Pacific alone had cost, taking into account all the facts then available, including, "All that appears in the evidence relating to the peculiar and difficult character of the work, to the excessive cost of building the road over the Sierra Nevadas, to the impediments offered by snow and stormy weather, to the unusual item of costs arising out of the construction of snow sheds, and to the increased cost resulting from the rapidity with which the work was carried on and the necessity of expensive and unusual transportation of all material required for the construction of the road."

The conclusion reached was that the road from Sacramento to Promontory, Utah, and the purchase from the Union Pacific Railroad Company of forty-seven and one half miles, a total distance of 737½ miles, did not exceed $36,000,000. This may be roughly compared with the cost from the table prepared by Mr. Miller. The total there given is $50,344,740. Deducting the two items of the Western Pacific road of $3,355,420, leaves a cost of the Central Pacific alone of $46,989,320, or an average cost of $64,000 per mile.

The difference between the two statements of cost merely represents differences that can occur when entirely different bases are used in determining the result. Miller's statement was made from the books of the railroad company, with which he had been familiar from the first. The details from the original records of costs would merely repeat the story with the same result. The commission's estimate was made after more than twenty years had passed from the time when the road was built and the money spent. While the engineer who prepared the

[108]

estimate may have labored in good faith, it must be recognized that no man can, by any stretch of the imagination, rebuild the actual circumstances under which the builders labored. Again, the commission sat with the fixed purpose of showing that the four men of the railroad company, by employing the device of the construction company, had robbed the railroad of large sums of money. The commission's adherence to this purpose detracts from the validity of its conclusions.

The subject was complicated further by the difference in money value at that time. Government bonds were currency bonds with interest and principal payable in paper money, which was subject to wide variation. At one point during the Civil War, paper dollars were worth only forty cents in terms of gold, with transactions on the Pacific Coast, a gold mining country, being made mainly in gold. After the close of the Civil War there were boom times, with the result that prices rose. Therefore labor costs and efficiency were considerably different in the decade of the sixties from what they were twenty years later. The meaning of the word "costs" depended entirely on the position of the estimator.

### FINANCIAL

It remains to consider the means by which the necessary funds were obtained to carry out the work of construction. Senator Stanford gave the only statement of the major arrangements, which was supplemented by a statement by Mr. Miller. Combined, the statement is as follows, the record being dated January 1, 1870, and including the Central Pacific and Western Pacific:

## COMBINED STATEMENT

| | Face Value | Sum Realized |
|---|---|---|
| United States bonds, C. P. and W. P... | $27,855,680 | $20,735,000 |
| Railroad company bonds .......... | 27,855,560 | 20,750,000 |
| Central Pacific | | |
| Convertible bonds .............. | 1,483,000 | 830,000 |
| State aid bonds ................. | 1,500,000 | 980,000 |
| County bonds | | |
| San Francisco to Central Pacific.... | 400,000 | 300,000 |
| Sacramento to Central Pacific ..... | 300,000 | 190,000 |
| Placer to Central Pacific .......... | 250,000 | 160,000 |
| San Francisco to Western Pacific... | 250,000 | 175,000 |
| San Joaquin to Western Pacific.... | 250,000 | 125,000 |
| Santa Clara to Western Pacific..... | 150,000 | 100,000 |
| Land sales to Central Pacific........ | | 107,000 |
| Profit and Loss balance, Jan. 1, 1870 | | 1,610,000 |
| Total ................. | $60,294,240 | $46,062,000 |
| To the above must be added the debt at that time, including sums due the Contract and Finance Company of. | | 12,500,000 |
| Total ................. | | $58,562,000 |

From this must be deducted the following bonds after issued:

| | | |
|---|---|---|
| U. S. bonds not received by Central Pacific.... | $1,514,120 | |
| U. S. bonds not received by Western Pacific... | 322,000 | |
| Central Pacific bonds not issued ............. | 8,203,000 | |
| Total ........ | 10,039,120 | 10,039,120 |
| at a sale of 75 cents on the dollar... | | 7,529,340 |
| Total receipts to December 1, 1869 from bonds ..................... | | 51,032,660 |
| Add to this stock subscriptions paid.. | | 1,001,400 |
| | | $52,034,060 |
| Total of bonds issued or to be issued.. | 70,333,360 | |

It will be noted from the above table that the floating debt and amounts due the Credit and Finance Company of $12,500,-000 were not extinguished by the sales of the $10,039,120 of land bonds, which brought to the company $7,529,340. In round numbers, at the end of 1869 there remained a debt of $5,000,000 owing to the Contract and Finance Company. It also seemed that the contracting company owed the Associates $5,700,000 for money advanced, probably to form the capital of the company. The debt of the railroad company to the contracting company was apparently liquidated in 1871 by money obtained from the sale of the land grant bonds that were authorized in 1870. The railroad company had given the contracting company its notes, dated October, 1869, and May, 1870. To liquidate these notes, 8,953 land bonds were sold at a rate of $865 per bond, which represented a return of $7,744,345 of cash and a discount of $1,208,665. It may be assumed that substantially all of the return from the sales of these bonds was to pay for work on the railroad prior to January 1, 1870. The return is probably included in the item of $12,500,000 in the preceding table, together with other floating debts. The face value of these land bonds, $8,650,000, must be added to the total of other bonds of $70,333,360, making $78,983,360, which represents the face value of the bonded debt of the railroad as of January 1, 1870.

The $7,744,45 received from the land bonds thus sold must be added to the total receipts of $52,034,060 from the other bonds and stock, making the total $59,778,405. The sums realized from the sale of bonds were somewhat less, since there is included in the above amount direct land sales of $107,000, and profit and loss of $1,610,000. It should be noted that the issue of land bonds was for $10,000,000, the total sum realized was $8,643,661.82, and the discount was $1,356,338.18. These latter sales were made mostly from 1874 to 1878 and had nothing to do with the original railroad. They indicate the relatively high rates paid for money at that time, as the bonds bore 6 per cent interest.

These statements of bond issues and of the sums realized have been given to show the magnitude of the transactions that were necessary to build the Central Pacific and Western Pacific. However, the statements are not necessarily exact. The work of building the road did not cease when the last spike was driven at Promontory. Much work remained to be done all along the line, and in the next five years it was necessary to replace the iron rails with steel. A railroad is never finished, and as standards change, bridges must be rebuilt, ties removed, wooden trestles filled, new rolling stock added, and old, worn-out stock discarded. Only a general statement can be made, and from the cost and other figures given by the railroad officials it may be stated that the cost of the 860.66 miles of railroad from San Jose to Ogden was $58,000,000. Of this sum, the Central Pacific cost $52,000,000; and the Western Pacific, $6,000,000. The bonded debt attributed to this stage of the development was about $79,000,000, of which sum, a portion not known may have been devoted to other purposes, such as building the line from Niles to Oakland. The work of building feeder lines and absorbing other lines already constructed went on even while the main line was under construction, and to arrive at any exact figures of the cost to the railroad company from the general figures available is impossible.

The operation of completed portions of the line was an important element in furnishing money for the construction forces and in meeting the growing interest on the company bonds and borrowings. As soon as the road reached the junction with the line leading north at Roseville, passenger and freight trains operated. At Newcastle there was a long delay in construction, and so trains from Sacramento met stages that ran to the mining towns. The same was true at Colfax. At Dutch Flat, passengers and freight were transferred to stages running over the mountains to Reno and the Comstock towns. At Cisco, where there was another long building delay, a similar arrangement was made.

The earnings and operating costs summarized by Miller for the Commission of 1873 are as follows, the figures being for gold coin:

| Year | Receipts Total in coin | Expenses | Net Income | Interest Payments |
|---|---|---|---|---|
| 1864-65 | $ 519,095.84 | $ 190,886.14 | $ 328,210 | $ 225,033 |
| 1866 | 864,268.16 | 200,722.96 | 663,545 | 568,827 |
| 1867 | 1,433,645.74 | 333,623.92 | 1,100,022 | 810,761 |
| 1868 | 2,312,017.15 | 843,166.54 | 1,468,851 | 474,766 |
| 1869 | 5,670,822.25 | 2,993,523.19 | 2,677,299 | 1,507,147 |
| | $10,799,849.14 | $4,561,922.75 | $6,237,927 | $3,586,534 |

### SUMMARY

| | |
|---|---|
| Total receipts, six years | $10,799,849 |
| Total expenses | 4,561,922 |
| Net income | 6,237,927 |
| Deduct interest paid | 3,586,534 |
| Net amount available in cash | $2,651,393 |

The operation of the road thus furnished money that not only paid bond interest but also contributed a substantial amount of cash for paying construction costs. The profit and loss balance of $1,610,000 included in the table of available funds was without doubt made up of cash received from operations.

In 1862, when the road was organized, the capital stock was set at $8,500,000, the shares having at all times a par value of $100 a share. The California law required that the capital stock should equal in value any bonded debt incurred. As the work proceeded and the scope of the enterprise enlarged, it became evident that an increase in the capital was necessary, so in 1864 the capitalization was raised to $20,000,000. Later, in 1868, it was found that this amount was not sufficient and it was raised to $100,000,000.

The disposal of the stock during the period to January 1, 1870, together with issues to care for debts incurred, was as follows, the amounts being expressed at par value:

Charles Crocker & Company contracts:

| | | |
|---|---:|---:|
| Sections 1 to 18 inclusive | $50,000 | |
| Sections 30 to 31 | 11,600 | $61,600 |
| Sections 32 to 54 | 1,044,767 | |
| Sections 55 to 138 | 13,612,930 | 14,657,697 |
| Contract and Finance Company | | 23,736,000 |
| | | |
| Total on Central Pacific contracts | | 38,455,297 |
| Issued under subscriptions | | 1,999,700 |
| Western Pacific Consolidation | | 7,900,000 |
| | | |
| Total stock issue, Central and Western Pacific | | $48,354,997 |

In his testimony before the Commission of 1887, Senator Stanford testified that the stock issue was about $54,000,000. That figure was reached by including stock issued on the construction of other roads as extensions to the Central Pacific, the account being carried forward from the above tabulation:

| | |
|---|---:|
| California and Oregon Railroad | $1,838,300 |
| San Joaquin Valley Railroad | 305,000 |
| San Francisco, Oakland and Alameda Railroads | 706,300 |
| Contract and Finance Company, February 24, 1871 | 1,281,500 |
| Contract and Finance Company, April 29, 1871 | 2,000,000 |
| | |
| Combined total | 54,486,097 |
| Deduct forfeited shares | 283,000 |
| | |
| Net total issued | 54,203,097 |

In considering only the Central and Western Pacific Railroads, the figure of $48,355,000 should be used, although it is uncertain for what construction the two payments were made to the Contract and Finance Company. The assumption is that it was for the branch roads mentioned.

It was freely admitted that the stock had little or no value when issued. In the first contracts Crocker rated the stock at fifty cents on the dollar, but this was soon reduced to thirty cents. Attempts were made, without success, to sell the stock, and the general opinion now is that it was worth only ten cents per share. When Crocker sold his holdings in the fall of 1871, the stock was rated at thirteen cents a share. Attempts of the Associates to sell out to San Francisco capitalists failed, so that when Crocker returned from Europe in 1873, he was forced take his stock back and resume his place in the directorate. At that time the $48,000,000 of stock was probably worth less than $5,000,000, with no one to purchase it. The stock in those days merely represented the chance for future profit, provided the railroad became a paying proposition. When on September 13, 1873, the first dividend on the stock was paid, the rate was 3 per cent. The one on April 1, 1875, was 6 per cent, after which the annual rate declined to 3 per cent. Including the dividend of January 15, 1884, the sum of $34,308,055 was paid, most of which went to the Associates. Naturally the stock rose in value, and much of that belonging to the Associates was sold. This constituted the major reward of the four men who built and financed the Central Pacific.

Even at the time the railroad was built, it was well known that the device of the construction companies made up of the railroad directors was a subterfuge. Its obvious purpose was to secure the stock as a bonus for the risk that the Associates took in the enterprise. The idea was for Crocker to make over the stock he received on his contracts to the Credit and Finance Company, and later when that company was dissolved, each of the Associates received his share of the stock, about $13,000,000 at face value. Whatever real return the stock made to the individuals is not known.

The same procedure was followed in the construction of the extensions of the Central Pacific, the absorption of other roads, and finally in the building of the Southern Pacific. To say that by this practice Stanford, Huntington, Hopkins, and Crocker became wealthy is something of an understatement. Nevertheless, it is equally true that the Associates built one of the great railroad systems of the West, which still operates to the great benefit of the region through which it runs.

## LANDS

The original Act of 1862 gave the company five 640-acre sections on alternate sides of the railroad line. The Act of 1864 doubled the grant, making it twenty sections or 12,800 acres per mile, extending ten miles on alternate sides of the line. Owing to the line's irregularities, the actual amount of land granted was less than the theoretical amount. In addition, mineral lands were excepted from the grant as well as all lands already preempted. Since the extent of mineral lands could not be determined in advance, there was some uncertainty about the total acreage. The amount of land remained indefinite until the actual route was determined by definite surveys. For these reasons, statements of the acreage allotted to the railroads varied from time to time.

In 1883, the Commissioner of Railroads, in reporting to the Secretary of the Interior, stated that the land grants were as follows:

Central Pacific—subsidized line, 737.5 miles, Sacramento to Ogden, total grant, 9,440,000 acres less estimated amounts previously disposed of 1,440,000 acres, leaving net granted lands .................................... 8,000,000 acres

Western Pacific—subsidized line, Brighton to San Jose, 123.16 miles, lands 1,576,448 acres, of which the company would obtain.......... 1,100,000 acres

Total .......................... 9,100,000 acres

The Western Pacific had disposed of its lands before its absorption by the Central Pacific. At the date of the report in 1883, the company had disposed of 780,879 acres. In fact, it was the policy of the company to dispose of its lands as rapidly as possible. The prices to settlers varied from $2.50 per acre up to $20 per acre, the latter figures being for land covered with timber. The benefit to the railroad came from traffic developed by the settlers on the land rather than from the sale of the land itself, which was sold on very reasonable terms. The best land was in California, where about 1,000,000 acres were available after deductions. The Nevada and Utah lands were mostly desert. At the present time unsold land amounts to approximately 5,000,000 acres.

Everything considered, the land grant was of little direct assistance to the Central Pacific during construction, since the total sum available therefrom was only $107,000. Notwithstanding ,the land grant was a big help in selling the company's first-mortgage bonds. Later, in 1871, a land-grant mortgage of $10,000,000 was executed, from which funds became available to pay off the floating debt.

Disposal of the lands would have moved more rapidly had the General Land Office been provided with sufficient personnel to make the surveys and to attend to the detailed work. However, unless the lands were under contract for sale, the company was in no hurry to patent the lands, because they then became taxable by the states. It took a lawsuit, together with a decision of the Supreme Court, to determine this liability.

# CHAPTER 6

# Locating the Central Pacific Railroad

On account of the magnitude of the undertaking of building the Pacific Railroad, both because of the length of nearly 1,800 miles and the remote and difficult country it traversed, certain principles which governed its location may be mentioned. In the case of railroad terminals as widely separated as Sacramento and Omaha, the shortest distance between the two is measured on the trace of a great circle. This trace cannot be drawn as a straight line upon an ordinary map, which is meant to represent the surface of a sphere on a flat surface. For short distances, the variation would be of no great importance, but over a spread of 1,800 miles there would be a wide difference between the shortest distance as measured on an ordinary map and as measured on a great circle. The topography of the country will rarely, if ever, permit a railroad to follow a great circle trace exactly, but it is remarkable how closely the located lines of the Pacific Railroad adhered to the trace of a great circle drawn between Sacramento and Omaha. The greatest divergence, some 110 miles, was found at the north end of Great Salt Lake and at the big bend of the Humboldt River,

On the line as built, seven topographical divisions of the country were traversed that were of major importance in fixing the route of the railroad. From west to east, these divisions were as follows:

(1) The Sierra Nevada, with passes at elevations of 7,000 feet or more;

(2) The valleys and basin ranges of Nevada and Utah having a north and south trend;

(3) Great Salt Lake, a body of water about eighty miles in length, north and south, lying directly across the route;

(4) The Wasatch Mountains, located directly across the route and bordering Great Salt Lake on the east;

(5) The high rolling plains of the Wyoming Basin, situated between the Wasatch Mountains on the west and the Black Hills (Laramie Mountains) on the east;

(6) The Black Hills of Wyoming, now called the Laramie Mountains, an extension of the Front Range of the Rocky Mountains;

(7) The Great Plains and the Central Lowland, extending from the eastern base of the Black Hills over 500 miles to the Missouri River.

The great mass of the southern Rocky Mountains also had an important bearing upon the location of the railroad. These mountains were regarded by the locating engineers of that time as practically impassable, from both financial and physical points of view. These factors determined that the location of the railroad should be across the Wyoming Basin, thus passing around the northern end of the southern Rocky Mountains.

### TOPOGRAPHIC FEATURES

Sacramento, from which city the Central Pacific Railroad was built, lies on the alluvial plain of the Valley of California. The city is located on high ground above the river, at an elevation of

[119]

twenty feet or more above sea level. The river, which is affected by the tides, furnishes a route for transportation by boat to San Francisco, about 130 miles to the west.

The plains extend eastward from Sacramento to merge without break with the Sierra Nevada. The rising ground of the mountains becomes apparent at a distance of fifteen to eighteen miles from the city. Along the line of the railroad there is a fairly uniform rise in 103 miles to the 7,018-foot summit of the Sierra. In the vicinity of Donner Pass, the mountains on the south rise to elevations of 10,000 feet, while to the north the elevations are somewhat less.

The Sierra Nevada is a tilted fault block, the central mass of which is granite. There is a long uniform slope on the western side, where rivers have incised deep canyons. On the eastern front there is a steep escarpment, with a drop of 2,500 to 3,000 feet from the high passes to the floor of the valleys that border the foot of the mountains.

The fact that there were two ranges of about equal height in the mountain chain to be crossed was important in fixing the railroad location. North of the headwaters of the South Fork of the American River, the mountains divide into two ranges, between which lies Lake Tahoe and the surrounding level lands. At the lake, the east and west distance between the two ranges is about twenty miles. The Truckee River drains Lake Tahoe and much of the surrounding watershed. This river runs northward from the lake, and then pursuing a generally eastward and northward direction for some fifty miles, reaches Big Bend, where it makes a sharp turn to the left and flows northwestward into Pyramid and Winnemucca lakes.

This favorable situation was recognized by Judah when investigating the route for the Central Pacific Railroad. He also expressed himself in favor of a route up the valley of the Humboldt River to reach Salt Lake City, a route that had been used for years by emigrants and was generally well known. It terminated at Humboldt Wells, from which point there was a choice of routes across the intervening mountains to Great Salt Lake, and then around the lake, either to the north or to the south.

### LOCATIONS

By the time Theodore Judah was ready to present the plan for a Pacific Railroad to investors, the main outlet had been determined. The road was to be built from Sacramento, California, to a point on the Missouri River, preferably Omaha. It was to cross the Great Plains, the Wyoming Basin, pass Great Salt Lake, cross Nevada, and go over the Sierra Nevada. Judah visualized the road as far east as Great Salt Lake and the road was built along the route he outlined.

Judah's final decision to cross the Sierra Nevada by the route that the railroad followed was not reached until after he had considered a number of other routes, each of which had its advocates. The investigations were made at various times from 1860 on, and were summarized in Judah's report of June 1, 1863.

Five routes were examined. The first was from Folsom, at the terminus of the Sacramento Valley Railroad, up the ridge via Georgetown to the summit of the mountains at the headwaters of the Middle Fork of the American River. This route was rejected because of the heavy grades required—150 feet to the mile. The second route was the one upon which the railroad was built. The third route led by way of Nevada City and the ridge between the North and Middle forks of the Yuba River. It was known as the Henness Pass road. This route involved crossing deep mountain canyons on the western slope of the mountains and a bad location to reach the Truckee River on the eastern side. For these reasons it was rejected. The fourth route crossed the canyons of the South and Middle forks of the Yuba River and continued up the North Fork of that river via Downieville and the Yuba Pass, and through Sierra Valley to the Truckee River. The fifth route led via Oroville, and up the Middle Fork of the Feather River, crossing the highest mountains at Beckwourth Pass. This route had the advantage of lighter grades and crossed the mountains by a lower pass, but it involved such heavy and costly construction that it was rejected. Years afterward, in 1903, the modern Western Pacific Railroad was built over practically the same route, excepting that it followed the North Fork of the Feather River. It was a costly line because between Sacramento and Winnemucca, common points on the two lines, the Western Pacific is sixty-five miles longer than the route of the Central Pacific. It was also true that to have built on this fifth route would have meant abandoning the lucrative traffic of the Comstock mines. The fifth route was therefore rejected by Judah, and his decision was sound.

After making his investigations, Judah decided that the railroad should be built directly across the Sierra Nevada by way of a ridge that lay between the Bear and South Yuba rivers on the north, and the North Fork of the American River on the south. He had made reconnaissance of the route in company with Dr. Strong of Dutch Flat in 1860, just as he had made a preliminary survey across the mountains to a junction with the Truckee River in 1861. The results of his work were embodied in a report to the president and directors of the Central Pacific Railroad, dated at Sacramento, October 1, 1861. Some excerpts from the report will explain his conclusions. Speaking of the survey he said:

"These observations demonstrated the existence of a route from Sacramento across the Sierra Nevadas, by which the summit could be obtained with grades of 105 feet per mile; accordingly, field parties were organized early in the spring, and a thorough Railroad Survey made, the results of which are embodied in the following Report, developing a line with lighter grades, less distance, and encountering fewer obstacles than are found upon any other route or line hitherto examined across the Sierra Nevada Mountains; and proving, by actual survey, that the difficulties and formidable features of this range can be successfully overcome for Railroad purposes."

[122]

Referring to the problem of reaching an elevation of 7,000 feet in the distance from base to summit, Judah said:

"When it is considered that the average length of the western slope of the Sierra Nevada Mountains, from summit of base, is only about 70 miles, and the general hight of its lowest passes about 7,000 feet, the difficulty of locating a Railroad line with 100-foot grades is correspondingly increased, as it becomes absolutely necessary to find ground upon which to preserve a general uniformity of grade.

"In the present instance, the elevation of summit 7,000 feet above Sacramento, is reached by maximum grade of 105 feet per mile; showing a remarkable regularity of surface, without which the ascent could not have been accomplished with this grade."

Judah set forth the general characteristics of the Sierra Nevada and described the ridge up which the railroad was located:

"These rivers run through gorges or canons, in many places from 1,000 to 2,000 feet in depth, with side slopes varying from perpendicular to an angle of forty-five degrees.

"The ridges formed by these rivers are sharp, well defined, and in many places so narrow on top, as to leave barely room for a wagon road to be made without excavating surface of ridge.

"The branches, also, of many of these rivers have worn out gorges as deep as those of the rivers, and present physical barriers to a line of communication either crossing them, or extending in a northerly and southerly direction.

"The line on top of crest of ridge being far from uniform, of course the lowest points or gaps in the ridge become commanding points, and it was found necessary to carry the line from gap to gap, passing around the intervening hills, upon their side slopes."

The most important controlling gaps were Clipper Gap, forty-two miles from Sacramento; New England Gap, six miles farther on; Long Ravine, about four miles from Illinoistown (Colfax); and Emigrant Gap, eighty-two miles from Sacramento. Beyond the last gap the line was on the side of a mountain and the gaps no longer controlled the surveys. The most characteristic portion of the ridge as described by Judah lies between Colfax and Emigrant Gap, an air-line distance of about twenty-one miles. In this section the distance between the Bear River and the North Fork of the American River is about four miles, the rivers running parallel and more or less southwest. The ridge between the two streams may average from one to two miles in width and is the remnant of an ancient peneplain. The ridge is cut by numerous small canyons, tributaries of the main streams. In following up the ridge it was necessary to pass around these gullies so that the distance of the railroad between the points mentioned would be about twenty-nine miles. This twisting of the location increased the length of the line by approximately eight miles.

The North Fork of the American River runs in a canyon much deeper than that of the Bear. At Cape Horn the depth from the railroad to the river is about 1,500 feet. Above Towle station, the railroad runs on the edge of the canyon, where the drop to the river is some 2,000 feet, while on the opposite side the Bear River runs 1,000 feet below. At Emigrant Gap, where the ridge narrows to a knife edge, Bear Valley is nearly 600 feet below the track, while several miles away the North Fork of the American is more than 2,500 feet below the railroad. These data give some idea of the favorable location selected by Montague for the railroad after Judah's death.

In the surveys directed by Judah, it was his opinion that the line could reach the South Yuba River bottom from Bear Valley on Bear River and follow it generally to Summit Valley and across that valley to the summit. However, it was determined later to keep to the side of the mountain above the Yuba bottoms and the line reaches the river only at Summit Valley, elevation 6,800 feet. Above the eastern end of Summit Valley, where the summit was reached, a tunnel 1,659 feet long was excavated through the culminating ridge, 124 feet below the summit. The highest point reached was an elevation of 7,042 feet in the tunnel.

After crossing the summit of the Sierra Nevada, Judah's problem was to drop down to the Truckee River. He describes the situation in the following words:

"From the summit looking easterly, you appear standing upon a nearly perpendicular rocky wall, of 1,000 feet in hight.

"Immediately below is seen a valley, from one to two miles wide, extending up from the Truckee River, to nearly beneath your feet. Donner Lake, (about three and a half miles long, by one mile in width) occupies the upper portion of this valley, and its outlet is seen pursuing its course down to a junction with the Truckee. Two long ranges or spurs are seen, on either side, parallel with and inclosing the lake, reaching from the summit to Truckee River. Immediately beyond the river is seen the second summit of the Sierra Nevada, while still further in the distance the Washoe Mountains are plainly visible."

The line was continued down from the summit along the mountainside above Donner Lake with maximum grades of 105 feet per mile. In order to reach the Truckee River as quickly as possible, advantage was taken of two ravines, the largest being the ravine of Coldstream Creek. Truckee River was reached after eleven and one half miles of maximum grades, the direct east and west distance being about eight miles.

The first surveys demonstrated that a line could be found up the ridge to the summit and thence to the Truckee River with maximum grades of 105 feet per mile. In discussing the merits of this location, Judah mentioned some important and favorable elements of the line:

"Running at first north-westerly about eight miles, thence northerly about ten, and then north-easterly about twelve miles, the Truckee passes down between these two summits with a nearly uniform fall of about thirty-five feet per mile; thence sweeping round to the eastward, it passes *through* the second range or summit, at a depression where it seems to be entirely worn away down to the level of the river, thence pursuing its way through an extensive plain known

[125]

as the Truckee Meadows; thence through the Washoe Mountains to the Big Bend; thence northerly about twenty miles, finds its way into Pyramid Lake.

"By avoiding the Second Summit of the Sierras and Washoe Mountains you are not only enabled to save the grades required to overcome these ranges, but also encounter a much narrower snow belt—the eastern limit of deep snow upon this line being the Truckee River, at a distance of twelve miles from the summit."

Judah also investigated the possibility of a line leading southward through the Truckee Meadows and Washoe and Eagle valleys to the Carson River, and by way of that stream to the open plains near Humboldt Lake. He rightly concluded that such a line was feasible but much longer than the one down the Truckee.

The reports by Judah give details of the location of the line up the Sierra Nevada, based upon his preliminary survey. Later location surveys varied from the original location at a number of places, but the line as built followed his first selection of the ridge between the Yuba and Bear rivers on the north and the North Fork of the American River. The route down the Truckee to the Big Bend at Wadsworth was also followed and it remains today the line of the Southern Pacific eastward from California.

On one point only was Judah incorrect. He believed that the snow could be handled in winter by snow plows, but experience during construction showed that this was impossible and that snow sheds were an absolute necessity in order to keep traffic moving.

Judah did not live to complete the location surveys eastward from the Truckee River, but he had urged the necessity of continuing them to Salt Lake City. In his cost estimates, he added to his own those of Lieutenant Beckwith as far as Salt Lake City and also those of the other government estimates to Council Bluffs. The total was $99,870,000. He pointed out important considerations that gave the route up the Humboldt manifest advantages over any other route for a railroad line. It was left to Montague and his corps of assistants to finish the line to a junction with the Union Pacific at Promontory.

The final location on which the road was built was made by Judah as far east as Dutch Flat, sixty-six miles east of Sacramento. His preliminary location beyond led into Bear Valley on Bear River, and thence up the canyon of the Yuba River. When Montague took charge, he made a more detailed study of the mountains and became convinced that a better line would be found by continuing along the mountainside well above the Yuba River instead of in the canyon near the stream. Had Judah lived, it is certain that he would have ordered additional surveys of this particular location and it is likely that he would have reached the same decision as did Montague. During 1864 and into 1865, further detailed studies of the location were undertaken, with the result that Montague submitted his findings to the management and advocated his location as having better grades and easier construction. Naturally, there was some question of adopting the new line rather than that made by Judah. To settle the matter, Stanford employed George E. Gray, who came out from the New York Central Railroad and examined the situation. Gray reported on Montague's location in the following terms:

"Mr. Montague leaves Mr. Judah's line a short distance above Dutch Flat, thence diverging to the right and crossing the dividing ridge to the North Fork of the American River . . .

"I did not pass over all of Mr. Judah's line through Bear Valley, but from a comparison of his maps and profiles and a personal examination of the line surveyed by Mr. Montague, I have no hesitation in pronouncing the latter decidedly preferable in all respects; it being more economical of construction, including only six tunnels of an aggregate of about 2,350 feet, and averaging less than 400 feet each. Besides, no loss of elevation is suffered, the grades are no heavier and the line is shorter by about 5,000 feet

[127]

between Dutch Flat and Crystal Lake, a distance of twenty-two and one third miles.

"From Crystal Lake to Summit Valley, and thence to the summit at Donner Pass, the grades of the new line will be much less than the maximum, far less than on Mr. Judah's and without any loss of distance or requiring a tunnel of more than 1,350 feet at the summit."

Gray also commented on the general excellence of the location up the mountains and assured the management of the railroad that the line as laid out could be built. Gray's decision settled the matter, and Montague's location was adopted. It was decidedly the best possible route.

The work of locating the line up the Sierra Nevada engaged the engineers up to the end of 1865. In his first report, dated October 8, 1864, Montague stated that an experimental survey line had been run late in 1863 to the Big Bend of the Truckee from the terminus of the Judah surveys. The result was "highly satisfactory, developing a line with easy grades and curves, and for the greater portion of the distance with very light work." Montague states that "from the Big Bend, the choice of routes must be hereafter determined by proper exploration and surveys."

In 1866, active work was undertaken to determine the route through Nevada and Utah to a possible junction with the Union Pacific. In his report of February 8, 1867, Montague says that the line had been finally located beyond the eastern boundary of California to a point thirty-four miles into Nevada toward the Big Bend of the Truckee River. Lines of exploration across central Nevada and through Utah were made by several parties under Mr. Ives, Mr. Eppler, and Mr. Buck. Two lines south of Great Salt Lake, together with the same number north of the lake, were investigated as far as the mouth of Weber River at the foot of the Wasatch Mountains near Ogden. The records show that a total of 3,623 miles of line were examined, either as a reconnaissance or by preliminary surveys. No portion of the central part of Nevada was omitted from the examination, and the same was true of the region of Utah westward from the Wasatch Mountains. The instrumental surveys extended from the Big Bend of the Truckee, "via Say's Station, Truckee Desert, Desert Gate, Sink Humboldt, north side of Humboldt Lake, and thence following the valley of Humboldt River to Humboldt Wells."

The result was that the original idea of a location up the Humboldt was confirmed. A glance at the map would seem to indicate that a direct line across Nevada south of Great Salt Lake to Salt Lake City might be the best. It was, in fact, the route of the overland stages. However, the physical obstacles were too great. The isolated mountain ranges scattered in that region would have made necessary a zig-zag line to round the ends of the ranges that lead through narrow passes. In addition, a uniform grade could not be obtained because the mountains, with desert valley between, gave an up-and-down profile that made such a location impossible. A line might have been run from Humboldt Wells south of Great Salt Lake, but lack of water along the route, the necessity of crossing twenty miles of Great Salt Lake Desert, which might again be flooded by the waters of the lake, and the twenty-five miles additional distance to the mouth of Weber Canyon determined the selection of the northern route. Montague's report summarizes the conclusions from the 1866 surveys and investigations:

"The route adopted for the location of the Central Pacific Railroad is via the line referred to above and also in the report for the year 1865 . . . following the valley of the Truckee River from the point where the line first reaches it (near Donner Lake) to the Big Bend. Thence via Truckee Desert, Humboldt Sink, and lake and valley of Humboldt River to the Wells (near the source of the stream), thence in an easterly direction on line surveyed by Mr. Ives, via north end of Peoquop Mountains, north pass of Toana Mountains, passage between Goose Creek and Ombe Mountains, skirting north margin of the Great Desert, to north end of Great Salt Lake; thence through the South Pass of the Promontory Mountains, skirting Mud Plains north of Bear River Bay to Brigham City; thence along the west base of the Wasatch Mountains to Weber River, and up said stream to the mouth of Weber Canyon. Distance from easterly boundary of California to Weber Canyon, 588 miles."

During 1867 the explorations were continued for a line to the north of Great Salt Lake at the same time that location surveys were being extended into Nevada and additional preliminary lines were being run. One of these preliminary lines extended from Wells across the eastern border of Nevada to the Salt Lake Valley. Another was carried from the mouth of Weber Canyon across the ranges to a tributary of the Green River at Granger. Trial lines were also run up the valley of Utah's Bear River, by way of the river and also across the mountains from Bear Lake to Cache Valley on Little Bear River. The country through the eastern mountains by way of Weber and Echo canyons, Chalk and Sulphur creeks, and along the northern base of the Uinta Mountains was explored by trial lines that extended to the tributaries of Green River. Together with running reconnaissance lines, the company explored the country from the western base of the Wasatch Mountains to Green River over a north and south distance of 150 miles.

The transit party starting at Humboldt Wells and ending at Salt Lake City covered 950 miles, while the exploring party traveled 1,430 miles. In addition, large-scale triangulation nets were made from the Big Bend of the Truckee River to the Reese River in Nevada.

It was quite evident from the wide extent of the surveys of 1866, 1867, and 1868 that the Central Pacific intended to build across the mountains into Wyoming as far east as the Green River. In fact, President Stanford stated later that they had hoped to meet the Union Pacific at a point as far east as Cheyenne.

By the end of 1867, the twenty miles of final location across

Nevada had been finished and in the first six months of 1868 it had been completed for 248 miles eastward of the Big Bend of the Truckee. In addition, final location east of Humboldt Wells had been completed to Independence, while locating parties were working on both sides of Promontory Point. When the roads were joined, after Central Pacific grading had been carried eastward to Bear River and Ogden, final location had been completed as far east as Ogden. Surveying expenses on reconnaissance, preliminary, and location surveys had risen progressively from the start. The amounts were: June 1, 1863, $33,889; March 1, 1864, $59,457; February 8, 1867, $181,121; June 30, 1868, $271,182.

It was the practice of the national government to have the railroad examined by special commissioners from time to time. One such commission composed of G. K. Warren, Brevet Major General U. S. A., J. Blickensderfer, Jr., civil engineer, and James Barnes, civil engineer, made a report to O. H. Browning, Secretary of the Interior, on November 23, 1868, in which the following statement occurs:

> "Ample surveys and examinations made by the Government, and by both the Central and Union Pacific Railroad Companies, show that the valley of the Humboldt River is a controlling feature of the direct central route to San Francisco. A line from the sources of the Humboldt River eastward by the north end of Great Salt Lake is more direct, and passes through a country, superior in many respects to that through which a line must be located leading to the south end of this lake, and consequently the line by the north end is the best, if the best location for the line through the Wasatch Mountains permits it."

The problem of location had been solved, but there were other details that required attention. The law granting a subsidy to the railroad had provided that grades and curves as used on the Baltimore and Ohio Railroad should not be exceeded. These limits were grades of 116 feet per mile and curves as sharp as 400 feet radius. However, principles of economy in operation dictated that grades of the least possible rise be obtained and that curves of larger radius be used whenever possible. The location had been made with these limitations in mind.

The line from Sacramento to the summit of the Sierra Nevada was the most difficult, because it had to reach an elevation of over 7,000 feet in 105 miles, of which about fifteen miles was across the nearly level valley floor. Therefore, the line was located diagonally across the mountains in order to gain distance. From Sacramento to the summit, there were 11.2 miles of level track, 20.9 miles of 105 feet per mile grade, and 9.55 miles of maximum grade of 116 feet per mile. Lighter grades intervened, the average grade in 195 miles to the summit being 66.97 feet per mile.

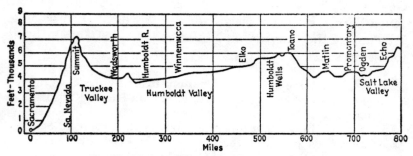

Profile view of the Central Pacific Railroad

From the summit, for 11.5 miles the line descended to the Truckee River, with maximum grades of ninety-five feet per mile. From that point for over seventy-two miles to the Big Bend of the Truckee, 189 miles from Sacramento, the line followed a descending grade along the river, the average grade being 35.12 feet per mile. Beyond the Big Bend of the Truckee River the average grades were all lighter, the heaviest, however, being 52.8 feet per mile. The Big Bend of the Truckee, where the town of Wadsworth was established, was at the western end

[132]

of the Truckee and Humboldt Desert. For forty miles the route led across the open desert to the west shore of Humboldt Lake. Skirting the low grassy shores of the lake, the line then followed up the valley of the Humboldt River for 291 miles to Humboldt Wells, 520 miles from Sacramento. The line was located away from the river in most places to avoid the bottom lands that were apt to be flooded. As far as Golconda, the river runs in the sediments of the former Lake Lahontan, a good region for a railroad to avoid. In this stretch of the line to Humboldt Wells there were several canyons and narrow gaps, as at the Palisades, but these offered few difficulties to the locating engineers.

At Humboldt Wells the valley of the river came practically to an end, so it was necessary to cross the intervening mountains toward Great Salt Lake. The location was not difficult, as the several basin ranges had wide gaps between them and there were also open valleys. The route was somewhat zigzag for this reason. About nine miles east of Wells, the highest point, with an elevation of 6,166 feet, was reached in a pass through the Independence Range. From that point on, there was a gradual down grade for sixty-two miles to Umbria Junction, near the present station of Lucin, where the Great Salt Lake Desert was reached. In that stretch of the line, such open valleys as Thousand Springs Valley were followed on through open passes in the Pequop, Toana, and Pilot ranges. The lowest point in the line into the desert was reached some twelve mile east of Umbria, where the elevation was about 4,340 feet. From there the line climbed the Ombe Mountains, a range of low hills about 375 feet high at the pass at Ombe, and then descended 500 feet to the flats at the upper end of Great Salt Lake. For about twenty-five miles along the shore of Spring Bay, the line was practically level. Monument Point, at 4,220 feet, was rounded in this stretch of line, 142 miles from Wells and 662 miles from Sacramento. About seven miles east of Monument Point the line commenced to climb the Promontory Mountains. The pass was through another open valley where the mountain breaks down from the north and then rises into the high range that extends southward into Great Salt Lake. The climb of 685 feet to Promontory Summit was made in sixteen miles, and from there the line descended the eastern slope of the mountains to the flats across Bear River Valley. The Bear River was crossed about ten miles north of Bear River Bay, the upper section of Great Salt Lake. Turning southward and eastward, the line followed the plains at the base of the Wasatch Mountains until it finally reached the mouth of Weber Canyon, 752 miles from Sacramento.

The valley on Promontory was where the line met the rails of the Union Pacific, but the Central Pacific line was graded into Ogden. The location of the two lines over the Promontory Mountains was practically the same, and, as both were graded, the observer can still see the unused grade, sometimes within 100 feet of where the rails were later laid.

Some statistics are available. In a distance of 450 miles from Sacramento, the location was based on 264 miles of tangent or straight lines and 186 miles of curved lines, of which the curves of minimum radius (573 feet) made up less than 1 per cent of the total length. East of Wells, for 219 miles the grades were less than 25 feet per mile for 133 miles; from 25 to 50 feet for 35 miles; and 50 to 75 feet for 50 miles. These results were obtained only after careful surveys had been made.

The railroad was built along the line as located, and with one major exception is still there today. The exception is the Lucin Cutoff crossing Great Salt Lake. That was finished in 1903, a third of a century after the completion of the road over the Promontory Mountains. The plan of building directly across the lake was indeed considered by the early engineers, but rejected on account of cost, lack of information regarding the lake bottom, and uncertainty as to the lake levels. Some records then available indicated a rising lake in the years from 1850 to 1868. To this day traces of ancient Lake Bonneville are in evidence that show that prehistoric water levels were at least 1,000 feet above the modern lake. To have crossed the lake where the modern line was built would have saved forty-five miles of distance and a climb of 680 feet over the Promontory Mountains, but it was just not possible in 1869. There is no question that the early engineers found and used the best route there was from Sacramento to Ogden, and their work remains today as evidence of great ability and far-seeing vision.

# CHAPTER 7

# Constructing the Central Pacific Railroad

THE CONSTRUCTION of the Central Pacific Railroad through uninhabited regions involved tremendous problems absent in building roads in more settled parts of the country. However, in the major items, the procedure was much the same.

Financing construction, while a part of general management of a railroad, played an important role in determining the speed at which the work went forward. Once the location surveys had been made, rights of way had to be obtained, and after that final construction surveys were needed. These surveys continued throughout the construction period and required surveying parties at frequent intervals along the line. The roadbed in cuts and on fills passed over uneven ground and through all kinds of earth materials where ditches had to be dug and provisions made for the discharge of storm water. Tunnels in solid rock could be left as excavated, but many other tunnels had to be lined with timber, brick, stone, or concrete. Bridges had to be designed and erected ahead of track laying. Culverts of stone or concrete were built under fills. Snow sheds, in the case of the

Central Pacific, and snow fences on the Union Pacific, were essential in keeping the line open in winter.

The track, rails, switches, and other items were transported to the construction depots from distant locations and carried from there to the end of the track. Sidings and station tracks were built along with the main line. Ballast was brought from distant quarries, placed in position, and the track brought to line on an even grade. Station houses with water tanks for the locomotives, eating houses on long lines, and similar structures were also vitally necessary. Machine repair shops and engine houses were located at carefully selected points. Provision had to be made for fuel to be stored in quantity at division points. Rolling stock of locomotives, freight and passenger cars, and construction trains were also an important and costly item in Central Pacific construction. A telegraph line had to be built as an adjunct to the construction forces. In many places a wagon road reaching ahead of the track was required. Then, too, there had to be an organized force of trainmen, graders, bridge builders, teams, earth-moving equipment, and finally the force that maintained and operated the railroad when construction was finished. Over all, there was the company organization, the engineering staff with the chief engineer and his principal assistants, the construction superintendent and assistants, contractors for various kinds of work, and many other groups of skilled men for performing special tasks.

### CONSTRUCTION STANDARDS

When the Law of 1862 was passed it contained a clause stating that "the track upon the entire line of railroad and branches shall be of uniform width to be determined by the President of the United States, so that when completed, cars can be run from the Missouri River to the Pacific Coast." President Lincoln, harried by the worries of the Civil War, set the gauge at five feet, but an Act of Congress of March 3, 1863, established the gauge as four feet, eight and one half inches, which is the standard gauge today.

[137]

The previously mentioned clause of the law, which stated that standards of the Baltimore and Ohio had to be used, was indefinite, and for this reason Secretary of the Interior James Harlan in 1865 appointed a board made up of government commissioners, government directors of the Union Pacific Railroad, and a number of representatives of the companies constructing the Pacific railroads. A circular was sent out to prominent railroad engineers, among whom were Major General M. C. Meigs, John B. Jervis, George Lowe Reid, Ashbel Welch, Benjamin H. Latrobe, G. A. Nicholls, W. W. Evans, Philip S. Justice, J. L. Williams, and Silas Seymour, the last two being government director and consulting engineer of the Union Pacific respectively. The comments of these men constitute an excellent summary of railroad building as it was understood in 1865. The men from the eastern states favored solid, permanent construction, such as stone bridges, but on most of the other items of construction there was a general agreement. It is interesting to note that Silas Seymour, whose name appears elsewhere in this work, advocated a road built on rails resting upon longitudinal timbers instead of upon crossties, a plan that had been abandoned everywhere long before. He favored Howe truss bridges, built mainly of wood, and said that he had never been in favor of iron bridges for railroads. This was the type of man with whom General Dodge of the Union Pacific had to contend.

The weight of locomotives suggested by the advisers ranged from twenty to forty tons, the weight being limited by the carrying capacity of the fifty- to sixty-five-pound rails then available. Today steel rails are double these weights, and locomotives weigh ten to fifteen times more than was then deemed safe. It is true that steel rails made by the Bessemer process were then coming into use, and the possibility of using them was discussed, but they were not adopted on the first Pacific Railroad.

The Board brought in recommendations on location, grades and curves, embankments and excavations, mechanical structures, ballasting, crossties, rails, sidings, rolling stock, and buildings. It properly stated that grades and curves should be adapted to the country, and that while grades of 116 feet to the mile, (2.2 per cent) had been used on the Baltimore and Ohio with curves of a minimum radius of 400 feet, the situation in the Platte and Kansas valleys was such that grades should not exceed thirty feet per mile. The roadbed should not be less than fourteen feet wide at the grade line, excavation in long cuts should be twenty-six feet wide, and in shorter cuts, twenty-four feet wide to allow room for side ditches. Earth slopes should be one and one half base to one of rise. Rock slopes could be steeper. Tunnels in rock should be made for double track, but this provision was never enforced. Culverts were to be of stone or brick, but could be made of wood and replaced later with permanent materials. Bridges were to be built of stone, iron, or wood, at the discretion of the railroad company. Ballast should be of broken stone or gravel, twelve to fourteen inches thick. Crossties should be of oak or other suitable timber; if of soft wood, such as cottonwood, they should be treated by the Burnetizing process. They should be six inches thick, at least six inches on the face and eight feet long, and laid 2,400 to the mile. Rails were to be of American iron and should weigh at least fifty-six pounds to the yard on ordinary track, and sixty pounds per yard in the mountains. Rails should be fastened by fishplates and bolts at the joints and should be spiked to the ties on each side of the rail at each tie. However, wrought-iron chairs could be employed at the joints if the use of fishplates would delay the work. Sidings should be at least 6 per cent as long as the line. Buildings should be of brick or stone.

The specifications were liberal and allowed for plenty of leeway in construction, depending upon the country. Much was left to the judgment of the railroad officials, and of the directors and commissioners who had charge of the work for the government. In accordance with the standards, a first-class road was constructed.

At Sacramento, the starting point of the line, the railroad was located on an embankment, which formed a levee that protected the city of Sacramento from the flood water of the American River, one of the broadest streams flowing from the Sierra Nevada. About three and a half miles from the initial point, the river, flowing nearly due westward, was crossed by the largest bridge on the entire Central Pacific line. At the crossing point the American River is about 700 feet wide, and on both sides there are wide bottom lands, flooded in times of high water.

Geologically, the mountains begin at Arcade Creek. In the vicinity of Rocklin, granite is encountered, but the road for seventy miles up the mountains to a point near Cisco runs mostly in gravels, sedimentary rocks, slates, cemented gravels, and volcanic rocks of various types. From Cisco to the summit and down the eastern slope of the mountains, the rock is a hard granodiorite. In the vicinity of Truckee there are glacial deposits, but between Truckee and Verdi a canyon is encountered where the river runs through a lava flow for about ten miles. Through Reno and the Truckee Meadows the construction was easy, but when passing over the Virginia Range the road had to follow an open canyon to Wadsworth, at the Big Bend of the Truckee. From Wadsworth to Ogden the railroad was built over the desert, which at places borders the Humboldt River, and across the mountains that were not difficult to surmount. In this distance of 550 miles, there were a few stretches of difficult construction, the most troublesome being at Palisade Canyon, where for some twelve miles the line was built beside the river between basalt cliffs. In the sections across Nevada and Utah, the country was similar to the terrain where the Union Pacific crossed the Wyoming Basin. It was here that great progress was made during the last year of building.

### TRANSPORTATION

As the Central Pacific began at Sacramento and built eastward, all supplies other than those obtained from California or from along the road had to be brought from the eastern states.

The usual route from Atlantic ports was around Cape Horn, a distance of 18,000 miles, which took a sailing ship some four months in passage. Some freight, mainly locomotives and rail, was sent across the Isthmus of Panama, but this route, while shorter in distance and time, was extremely costly, owing to high freight rates.

Mr. Clement stated that shipping rail by way of the Isthmus in 1868 cost $51.97 per ton, making the cost of rail delivered at Sacramento $143.67, which did not include transfer charges to lighters at San Francisco or transportation up the Sacramento River. The corresponding Isthmus freight on one locomotive was $8,100, and the average freight cost for eighteen locomotives was $4,692.50 each. Freight charges on the first locomotive sent by way of Cape Horn was $2,282.25. Much of the high freight cost was due to high war-risk insurance during the period of the Civil War.

When material reached San Francisco, it was loaded on river steamers or barges and carried up San Francisco Bay and the Sacramento River, 130 miles to Sacramento. In flood seasons the river furnished a reliable means of transportation, but at low water, even with the help of the tides, the passage was difficult. Thus all equipment for building and operating the Central Pacific had to be shipped from eastern mills to Atlantic ports, loaded on vessels, taken on a long sea voyage by way of Cape Horn, or across the Isthmus, to San Francisco, there to be transferred again to river craft and by way of the bay and river carried to its destination. There it was again loaded on cars and forwarded to the place of use at the end of track.

### MATERIALS

Iron for the track, in accordance with the Law of 1862, was manufactured in American mills in the East. The rail varied from fifty-six to sixty-six pounds per yard, the heavier rail being used on the mountains where the height of the rail section was raised in order that the head would be above snow. Wrought-iron chairs to connect the ends of two rails were used on 115 miles of road, but the remaining length of the line was laid with fishplate joints, which were much superior.

Ties and bridge timbers were cut from California forests. Redwood ties from the Coast Mountains were brought by steamer to San Francisco and were used from Sacramento to the summit. From there on, the native lumber, sawed in mills at Verdi and elsewhere on the eastern side of the mountains, was used. All of this timber was of a quality that made special treatment unnecessary. The number of ties varied from 2,260 to 2,640 per mile, depending upon alignment and grade. The forests also provided wood for bridges and trestles, some timber being hewn but most of it being sawed. From the forests, too, came fuel, since wood-burning locomotives were used during the entire construction. In this respect, the Central Pacific had a great advantage over the Union Pacific, but the Union Pacific had a similar advantage later when coal deposits were discovered along its line in Wyoming.

Stone of good quality for culverts, bridge piers, and building foundations was found along the Central Pacific line through the mountains; and for the long stretch across Nevada and Utah, stone for replacement of temporary structures could be brought from quarries along the part of the line that had already been built.

Ballast, also, was usually obtained from pits along the line. Up the Sierra Nevada and down the Truckee River there was an ample supply. Across the deserts, where the railroad was kept away from the Humboldt River in order to avoid the sediments of the former Lake Lahontan, material from the excavations was used as ballast. It generally consisted of coarse sands and gravels washed down from the near-by mountains.

### CLEARING

On the open plains east of the Sacramento Valley and from Reno eastward to Promontory, no clearing or grubbing was necessary. On the slopes of the Sierra Nevada, especially in the center portion, the line passed through dense forests where trees 100 to 150 feet in height were common. Brush was also abundant. In some sections the cost of cutting trees and brush and grubbing out stumps was an item of considerable expense.

### GRADING

For eighteen miles eastward from Sacramento to Roseville, the grading was light, inasmuch as the road was located over the flat lands of the Sacramento Valley. Beyond Roseville, then called Junction, where the line crossed the railroad leading northward from Folsom, the work became heavier; and from Newcastle, thirty-two miles from Sacramento, to a point near Truckee, a distance of nearly ninety miles, grading work was the heaviest order of construction. In order to keep within the ruling grades, deep cuts and high fills were essential over most of the distance. Bloomer Cut, west of Auburn, about 800 feet long and sixty-five feet in average depth, had to be blasted through a mass of cemented gravel. Higher in the mountains the excavation was through stained earth and shale, or sometimes sandstone; and when beyond Emigrant Gap the line passed to side-hill construction the material encountered was granite. Wide ravines were passed by trestles that were afterward filled, and in the upper region, tunnel succeeded tunnel. From Truckee eastward the work was lighter, except in the two canyons of the Truckee River. Out on the plains of Nevada and Utah the grading was all light, except for rock work in narrow canyons.

All earth work was done with pick and shovel in the hands of laborers, who loaded the material in wheelbarrows or on one-horse wooden dump carts. Animal traction was the only power used. Blasting was mainly done with black powder, which was far less expensive than the newly patented nitroglycerine that was just coming into use. Nitroglycerine was put to good use, however, in some of the tunnel blasting operations.

[143]

## LABOR

The Central Pacific was built largely by Chinese laborers, imported for that purpose from southern China. The Chinese had a well-developed system of contracting for labor, which was used on the railroad. As organized by Strobridge, the work was under the supervision of riding bosses, whose responsibility it was to keep the work going and to provide supplies for the workmen.

At first Strobridge was opposed to the use of Chinese laborers, but later changed his mind, since white laborers were not available. Clement thus described the situation: "California laborers were mainly miners accustomed to work in placer mines or not, as it suited them. Mining was more to their liking than the discipline of railroad work. They were indifferent, independent, and their labor high priced. Labor sufficient for the rapid construction of the Central Pacific was not then on the coast and the labor as it existed could not be depended upon—the first mining excitement meant a complete stampede of every man and a consequent abandonment of all work."

Strobridge expressed his revised opinion of the Chinese when he said: "They learn quickly, do not fight, have no strikes that amount to anything, and are very cleanly in their habits. They will gamble and do quarrel among themselves most noisily—but harmlessly."

The Chinese, who numbered about 12,000 at the most, worked in groups, each with his own cook, who also provided hot water for bathing. Their drink was tea, which, being made with hot water, avoided the danger of disease to which white men were subject from drinking all kinds of water along the line. The pay of the Chinese ranged from $30 to $35 a month, on which they boarded themselves. They were paid in coin, brought to them by the railroad paymaster, the payment being made to the Chinese labor boss of the gang, who kept the time of the men during the month. The Chinese gave very little trouble, but out in Nevada they sometimes wanted to quit. The

[144]

Piute Indians spread the story that in the desert toward which they were heading there were snakes big enough to swallow a Chinese whole, which of course had its effect. However, the Chinese were kept on the work to the finish, and years later the people of California came to recognize the splendid character of the Celestials.

White labor, as stated, was difficult to obtain and was used only on important tasks. After the Civil War, white labor was more readily available with the Irish predominating. White common laborers were paid about the same as were the Chinese but were provided with subsistence and living quarters by the contracting company. The number of whites employed ranged from 1,200 to 1,300, the largest number being used in the years 1866-1868. Expert workers, such as carpenters, track layers, and stone masons of which some 500 were used, were paid higher wages, ranging from $3 to $5 a day. All wages were paid in coin, usually gold.

### TUNNELS

In contrast to the Union Pacific, the tunnels on the Central Pacific were one of the major problems of construction. In all, there were fifteen tunnels, with a total length of 6,213 feet. The shortest was the Red Spur Tunnel, ninety-two feet long, and the longest was the Summit Tunnel, 105 miles from Sacramento, which was 1,659 feet in length. Some of the tunnels were built on curves and some were on tangents, the long tunnel at the summit being constructed on a tangent.

All of the tunnels were located over a distance of sixty miles on the upper reaches of the Sierra Nevada, but the heaviest tunnel work was in the twenty miles from Cisco eastward to the summit. Nine tunnels, having a total length of 5,158 feet, were necessary in this stretch of the road, which lies at elevations of from 6,000 feet to 7,000 feet above sea level in the region of heaviest snowfall. Here the road was built along the sides of steep mountains, with an average slope greater than forty-five degrees, sometimes on the side of bare granite cliffs that were

[145]

broken by projecting ledges and boulders. Embankments were impracticable, as the excavated material from cuts slid far down the mountainside. Under such conditions it was best to locate the road inside the mountain, since tunnels made snow sheds unnecessary, heavy retaining walls were avoided, and work could be carried on in the wintertime. In one place there were seven tunnels in two miles of line.

Most of the tunnels were excavated in solid granite. The cross section of a tunnel was a rectangle at the bottom, sixteen feet wide by eleven feet high, above which the section was arched with a diameter of sixteen feet. Grade was at the center of tie, being one foot three inches above subgrade. Tunnel 11 was partly lined, and Tunnel 13 wholly lined with timber. Sills were 12 inches by 12 inches, posts were 12 by 16, and the arch was formed of three 5- by 12-inch planks bolted together at breaking joints. The distance between the centers of the timber supports varied from one and one half feet to five feet, according to the type of earth material to be supported. Wall and ceiling clearance in mixed soil tunnels was greater than in rock tunnels, allowance having been made for future lining with masonry. However, after completion of the road, the size of rolling stock increased so rapidly that the original tunnel sections had to be enlarged.

Tunnel 6 at the summit, the longest on the road, was 1,659 feet in length, and was the greatest depth below the surface, 124 feet. It was built through granite of medium hardness, crossed by seams. The excavation of this tunnel caused such a serious delay that to expedite matters a shaft was sunk about halfway between the tunnel openings, a hoisting engine was installed, and the tunnel was simultaneously excavated from both ends and from the middle.

It was at Tunnel No. 6 that nitroglycerine was first used on the road. It had been discovered in 1846, but it was not until 1867 that Alfred Nobel patented it as being usable for blasting. It was made by treating glycerine with nitric and sulphuric acids, which produced a light yellow-colored oily liquid that was highly explosive. It was possible to use nitroglycerine in small holes, thereby reducing drilling costs and correspondingly increasing the speed of excavation. At Tunnel 6, and to some extent at Tunnel 8, nitroglycerine was used, being prepared on the spot by James Howden at a cost of about seventy-five cents a pound. It was thought to be eight times as effective as powder, and building progress was increased by 50 per cent.

Work on the tunnels was carried on throughout the winter of 1866-1867, although Tunnels 1 and 2, both west of Cisco, were finished in 1866. Some work had been done on the approach cuts to the Summit Tunnel late in 1865, but winter set in before much was accomplished, and the work gangs were driven out. During 1866 the tunnel approaches swarmed with men working night and day in three shifts of eight hours each. Some storms occurred in November and December, but by the time winter arrived the headings were all under ground. The work was then independent of the weather, except as storms would block tunnel entrances or avalanches would sweep over the work camps. In spite of these difficulties, excavation went on inside and much was taken out through tunnels in the snow. Tunnel 6 took longest to complete on account of its length and its position at the head of Donner Pass, but it was finally holed through in November, 1867.

Much of the foregoing information regarding tunnels was obtained from an account contributed to the American Society of Civil Engineers in 1870 by John R. Gilliss, engineer in charge under L. M. Clement.

In describing the work, Gilliss dwells on the snowstorms of the high Sierra and the difficulties of carrying on work. All accounts of the winters emphasized the violence of the storms and the deep snows. Speaking of the winter of 1866-1867 Gilliss says:

"These storms, forty-four in number, varied in length from a short snow squall to a two-week gale, and in depth from a quarter of an inch to ten feet—none less than the former number being recorded, nor had we occasion to note any greater than the latter. This, the heaviest storm of the winter began February 18th at 2 P. M. and snowed steadily until 10 P. M. of the 22nd, during which time six feet fell . . . . It snowed steadily until March 2nd, making ten feet of snow and thirteen days of storm. It is true that no snow fell for five days, but it drifted so furiously that in time the snow tunnel at the east end of Tunnel No. 6 had to be lengthened fifty feet.

"The storms were grand. They always began with a fall in the barometer and a strong wind from the southwest . . . . The thermometer was rarely below twenty degrees at the beginning of a storm, and usually rose to thirty-two degrees before its close so that the last snow would be damp and heavy, sometimes ending in a rain. The storms ended and clouds were scattered by cold winds blowing over the eastern range of the Sierra Nevada; these raised the barometer and dropped the temperature at once. The lowest temperature of the winter was from a wind of this sort, five and a half degrees above zero."

Gilliss gives a picture of the furious winds that roared through the pass, piling the snow into towering drifts. He tells also of the difficulties in breaking roads, and of the use of snowshoes by the men. Of the snow slides or snow avalanches, he gives the following graphic account:

"Snow slides or avalanches were frequent. The storm winds being always from the southwest, form drifts or snow wreaths on the northeast crests of hills. When these become too heavy, which is generally towards the close of the storms, they break off, and in falling start the loose snow below. This slides on the old crust. I never knew of a slide from the ground.

"Near the close of one storm, a log house with board roof, containing three Scotchmen, brothers, and sub-contractors with their gang, some fifteen or sixteen men in all, was crushed and buried up at day-break. The storm ended at noon. Towards evening a man coming up the road missed the house and alarmed the camp, so that by six o'clock the men were dug out. The bulk of the slide had passed over and piled itself up beyond the house, so that it was only covered fifteen feet deep. Only three were killed; the bunks were close to the log walls and kept the rest from being crushed. Most of them were conscious and strange to say, the time had passed rapidly with them, although about fourteen hours under the snow ..... (The snow slides) were so frequent across the trail leading to Tunnel No. 9, some fifteen or twenty Chinamen were killed by a slide about this time. The year before, two road repairers had been killed and buried, too, by a slide, and their bodies were not found until spring."

Dirt and rock from the tunnels were carried out to the waste banks through tunnels dug through the snow that filled the approach cuts. The length of the snow tunnels varied from 50 to 200 feet, and some of the tunnels were big enough for a two-horse team to walk through. At Tunnel 8 a snow tunnel for the men was dug around the outside of the rock ledge through which the tunnel was being excavated. As the rock tunnel was 375 feet in length, the snow tunnel must have been at least 500 feet long. In the spring, when the wagon roads down the mountain had begun to be bare, snow had to be dug out of the cuts in order that the road could be used. One such snow bank was twenty-five feet deep.

The snowfall in the winter of 1866-1867 and also in the following winter was extremely heavy. Over forty-four feet of snow fell and the depth of hard packed snow in Summit Valley was eighteen feet. This extraordinary snowfall comes from the storms that sweep in from the Pacific Ocean and break against the high mountains. The rain precipitation increases about one inch for each 100 feet up to 5,000 feet as a storm climbs up over the Sierra. While the average rainfall may be eighty inches, it has occasionally reached more than 100 inches. Once the storm passes over the summit of the range the snowfall rapidly decreases. At Truckee there may be from two to three feet, and at

Reno, at the base of the mountains, only a few inches of snow may fall.

### SNOW SHEDS AND GALLERIES

As has been mentioned, when the railroad over the Sierra Nevada was projected by Theodore Judah, he believed that the railroad line could be kept open during the winter by using the ordinary snow plows of that period. Such plows only shoved the snow to each side of the tracks, where it packed. In the fall of 1866 the road had reached Cisco, where experience during the following winter proved that snow plows would not solve the problem. Most of the snow had to be removed by hand and it was therefore necessary to keep a small army of men shoveling all the time. It was obvious that some other method had to be found to keep the road open.

Much discussion followed before it was finally decided that snow sheds and galleries were the only solution. To build fifty-odd miles of these structures was unprecedented in railroad work and the cost would be heavy, but there was no alternative. The work was entrusted to Arthur Brown, Engineer of Bridges and Buildings.

In the summer of 1867 some experimental sheds were erected from a design that was later modified. In 1868 the building of the sheds was begun, all the cuts were covered with sheds, and at the points where there was danger of avalanches, snow galleries were built. As the great rush across the deserts of Nevada and Utah was then under way, it was vitally necessary to keep the railroad open for through traffic in order that supplies would reach the builders at the end of the track without interruption. Men were gathered from every source and were paid high wages for the work. About 2,500 men were employed and six trains were used to bring material. It was not until the fall of 1869, months after the rails had been joined at Promontory, that work on the snow sheds was finished.

The sheds were built with two sides and a steep peaked roof. Owing to the lack of sawed timber, hewn timber and round logs were often used. The galleries differed from the sheds in that they had but one side and a roof that sloped upward until it met the mountain side. This design permitted avalanches to slide over the gallery, some of which extended up the mountainside as much as two hundred feet. In some places, masonry walls were built across canyons where avalanches occurred, to prevent an avalanche from striking the side of the vulnerable wooden construction.

The total completed length of the sheds and galleries was about thirty-seven miles, the building of which consumed 65,000,000 feet board measure of lumber and 900 tons of bolts, spikes, and other iron. The cost was over $2,000,000, but the sheds and galleries did accomplish the purpose of protecting the line from snow blockades. Maintenance experience since 1869 has brought about changes in the design of snow sheds, but the railroad still depends upon such works to keep the line open for traffic throughout the entire year.

### BRIDGES, TRESTLES, AND CULVERTS

With the exception of the great bridge over the American River at Sacramento, spans were of moderate size on the Central Pacific. However, over the Sierra Nevada the location of the line was such that long, high trestles were often necessary. They were employed as an economy measure on the first construction, but it was also true that they speeded up the progress of the road. For a number of years after the opening of the road to traffic, the work of filling the canyons crossed by trestles was carried on, the time for the fill-ins being determined by the condition of the individual wooden trestle. Where fills were made across small water courses, cut stone culverts were generally used, the stone being set in Portland cement.

The bridge over the American River was a work of considerable magnitude. As first built, there were two spans of 192 feet each, the two spans covering a length of 400 feet. In addition, there was a trestle approach on the south or Sacramento side of 2,196 feet, and one on the north side of 2,890 feet over the bottom lands of the river. The total length of trestle was thus 5,086 feet, making the total length of the bridge 5,486 feet, or over a mile. Trusses of the bridge were simple Howe trusses, where all members, including the lower chord, were of timber, with only the vertical members being of iron. The original bridge was founded on pile piers that were later replaced by stone masonry piers. The stone piers rested on piles that had been driven into the bed of the river, cut off below low water, and covered with a timber grillage. The first bridge burned a few years after it was built.

Most of the bridges on the line were also erected with a truss span having trestle approaches at one or both ends. At Long Ravine there were three Howe trusses with a combined length of 428 feet, and at one end 450 feet of trestle of a maximum height of seventy feet, the total length of the bridge being 878 feet. Others of this type, with truss spans exceeding 100 feet, were the bridges at Lower and Upper Cascade Creek, each with spans of 204 feet; at Cold Creek, 126 feet; at Little Truckee and at Prosser Creek, each with spans of 105 feet; the first, third, fourth, and fifth crossing of the Truckee River, with spans of 150 feet; the first crossing of Humboldt River of 129 feet and the second crossing of the same stream of 150 feet. All of these truss spans were of the Burr type, which was the same as the Howe truss, with a wooden arch in addition, built alongside the trusses from end to end and abutting upon the piers or abutments. The Burr type was popular with bridge engineers at that time, but went out of use a long time ago. All of these bridges rested upon stone masonry piers, usually on rock sides of the river or canyon.

In addition, there were numerous trestles made with bents spaced about sixteen feet apart, with wooden stringers spanning the space between on which the ties of the track rested. The bents were made of four posts, one on the bottom, two inclined, and one as a cap at the top. Longitudinal girts connected the several bents, which were sometimes in two or more stages. The bents rested upon stone masonry foundations. In some cases, where the track was high above a gully, the trestles were made up of short spans of trusses, about forty feet in length. An example of this combination was the Secret Town trestle, where there were 280 lineal feet of forty-foot spans and 820 lineal feet of trestle, a total of about 1,100 feet of timber structures with a maximum height of ninety feet.

There were originally a number of long, standard-type trestles crossing low places or ravines. Among these, on the ascent of the Sierra Nevada were: Newcastle, 528 feet long; Auburn, 416 feet; Station 450, 568 feet; Station 470 near Lovells Gap, 496 feet; Clipper Gap, 464 feet; Clipper Ravine, 450 feet; and Butte Canyon, 48 feet. The height of the trestles ranged up to seventy feet.

At the time the road was nearing completion, culverts had been built on 375 miles of line. They were usually of stone, but some were of brick, and all were laid in hydraulic cement. The bottoms were paved, and some of large size were made to be used as cattle crossings. On the line across the desert, where stone could not be easily obtained, short trestles were built in place of culverts, although as a rule the water courses were small. Culverts were afterward built at these places.

A telegraph line and other adjuncts of a railroad were built along the main track. The track sidings and turnouts aggregated about 7½ per cent of the length of the main line. The necessary rolling stock was determined at first by the needs of construction. Near the close of the work there were on hand 162 locomotives, of which two had two drivers, 110 had four drivers, and fifty had six drivers, the number of drivers depending on the capacity of the locomotive. One locomotive had been constructed in San Francisco, the others had been purchased from various companies in the eastern states. At that time thirty-six additional locomotives were being shipped west and twenty-eight more were under construction. There were some passenger cars, but when the road opened there were not enough. The first sleeping car, the "Silver Palace Sleeping Car," arrived at Sacramento June 8, 1868. There were 1,694 freight cars of various types, with additional cars being manufactured at the company's shops at Sacramento at the rate of eight a day. Snow plows were provided for all the locomotives. Turntables had been built at section points, with principal shops being located at Sacramento, where all necessary machinery had been installed for repair and construction of both cars and locomotives. Passenger and freight stations had been built at depots, while at Sacramento a wharf and quay with a frontage of 1,150 feet were erected. Watering stations as far east as Wadsworth were easily found, but across the desert water had to be obtained from wells or from springs from which it was piped to the railroad. The wells at Humboldt Wells and in Thousand Springs Valley furnished much of the supply. One reason for locating the road north of Great Salt Lake was the fact that water was available on that route, whereas it was lacking on the salt deserts south of the lake.

### CONSTRUCTION AND PROGRESS

The Central Pacific Railroad of California was incorporated June 28, 1861, and a year and six months later, on January 8, 1863, ground was broken at Sacramento, marking the commencement of the actual work of building the railroad. As a local newspaper described the event, there were gathered on the water-soaked levee on Front Street near K, "Dignitaries of the state, representatives of every portion of the commonwealth and a great gathering of citizens to see Leland Stanford, newly elected governor and president of the Central Pacific Railroad of California, break ground for the commencement of the iron belt that was to make the United States for the first time a united country and open to California an era of great development."

Women looked on from near-by balconies, a brass band played, a preacher called for divine blessing on the work, and Stanford said that the work would go on with "no delay, no

[154]

halting, no uncertainty in its continued progress." He cast a few shovelfuls of earth from a cart and told his hearers that they could look forward with confidence to the completion of the road. He used more flowery terms that seemed appropriate for the occasion, and then followed a spate of oratory by a group of politicians whose names have since passed into oblivion. Charles Crocker, who was master of ceremonies, then said, in a more practical vein:

"This is no idle ceremony. The pile driver is now, while I am talking, driving piles for the foundation of the bridge across the American River. Tomorrow morning one of the subcontractors who owns these teams and has brought this earth here to deposit on the commencement of this road, will proceed across the river and commence the labor of grading. It is going right on, gentlemen, I assure you! All that I have—all of my own strength, intellect, and energy—are devoted to the building of this section which I have undertaken. Amen." A mural painting in the Southern Pacific depot at Sacramento idealizes the scene, which was more significant than many of those present could appreciate. It is probable that Judah was there, but there is no record of a speech being made by the man who had originated the project and to whom much credit was then due.

Grading and bridge building went forward slowly and it was not until October 8, 1863, that the ship, *Herald of the Morning,* arrived at San Francisco with rail. The first rail was laid on October 26, and the next month, on November 10, the first locomotive, the "Governor Stanford," moved over the rails. Grading across the level plain was easy, and by February 29, 1864, when the road had been finished to Roseville, eighteen miles distant, train service started. It had taken fourteen months from the time when ground was first broken to build those eighteen miles. Judah had been in his grave four months.

The fundamental trouble with the constructive progress, or rather lack of progress, was due to a lack of money. The Law of 1862 had not produced any securities that would sell, other than government bonds, and forty miles of road had to be built before those bonds became available. However, the builders went on slowly with the construction, and Newcastle, thirty-one miles from Sacramento, was reached on January 31, 1865. Two years had been consumed in building thirty-one miles of railroad under favorable physical conditions. But by that time the Law of 1864 had been passed, and the Civil War was soon to close, and from that date on until the line was completed to Promontory, four years later, progress was rapid.

The contract for constructing the first eighteen miles had been let to Charles Crocker, who had resigned from the firm's board of directors, and Crocker had sublet the work of grading to several other contractors. On the section as far as Newcastle, Crocker was given only two miles to construct, the remaining road being awarded to other minor contractors. This method was unsatisfactory from a number of standpoints. The contractors bid against each other for the scanty supply of labor; some work was finished and other parts left unfinished, as the small contractors failed to complete their work on time. For these and other reasons, a general contract was given to Charles Crocker to build to the California-Nevada line, and from that point on the work was in the hands of the Contract and Finance Company, which was the Big Four under a different name.

In building the railroad to Dutch Flat, the construction forces relied on local wagon roads that had been built by the mining interests, but beyond Dutch Flat there was no road of any importance. As a wagon road is a vital adjunct to the construction of a railroad through a new country, especially so across a high range of mountains such as the Sierra Nevada, the directors of the Central Pacific organized the Dutch Flat and Donner Lake Wagon Road. This was the basic reason for the road, but there were other reasons that were also important. At that time the mines of the Comstock Lode at Virginia City and Gold Hill were under intensive development and thousands of people had gathered in that region. All supplies had to be obtained in California, and therefore a highly developed system of animal-drawn freighting had been organized. It was a profitable business while it lasted. The route led from Folsom, at the terminus of the Sacramento Valley Railroad, and over the mountains by way of Placerville and the South Fork of the American River, across two summits to the Carson Valley, thence to Virginia City.

The ninety-mile Dutch Flat and Donner Lake Road, which was started in 1862, was built at a cost of $100,000, being completed in June, 1864. There was some profit from it but it was in full use for only about three years. When the railroad reached Reno in June, 1868, the highway was completely abandoned, but it had already served its principal purpose as a construction road.

The road was located over the Donner Summit, where the railroad was to be built, because no road crossed that rocky gap. There was some semblance of a road that led up Cold Creek and across Emigrant Pass to Summit Valley, but this pass was some 700 feet higher than Donner Pass, although easier for wagons to cross. Today, tourists traveling through the pass by automobile can see portions of the old construction road where it leads eastward from the summit.

The road could not be kept open for wagons during the winter, so animal-drawn sleighs were used for the transportation of men and animals for the construction forces. It was over this road that the rolling stock and materials were moved in the winter of 1866-1867. Three locomotives, forty cars, and material for forty miles of track, together with camp supplies, were hauled from Cisco across the summit and down to Donner Lake, a distance of over twenty miles. The locomotives were carried on sledges made from logs that had been split down the middle and rounded at the ends. This work was often done during raging blizzards and it was sometimes even necessary to transfer construction forces from the snowbound western side of the Sierra to the eastern slope, where the snowfall was less and work could go on. In this manner about fifty miles of road were com-

[157]

pleted down the eastern side of the mountains before the summit tunnel had been opened and the final track laid across the summit.

Track laying was organized under Strobridge as a part of the general construction contract, and not, as on the Union Pacific, as a separate contract. A camp train moved ahead with the track at the speed at which the track was being laid. Trains of track material came from Sacramento, with ties being obtained from mills along the Truckee River. Rails, fastenings, and ties were first dumped on the ground and were then loaded in horse-drawn cars that carried supplies forward to the end of track. The correct number of ties were then placed in position to hold the rail and the rail gang carried forward two rails to place them on the ties, where a spiking and bolting crew fastened them into place. The small car was then moved ahead and the operation was repeated. When the car was empty, it was tipped off the track so that another car could be pulled past it. The empty car was then returned to the track and sent back for another load.

It was on the track of the Central Pacific, near Promontory, that the laying of ten miles of track in one day of twelve hours was achieved on April 28, 1869. This accomplishment stands as a record even today. The Union Pacific under the able management of the Casement brothers, had stepped up track laying from one mile a day to an average of about three miles, and on one occasion, when everything was favorable, had laid eight and one half miles. The uncorroborated story runs that Durant bet Crocker $10,000 that the Central Pacific force would not exceed that record. In any case, Crocker was determined to beat the record of the other road. It was close to the end of the great race of the two roads across the country; therefore Crocker waited until the distance between the track was so short that there was no chance for the rival road to beat the record he hoped to make. An accident on April 27 delayed the start, but on the next day the contest was held, with a newspaper correspondent timing the movement of the track layers. The first rail was laid and others followed at the rate of about 240 feet of rail in one minute and twenty seconds. As the reporter said: "It may seem incredible, but nevertheless it is a fact that the whole ten miles of rail were handled and laid down this day by eight white men. These men were Michael Shay, Michael Kennedy, Michael Sullivan, Patrick Joyce, Thomas Dailey, George Wyatt, Edward Kioleen, and Fred McNamara. These eight Irishmen in one day handled more than 3,500 rails—1,000 tons of iron."

The rails were fifty-six pounds to the yard and weighed 560 pounds each. On curves, the rail was bent in the usual manner. In all, there were brought up and placed 25,800 ties, 3,520 rails, 55,000 spikes, 7,040 poles, and 14,080 bolts, a total of 4,362,000 pounds. The distance was ten miles and 200 feet, and representatives of the Union Pacific were present to measure the distance. The track was ballasted with the ties tamped, so that a train was run over the line that night. It was a notable achievement. That ten-mile stretch of track was later marked by signs recording the feat.

The telegraph line was built at the same time the track was laid. Poles were brought out on the material trains and distributed by wagons. The cross-arms were fastened to them, a gang of laborers under a foreman dug the holes, and a third gang erected them. The wire was then brought forward on a wagon and unwound from a reel as the wagon went ahead. A wire gang raised the wire and fastened it to the insulators. Great rivalry existed between the telegraph gangs and the track gangs, the former being sometimes delayed by lack of poles. However, at the end of a day the wires were connected to a temporary telegraph set and communication established with the supply points at the rear.

It is customary to indicate the progress of construction of a railroad by the position of the rail head, or end of track. That is the measure of the advance of the operated track but not of the progress of the entire project, as much difficult work may be in progress beyond the end of track that must be completed before track laying is resumed. The tunnels at the summit of the Sierra Nevada held the end of track at Cisco for over a year, but still work went on beyond Truckee. The following record of track should be of interest.

The first rail was laid at Sacramento October 26, 1863; and Roseville, eighteen miles away, was reached February 29, 1864. Newcastle, thirty-one miles from Sacramento, was reached June 6, 1864, and then there was a long delay. The line was in operation to Clipper Gap, forty-three miles, June 10, 1865, and to Colfax, fifty-five miles from Sacramento, September 10 of that year. Grading had begun beyond Colfax on August 1, 1865, when work was started on the Summit Tunnel. In July of 1866 trains were running to Dutch Flat, and by November 9 to Cisco, ninety-four miles from Sacramento. At this point the track was held up, although about fifty miles of track were laid east of the mountains. In August, 1867, the Summit Tunnel was completed, together with the other tunnels, leaving only a seven-mile gap in the track at the end of that year, between Coldstream and Tunnel 12. The completed track reached Truckee April 3, 1868; Reno, 154 miles, June 19; and Wadsworth, 189 miles from Sacramento, July 22. The road across the desert from Wadsworth to Promontory, a distance of 501 miles, was built between July, 1868, and the early part of May, 1869. Actually, 523 miles of line were built in ten months, July 1, 1868, to May 1, 1869, and about fifty miles of grading had been done beyond Promontory. Afterward the Central Pacific purchased forty-seven and one half miles and leased five miles of line from the Union Pacific so that a connection could be made at Ogden. In this manner the Central Pacific comprised 742 miles of line from Sacramento to Ogden, and the Union Pacific 1,032 miles of line from Omaha to the same place, a total length from Sacramento to Omaha of 1,774 miles.

Accounts differ as to the number of men that worked on the Central Pacific. On the western side of the Sierra Nevada there

[160]

were about 11,000 men employed at the time of maximum effort. It has been stated that, in the race with the Union Pacific, from western Nevada to Promontory, the Central Pacific employed from 5,000 to 6,000 men. Thirty vessels were at sea at one time carrying supplies, and numerous mills were at work along the Truckee River turning out ties, bridge timbers, and fuel.

The men on the western side of the mountains were moved eastward as the construction work progressed. The experience of one engineer, J. M. Graham, was typical of this progress. Employed first at the Summit, Graham moved progressively to the Truckee River, to the Truckee Meadows, to Wadsworth, to Humboldt Station, to Emigrant Canyon, to Palisade, and finally to the Toana Mountains.

In a report to Leland Stanford, Strobridge describes the construction work under his charge:

> I was superintendent of construction during the building of the road. The work was pushed with the utmost vigor; all the men were hired that could be found and no effort or expense was spared to complete the road as quickly as possible. In this way it was finished and in operation from Sacramento, Cal., to Ogden, Utah, about seven years sooner than was required by the act of Congress. During construction very high prices were paid for powder and all tools and supplies used on the work, and nothing was spared that would hasten its completion and the work was pushed regardless of the season. The winter of 1865 and 1866 was a very wet one, making the roads on the clay soils of the foothills nearly impassable for vehicles. Large numbers of pack animals had to be brought into use and on them were carried nearly all supplies and even hay and grain over steep mountain trails to the construction camps. . . . During the winter of 1866 and 1867 and the following winter of 1867 and 1868 there were unusual snowfalls in the upper Sierra Nevadas where the road was then under construction. The tunnels were got under way with as large a force as could be used on them and the remainder of the force was sent to the Truckee canyon on the east slope of the Sierras where the snowfall was not so great as to

[161]

prevent entirely grading during the winter, the total force being about 13,500 men at that time. . . . In the spring of each year the men were taken back from the Truckee into the mountains and an average depth of ten to twelve feet of snow was cleared away before grading could be commenced.

In crossing the deserts eastward from the Truckee River, water for men and animals was hauled at one time forty miles. It was necessary to have the heavy work in Palisade Canyon done in advance of the main force, and 3,000 men with 400 horses and carts were sent to that point, a distance of 300 miles in advance of the track. Hay, grain, and all supplies for the men and horses had to be hauled over the desert for that great distance, there being no supplies to be obtained on the entire route. The winter of 1868 and 1869 was one of severe cold. The construction was in progress in the upper Humboldt Valley, where the ground was frozen to a depth of two to three feet, and material required blasting and treatment like rock which could have been cheaply moved in a more favorable time.

The road from Wadsworth to Ogden, about 555 miles, was built between July, 1868, and May, 1869, about ten months, with a force averaging 5,000 men.

As the road advanced across the desert, the same procedure of sending men and supplies to advance points was followed. The final advance outfit was sent from Wadsworth to Promontory, as construction east of that point was done by the Mormons.

On the Central Pacific there was little or no trouble from liquor, gambling, and prostitution such as troubled the builders of the Union Pacific. The common laborers were Chinese, who kept to themselves. The white men were above the grade of laborers, but credit for the absence of saloons was due to Strobridge. He hated liquor, and whenever someone set up a tent to sell it, the superintendent sent men to destroy the tent and if objections were offered to destroy the liquor. His actions may not have been quite legal, but the railroad builders were the only law in that uninhabited region, and drastic action was deemed necessary.

[162]

There is no record of any particular Indian trouble on the Central Pacific, in contrast to the major difficulties with Indians experienced by the Union Pacific. In western Nevada the Piutes were the only tribe of any consequence, and they had been subdued in what was known at Virginia City as the "Indian War." In previous years Indians had murdered a number of emigrants and had robbed the pioneers' wagon trains, but much of the trouble should have been laid to the deeds of renegade white men, bad whiskey, and outrages committed by the whites against the Indians. In 1860, several white men were murdered by Indians at William's Station in revenge for assaults on Indian women. When a party of men under Major Ormsby was sent out after the redskins, the party was trapped on the Truckee River near Pyramid Lake, and a number, including Major Ormsby, were killed. A larger expedition soon afterwards defeated the Indians and drove them into the northern deserts.

In eastern Nevada and in Utah there were constant conflicts betwen the Indians and the operators of the stages, which finally led to the establishment of a number of military posts through central Nevada. To protect the construction forces on the Central Pacific, the federal government in 1867 established Fort Halleck near the north end of the Ruby Mountains, not far from the Humboldt River. The presence of troops at Fort Halleck and the operations of General Patrick E. Conner in cleaning out the Indians had its effect, and while brushes with the Indians occurred from time to time, this did not delay the building of the Central Pacific.

### THE MEETING OF THE RAILS

By the Law of 1862, the Central Pacific was authorized to build eastward as far as the Missouri River, provided the eastern roads had not built westward. The Law of 1864, inspired by the Union Pacific, limited the Central Pacific to building to a point 150 miles east of the California-Nevada line, the Union Pacific to meet with it at that point. Huntington was not especially worried by that provision, preferring to allow the matter to come up later. The subject was brought to a head in 1866, and by the Act of Congress of July 3 of that year the "Central Pacific Railroad Company of California, with the consent and approval of the Secretary of the Interior, are hereby authorized to locate, construct and continue their road eastward, in a continuous completed line until they meet and connect with the Union Pacific Railroad."

Each company was prohibited from working more than 300 miles in advance of their completed lines.

At all times it was the intent of the laws that the two railroads should join when and where they met. The men of each road, however, interpreted this statement to suit themselves. The Union Pacific graded a complete line to Promontory and a partial line to Monument Point, and did a small amount of work as far west as Humboldt Wells, about 168 miles west of Promontory. The Central Pacific made its surveys and filed its maps beyond Ogden as far east as the eastern end of Echo Canyon, and had graded to Ogden. Thus the grading of the roads, more or less complete, paralleled each other for about 200 miles. The struggle was for the trade of the Salt Lake region and for the subsidy bond and also to secure the greatest freight length of haul over the total distance. Over a million dollars were wasted in the struggle between the two roads. A compromise was finally offered to the Union Pacific by Huntington, by which the Union Pacific would build its road to Promontory and the Central Pacific would then purchase enough of the line to enable it to reach Salt Lake Valley. As an alternative, he would continue with his plans of extending the Central Pacific to Ogden. He seemed to hold the trump cards when he applied for and received over a million dollars in government bonds for the line east of Ogden. The struggle had reached a point where the grading crews of the two railroads were setting off blasts that killed men on the rival line, when Huntington's compromise was accepted by the Union Pacific. The Union Pacific agreed to join rails at Promontory and to sell forty-seven and one half miles of line extending to within five miles of Ogden for $4,000,224.96. When this agreement was reached, Congress ratified it on April 10, stating that the "common terminus of the Union Pacific and the Central Pacific Railroads shall be at or near Ogden; and the Union Pacific Railroad Company shall build, and the Central Pacific Railroad Company shall pay for and own, the railroad from the terminus aforesaid to Promontory Point, at which point the rails shall meet and connect and form one continuous line."

Later the price to be paid was reduced and the Central Pacific leased the remaining five miles into Ogden for 999 years. Thus, after much pointless struggle and waste of money, the meeting point was settled and the proper junction, Ogden, was determined.

The early building years of the two railroads did not interest the general public especially, but after the Civil War ended and as progress on the work was accelerated, the attention of the American people became focused on the great project. Prominent men journeyed into the West to see the work, and editors all over the country described it. In the year 1868, the race across the Utah and Nevada deserts by the Central Pacific and across the Wyoming Basin and over the mountains to the Salt Lake Valley by the Union Pacific was in full swing. Every day the newspapers of the country carried bulletins of miles laid and vivid descriptions of progress made. It soon became apparent that the meeting of the rails would take place some time in the first part of 1869, almost seven years sooner than the date set by Congress for completion.

In April came the last rush, and on the 28th of that month Crocker and his men laid the ten miles that set the track-laying record. The gap between the tracks grew smaller and smaller until finally early in May it was seen that it would close on or before May 8. The Union Pacific permitted the last of its rowdy construction towns to be established at Promontory, complete with saloons, gambling dens, and houses of prostitution. The celebration of the meeting of the rails and the driving of the last spike was set for May 8, but the Union Pacific train bearing the official delegation was late, and so the ceremonies had to be held on May 10.

The story of the event has been told by various writers, but the eyewitness account given by Sidney Dillon, then a director and later president of the Union Pacific, covers the essential points. He said:

> The point of junction was the level circular valley about three miles in diameter surrounded by mountains. During all the morning hours the hurry and bustle of preparation went on. Two lengths of rail lay on the ground near the opening in the roadbed. At a little before eleven the Chinese laborers began leveling up the roadbed preparatory to placing the last ties in position. About a quarter after eleven, the train from San Francisco [he should have said from Sacramento] with Governor Stanford and his party arrived and was greeted with cheers. In the enthusiasm of the occasion there were cheers for everybody, from the president of the Union Pacific to the day laborers on the road. The two engines moved nearer each other and the crowd gathered around the open spaces. Then all fell back a little so that the view should be unobstructed.
>
> Brief remarks were made by Governor Stanford on one side and by General Dodge on the other. It was now about twelve o'clock noon, local time, or about two P.M. in New York. The two superintendents of construction, J. H. Strobridge of the Central Pacific and S. B. Reed of the Union Pacific, placed the last tie on the rails. It was of California laurel, highly polished, with a silver plate in the center bearing the following inscription: The last tie laid on the completion of the Pacific Railroad, May 10, 1869, with the names of the officers and directors of both companies.
>
> Everything was then in readiness, the word was given and "Hats Off" went clicking over the wire to the waiting crowds at New York, Philadelphia, San Francisco, and all principal cities. Prayer was offered by Mr. Todd, at the conclusion of which our operator tapped out: "We have

got done praying. The spike is about to be presented," to which the response came back: "We understand. All ready in the East." The gentlemen who had been commissioned to present the four spikes, two of gold and two of silver, from Montana, Idaho, California, and Nevada, stepped forward and with brief appropriate remarks, discharged the duty assigned to them.

Governor Stanford, standing on the north, and Dr. Durant on the south side of the track, received the spikes and put them in place.

The operator tapped out, "All ready now. The spike will soon be driven. The signal will be three dots for the commencement of the blows."

An instant later the silver hammers came down and, at each stroke, in all the offices from San Francisco to New York, the hammer struck the bell.

The signal "Done" was received at Washington at 2:47 P.M., which was about a quarter of one at Promontory. There was not much formality in the demonstration that followed, but the enthusiasm was genuine and unmistakable. The two engines moved up until they touched each other and a bottle of champagne was poured on the last rail, after the manner of christening a ship at a launching.

There were several photographs taken, in one of which General Dodge and Montague, the engineers of the two roads, are shown shaking hands. It was fitting that Strobridge, superintendent of construction on the Central Pacific, and Reed, of the Union Pacific, should be there and take a prominent part in the ceremony. For some reason never explained, Crocker was not there to meet Durant of the Union Pacific, though they represented the driving forces that had pushed the construction over the plains, mountains, and deserts for nearly 1,800 miles. The memory of General Dodge must have gone back over the years to that day in 1853, sixteen years before, when he had crossed the Missouri River with his survey party on the first investigation of the Pacific Railroad. The other great engineer, Theodore Judah, had been dead for six years, but undoubtedly he was not forgotten by those at the ceremonies.

There were celebrations in many cities of the country. The telegraph company had arranged for bells to be rung in Washington, New Orleans, New York, Boston, and Omaha by the strokes of the hammer that drove the last spike. A gun was fired at Fort Point in San Francisco. In Chicago there was a parade. In New York a salute of 100 guns was fired, and the bells of Trinity Church were rung. There were celebrations at Omaha and Sacramento, and ministers throughout the nation preached sermons about the work. The importance of the great achievement was everywhere appreciated with the closing of the line at Promontory, being justly regarded as the greatest engineering and construction feat of the ninetenth century.

When the ceremonies were concluded a luncheon was held in Stanford's car, and then the trains separated. There was still work to be done, but in the weeks that followed the working forces gradually melted away. Many of the men went into the operating forces of the two railroads, but most of the engineers moved to other railroads and were active in later construction. Many railroads were to be built across the continent, but never again would there be a first one. That had been completed. It was not long before the shacks that formed the town of Promontory Point disappeared and nature reclaimed the lonely valley. Since that time some attempts at farming have been made there, but today the desert mountains with their sparse growth of stunted trees look down in silence upon the historic spot where the great enterprise was culminated. A concrete monument erected there bears this inscription:

LAST SPIKE

COMPLETING FIRST

TRANSCONTINENTAL

RAILROAD

DRIVEN AT THIS SPOT

MAY 10TH 1869

The line over the Promontory Mountains was operated for more than thirty-three years, but was largely discarded when the Lucin Cutoff across the Great Salt Lake was opened for service in 1903. Later, most of the western end of the line was abandoned, and in 1942, during the World War II, the entire line of rails from Corinne to Lucin was scrapped.

The railroads were not completed when the tracks were joined. There was still much work to be done, even to comply with the requirements of the government. To settle the legal requirements of the laws, an examination was made by a special commission of five men that was appointed by the Secretary of the Interior, J. D. Cox. The Central Pacific was examined in September, 1869, and the commission's report included a list of twenty-seven items to be completed at an estimated cost of $576,650. The inspection of the Union Pacific was made in the same month, and the cost of the sixty-four items listed was estimated as $1,586,100. The commission concludes its report, which is dated October 30, 1869, with the following statement:

"This great line, the value of which to the country is inestimable, and in which every citizen should feel a pride, has been built in about half the time allowed by Congress, and is now a good and reliable means of communication between Omaha and Sacramento, well equipped and fully prepared to carry passengers and freight with safety and dispatch, comparing in this respect favorably with a majority of first-class roads in the United States."

The actual date of the completion of the two roads was long the subject of controversy between the railroads and the government. The report of the commission was not conclusive, as it noted in the case of each road that additional work was necessary. In November, the Secretary of the Interior released to the companies the remaining bonds that were due them, but required that collateral securities be deposited with him. However, the Secretary refused for five years to issue patents for the lands. On request of the Union Pacific another commission,

[169]

this one of three men, was appointed, and after an examination rendered a report that the roads had been completed as required by law, by the report of the former commission, and by the instructions of the Department of the Interior on October 1, 1874. However, when the Secretary of the Treasury, acting under the Law of 1874, demanded payment of 5 per cent of the net earnings, he gave the date of completion for the Central Pacific as the 16th of July, 1869, and of the Union Pacific as the 6th of November, 1869. A suit was then brought by the government against the Union Pacific, in which the court held that the above completion dates would hold as far as payment of the 5 per cent was concerned, inasmuch as these were the dates when the last bonds were delivered by the government to the railroad companies.

# CHAPTER 8

# The Builders of the Union Pacific Railroad

IN THE group of men who built the Union Pacific, three were most outstanding for determination, natural ability, and force of character. They were Durant, the projector, vice president, and general manager whose incessant activity carried all before him; Dodge, the chief engineer, under whose direction the difficult location was made; and Oakes Ames, the financier without whose efforts financial failure would have been almost certain. Close behind these three were General Dix, Oliver Ames, Sidney Dillon, Peter A. Dey, the first chief engineer, Samuel B. Reed and James A. Evans, at first engineers on location and later superintendents of construction, and General J. S. Casement and his brother Dan. They were all strong characters and often clashed, but the situation required men of that type. There was no room for weaklings.

[171]

## JOHN ADAMS DIX

As the first president of the Union Pacific Railroad, mention must be made of General Dix, but as he performed none but the most casual duties of the office he was never a factor in the construction of the road.

Dix was born at Boscawen, New Hampshire, July 24, 1798, and joined the army at an early age, yet somehow found time to study law. He moved to Albany, New York, was a Democrat in politics, served an unexpired term as United States Senator, was postmaster at New York, and in 1861 became Secretary of the Treasury at Washington. He was active in war work and was appointed Major General in command of New York State troops. In 1862 he was in command of Fortress Monroe, and in 1863 was placed in command of the Union Army's Department of the East. He served with credit throughout the Civil War, and was appointed Minister to France in November, 1866, a position he held until 1869. He returned to America in 1872 to serve a term as governor of New York and was defeated for a second term.

General Dix had engaged in railroad work before the time of the Union Pacific, as president of the Chicago and Rock Island, and also as president of the Mississippi and Missouri Railroad. He was therefore the logical choice for president of the Union Pacific. However, the outbreak of the war, his services in the army, and his appointment as Minister to France, together with increasing age, made it impossible for him to attend actively to the affairs of the railroad. General Dix was an accomplished gentleman and a scholar, and was everywhere esteemed for his honesty of purpose. He died April 21, 1879.

The duties of active service on the railroad fell upon Thomas Durant, vice president, and later on Oliver Ames, who became president. General Dix was little more than a figurehead, having been given the position of president largely because of his excellent reputation.

[172]

## THOMAS CLARK DURANT

Of all the men who were connected with the building of the Union Pacific, Durant was the most important. It was he who conceived the project, fought for it during the years when its future was most uncertain, and remained with it through the rush of construction to the climax on that day in May, 1869, when the rails were joined at Promontory. Thomas C. Durant was born at Lee, Massachusetts, February 6, 1820, and died October 5, 1885. At the age of twenty he graduated from Albany College, where for the next two years he served as assistant professor in medicine. It is from this experience as well as from some practice that he gained the title of Doctor. From medicine he passed into trade in his uncle's firm, but it was not long before the young man became interested in railroads. The rush to extend lines into the West was on, and Durant was the kind of man who would never be satisfied with a humdrum existence at home.

Thomas Durant came into contact with railroad builders through his uncle's firm and quickly made his presence felt among them. The builders were older, but there was a place for an energetic young man such as Durant. In 1851 he was with Henry Farnam on the Chicago and Rock Island Railroad. Then, early in 1853, the Mississippi and Missouri Railroad was organized, with John A. Dix as president. Other men connected with the enterprise were Sheffield, Jervis, and Farnam. It is not apparent what part Durant played in the organization, but it is known that he was active in raising money for the work. Peter A. Dey was chief engineer of the road, and his principal assistant was the young Grenville M. Dodge. Surveys were made in 1853 and reached Council Bluffs in November of that year, after which Dodge crossed the Missouri to examine the possibilities of extending the line westward up the valley of the Platte. The result was that the construction of the M. and M. Railroad was awarded to the firm of Farnam and Durant, as by

[173]

that time Sheffield had tired of the work and had given it up. The M. and M. struggled slowly across Iowa, only to be seriously delayed by the panic of 1857, when the original road went into bankruptcy. Reorganized, it was absorbed by the Chicago and Rock Island, and so did not reach Council Bluffs until May, or possibly June, 1869.

Henry Farnam, with whom Durant had formed a partnership after the withdrawal of Joseph Sheffield, continued his interest in western railroads, and was later named president of the Chicago and Rock Island Railroad Company. He was active in promoting a railroad to the Pacific coast, and became one of the incorporators of the Union Pacific. Not long afterward he became dissatisfied with the methods of conducting the affairs of that railroad, to a degree that he refused to have anything further to do with it. He lost money in the failure of the M. and M. Railroad in 1857, and in 1863 he left the Rock Island and retired from active work. From that time on, Durant acted alone.

During the latter part of the fifties Farnam and Durant furnished the money for surveys and reconnaissance work as far west as the Rocky Mountains, and after Farnam retired, Durant forwarded the project of a railroad west of the Missouri. He was one of the active proponents of the Act of Congress of 1862, was a subscriber for fifty shares at the incorporation of the Union Pacific Railroad Company in 1863, and became a member of the board of directors at the election on October 29, 1863. When the board organized, Major General John A. Dix was chosen president, Thomas C. Durant became vice president, Henry V. Poor, secretary, and John J. Cisco, treasurer. The burden fell upon Durant, as he was a member of two important committees, executive and finance. As vice president and general manager, he had charge of practically everything until the road was completed.

Durant wrestled with the problem of starting the road and with the organization of the construction forces. He had em-

[174]

ployed as his consulting engineer Silas Seymour, brother of the governor of New York, who was an engineer of some experience in railroad work. The conflict over the location from Omaha to the Platte Valley delayed matters for a year, and that, together with the Hoxie contract, led to the resignation of Dey. The Hoxie contract brought into being the device of the controlled construction company and the formation of the Credit Mobilier.

In July, 1865, Durant became president of the construction company that assumed the obligations that Durant and his friends had taken in financing the Hoxie contract. It was in 1865 that Oakes and Oliver Ames became interested in the Credit Mobilier through purchasing some of its stock. Later, in 1867, Durant was removed from the Credit Mobilier, which act marked the beginning of the struggle between the two factions. Several court actions resulted in the Oakes Ames contract and the formation of a board of seven trustees, which included Durant. When the Oakes Ames contract was completed, Durant made a contract with J. W. Davis, which was assigned to the same trustees, and the road was completed.

Durant at all times appeared on the railroad in a dual capacity. As vice president and general manager, he was supposed to represent the interests of the railroad company. Under the Hoxie contract, first with his associates and then under the Credit Mobilier, he was a contractor, and as trustee under the two following contracts he shared in the profits. He insisted in having all the stockholders of the railroad become equivalent shareholders in the construction company. His lawsuits, while ostensibly in the interests of the stockholders, were in reality attempts on his part to fight the other interests. As soon as matters were smoothed out, he joined with the others in the contracts.

Durant's character was such that he seems to have quarreled with nearly everyone with whom he came in contact. He was supposed to have made himself so objectionable to Henry Farnam as to cause that gentleman to abandon further activities in railroads west of the Missouri River. He treated his chief engineer, Dey, in ways that caused Dey to resign, and afterward Durant attempted to cast slurs on Dey's reputation. Oakes Ames, writing in September 17, 1867, to McComb, said:

"I do not think we should do right to put Durant in as a director, unless he withdraws his injunction suits and submits to the will of the majority. He cannot hurt us half as badly out of the direction as he can in, and there is no pleasure, peace, safety, or comfort with him unless he agrees to abide by the decision of the majority, as the rest of us do."

When Durant ran into General Dodge he met an antagonist worthy of his steel. Through his subordinates, Dodge had made the location up the slope of the Black Hills, and Durant had caused or permitted his consulting engineer, Silas Seymour, to change it, to the detriment of the road. Then on Rock Creek, west of Laramie, by changing the location already made, they added some twenty miles to the length of the line, with a resulting higher cost to the railroad company. When General Grant and others came west, the subject was reviewed, with the result that Durant lost the controversy and no more similar changes were made.

Durant also took a hand in directing construction, and S. B. Reed, superintendent of construction thus describes his interference:

"Dr. Durant is still here and of all men to mix accounts and business, he is the chief. . . . To illustrate, I will give you a short history of our work for the past two or three months. In October last I had a large force on grading, enough to have kept the work well out of the way of the track. Davis and his associates had teams enough in the timber to haul ties to the line of the road as fast as they could be laid. The Doctor took all of Davis' and his associates' teams down the road to distribute ties and timber. He also took one half of all the force of all the graders on the line and put them on the same service. This reduction of the grading and tie-hauling teams retarded the work so much that before it could be done the ground was frozen and a large amount of earth excavation, which should and would have been done before frost, had my arrangements not been interfered with, at a cost of not exceeding thirty cents per cubic yard, has now cost as much as any solid rock on the line of work, as it was done night and day by blasting frozen ground. Ties, of course, were all used up in a short time and then all the teams that could be obtained at enormous prices were rushed into the mountains to haul ties to the line of the road. Immense amounts of money were squandered uselessly and not as much work done as would have been done if we had kept steadily moving all branches, seeing that none were behind. Then no confusion would have occurred, each part of the work would have kept pace with the others and today more road would have been built than we now have and money enough saved to nearly complete the road to Ogden, thirty-eight miles. . . .

"A large amount of money has been spent during the past two months and the Doctor himself, I think, is getting frightened at the bills. He costs hundreds of thousands of dollars extra every month he remains here and does not advance, but retards the work. . . .

"No one can tell by Mr. Durant's talk what he thinks of a man, his best friends may not know what he means when talking to them."

These quotations are from a compilation of letters written by Samuel B. Reed to his wife and family covering the period of organization of the Union Pacific's construction, 1864 to 1869.

Durant kept in touch with the road until the rails met at Promontory. He then returned east and never again visited the scene of his labors. On November 18, 1870, he was elected a Fellow of the American Society of Civil Engineers. Durant sold his Union Pacific stock and with his large fortune engaged in building the Adirondack Railroad, of which he was chief stockholder, president, and general manager. The panic of 1873, however, greatly reduced his fortune. He died in 1885.

Thomas C. Durant was evidently neither better nor worse than his contemporaries. It is evident that he regarded the Union Pacific as a contracting job on which to make money.

However, his restless energy pushed the road to completion years before it was expected to be finished. While he spent money recklessly, rapid construction might have been justified by the fact that interest charges were thereby reduced and the road placed on an earning basis much sooner. Durant's dictatorial character repelled many who might have been his friends. His force of character, unceasing determination, and attention to all details in the office or in the field, justifies the conclusion that Durant was the man who above all others deserves credit as the driving force in the building of the great Union Pacific.

### OAKES AMES

Oakes Ames was also an indispensable man in the building of the Union Pacific. It was his task, which he took upon himself, to bring to the work sufficient cash resources to make the project financially possible.

Oakes Ames, the son of Oliver and Susannah Ames, was born at Easton, Massachusetts, January 10, 1804, and died at the same place May 8, 1873. His education was obtained in the public schools, with a few months being spent at Dighton Academy. He then entered his father's tool and shovel factory as a laborer. When his father retired in 1844, the factory was continued by Oakes and his younger brother, Oliver, who in later years became president of the Union Pacific. Shovels made by the Ames brothers were known over the entire country for their excellent quality.

Like many Massachusetts men, Oakes Ames was a "Free Soiler," with an interest in politics, so that in 1860 he became a member of the Executive Council of his state. In 1862 he was elected to the national House of Representatives, and was re-elected four times, serving until his death. In the House he was a member of the Committees on Manufactures and of the Pacific Railroads, where he became familiar with the transcontinental railroad project.

In 1865 Ames interested himself in the Credit Mobilier, and

[178]

by his efforts the capital of that company was brought up to $2,500,000, later to be increased to $3,750,000 in 1867. By that time it had become apparent that Durant and his friends did not have sufficient resources to carry on the work of building the road. In addition, a rupture took place between Ames and Durant. Durant was thereupon ejected from the Credit Mobilier, with Ames taking over the work of raising funds to complete the road. In this he was successful, although at times the brothers' shovel business was badly in debt. At one point their private affairs carried obligations amounting to some $8,000,000, which were liquidated only after Oakes Ames was dead.

In order to forward the work on the railroad, Ames took a contract in 1867 for the construction and equipment of 667 miles of road. This section extended from the 100th meridian westward over the Black Hills, and in the opinion of many at the time, the contract was an insane venture owing to the unknown costs that would be encountered in such a region. The venture was ultimately profitable, but Ames made himself responsible for a contract involving over $47,000,000. However, he assigned the contract to the seven trustees and thus personal liability was avoided. It was only by Ames's assuming a personal contract that financial interests in New England could be brought to the point where they were willing to buy the railroad's securities. When the Ames contract was completed, the road was so far advanced that the moneyed men saw the project through to the end.

It was Oakes Ames's policy personally to interview men of means to show them the chances of profit in the railroad, which was a difficult job at best because not even Ames himself was positive that it would pay out. However, the construction company that received the railroad securities as payment for work done, did offer a chance to make an immediate profit on the investment, an argument evidently used by Ames. It was with this inducement that he sold a few shares of Credit Mobilier to members of Congress in 1867 and 1868. Some of the most prominent members of Congress, twenty-two in all, purchased stock from Ames in small amounts, Ames's idea being, of course, that the railroad needed friends in that body. The road was being assailed from every side by a variety of enemies, some of whom were in Congress, at a time when the company was split by internal dissention. When, in 1872 and 1873, the storm broke in Congress with the Credit Mobilier investigation, most of the members of that august body who had bought stock, ran for cover. Some denied their transactions and all had excuses for being "accidentally" involved.

The result of the investigation was that the Poland Committee brought in a verdict of guilty and recommended the expulsion of Oakes Ames from Congress. Ames had given complete information regarding the transactions and throughout the inquiry had maintained his innocence. The House then changed the verdict to one of censure, which proved to be one of the most absurd verdicts in American history. By it, Ames was judged guilty of having given bribes, but Representative Schuyler Colfax, who was later Vice President, James A. Garfield who later became President, and other Senators and Representatives, were not guilty of having accepted the alleged bribes.

Oakes Ames returned to his home at Easton, a worn-out and disillusioned man, stung by the ingratitude of the people whom he thought he had served to the best of his ability. Ten weeks after the vote of censure, he died. His friends, however, did not accept the decision of the politicians in Washington. From all sides came expressions of confidence in Ames and belief in his innocence. A resolution to that effect was even put through the legislature at the time. At a later date the Union Pacific erected a granite pyramid sixty feet high on the Sherman Summit of the Black Hills, on which a bronze tablet records that it was erected to the memory of Oakes and Oliver Ames. The monument still stands, but the relocated line of the railroad today passes several miles to the south.

Oakes Ames was a strong, rugged, and tireless worker who gave his energies and his wealth to the building of the Union Pacific in what he believed was his patriotic duty. His method of handling the contracting company was bad for the railroad, since it loaded the road with debt, but it was the method common at the time and Oakes Ames took the situation as he found it. The chance of large profits was the only thing that could induce men of wealth to provide the necessary funds, and even so it required the example of Oakes Ames and his brother Oliver to induce them to subscribe. The condemnation of Ames by the House of Representatives was an ignoble example of politics brought about by the desire of the people for a scapegoat.

In later years, long after Ames was dead, the people of Boston erected a memorial hall to record his services. It was opened November 7, 1881, with a ceremony at which tributes by prominent men from various parts of the country were read. General Dodge expressed his opinion of Oakes Ames and the proceedings in Congress in the following terms:

"In 1865 Oakes and Oliver Ames of Boston became interested in the enterprise, bringing their own fortune and a very large following, and really gave the first impetus to the building of the road. There was no man connected with it who devoted his time and money with the single purpose of benefit to the country and Government more than Oakes Ames, and there never was a more unjust, uncalled-for and ungrateful act of Congress than that which censured him for inducing, as it is claimed, members of Congress to take interest in the construction company. . . . Oakes Ames once wrote me, when it seemed almost impossible to raise money to meet of expenditures: 'Go ahead; the work shall not stop, even if it takes the shovel shop.' . . . When the day came that the business of the Ameses should go or the Union Pacific, Oakes Ames said: 'Save the credit of the road; I will fail.' It took a man of courage and patriotism to make that decision and lay down a reputation and business credit

[181]

that was invaluable in New England, and one that had come down through almost a century."

Senator William Stewart of Nevada, who as a member of the Senate at the time of the investigation was familiar with the proceedings, said in his *Reminiscenses*:

> "I do not feel disposed to discuss or criticize persons who were involved in the Credit Mobilier investigation, but Oakes Ames, notwithstanding the errors he unwittingly committed, deserves well of the American people, and his name should be cherished by all as a brave, energetic, enterprising man.
>
> "The unjust and violent criticism of the press and of ambitious partisans will be deplored in view of the accomplishments of the great work under embarrassing and adverse circumstances and particularly in view of the fact that the Government has received back all of the subsidy granted, dollar for dollar, with interest at six per cent per annum, while the Government was borrowing money for less than four per cent per annum, making a net gain in interest of from two to three per cent."

### GRENVILLE MELLEN DODGE

The boy who was to become a major general of the Union Armies in the Civil War, and who afterward was chief engineer of construction on the Union Pacific and still later on other railroads, was born at Danvers, Massachusetts, on the 12th of April, 1831. He died at his home in Council Bluffs on January 3, 1916, after having lived eighty-five eventful years. In fact, he outlived most of his comrades of the Civil War, as well as many of the men with whom he had been associated during the building of the Union Pacific.

After the usual amount of schooling, Dodge was graduated from Norwich University in December, 1850, and in the following year underwent a six month's special military training. This training was to be of value when he entered the army at the outbreak of the Civil War.

[182]

SIDNEY DILLON

OLIVER AMES

OAKES AMES

THOMAS C. DURANT

OFFICERS OF THE UNION PACIFIC RAILROAD

SAMUEL B. REED
Superintendent of Construction.

PETER A. DEY
First Chief Engineer.

GEN. JOHN S. CASEMENT
Construction Contractor.

GEN. GRENVILLE M. DODGE
Chief Engineer after Dey's resignation.

LEADERS IN UNION PACIFIC ENGINEERING AND CONSTRUCTION

Railroad supplies brought from distant points by river steamer were often transferred to ox-drawn wagons for shipment to construction points along the way.

View of Omaha in the 'sixties taken from a bluff west of the city and showing the Missouri River in the background.

General Casement's twelve-car construction train, loaded with equipment and with wood piled high in the tenders, ready to roll west over newly-laid track.

The Union Pacific construction train joins a wagon party at end of track near Archer, Wyoming, in 1867.

The Union Pacific paralleled the old Oregon Trail in Echo Canyon, Utah, in 1869.

Burning Rock Cut showing rock stratification before the tracks were laid.

Carmichael's Cut at Granite Canyon, Wyoming. This sixty-foot deep cut was blasted through solid red granite for a distance of almost eight hundred feet.

Granite Canyon, nineteen miles west of Cheyenne. Compare height of grading and fill with telegraph poles at left and figure of man at right.

Eastern portal of Union Pacific Tunnel No. 3 in the Weber River Canyon not far from the city of Ogden, Utah.

## BRIDGES OF THE UNION PACIFIC
Pile trestle bridge more than a third of a mile long over the Platte River.

The first Omaha Bridge across the Missouri River to Council Bluffs cost $1,750,000 and its spans totaled over half a mile in length.

Green River Bridge at Green River, Wyoming, is overshadowed by Citadel Rock towering high in the background.

Dale Creek Bridge, owing to its height, was the most important crossing in the mountain section of the Union Pacific line.

Devil's Gate in Utah's Weber Canyon was one of the few places on the Union Pacific route where heavy rock excavation was necessary.

View of Echo City, Utah, showing layout of a Union Pacific construction town.

Engine No. 119 represented Union Pacific motive power at the ceremonies when the rails were joined at Promontory.

The sturdy "Vice Adm. Farragut," one of the first locomotives on the Union Pacific, was built by the Norris Locomotive Works at Lancaster, Pennsylvania.

Locomotive No. 75, a typical passenger engine, was a product of the Rogers Locomotive Works of Paterson, New Jersey.

Union Pacific Engine No. 121 heads east along the track from Ogden.

Engine No. 86 is shown at Green River Station in western Wyoming.

The track-laying crew were slightly ahead of these telegraph linemen when this picture was taken in Weber Canyon.

The Union Pacific's famous 1,000 Mile Tree (one thousand miles from Omaha) was located thirty-two miles east of Ogden.

Officers of the Union Pacific hold a conference in their private car at Echo City, Utah. Scated at the table left to right are Silas Seymour, Sidney Dillon, Thomas Durant with Samuel Reed standing behind Dr. Durant. Note firearms crossed over doorway.

Union Pacific Engine No. 119 crosses a Central Pacific trestle near Promontory, seven hundred and seventy-eight miles from Sacramento.

Abandoned Central Pacific and Union Pacific grades parallel each other in this modern photograph taken near Promontory.

The author standing beside the Last Spike Monument at Promontory, marking the spot where three-quarters of a century earlier America's dream of a Pacific railroad became a reality.

On leaving school, Dodge yielded to the fever that drove able men out of the civilized East into the undeveloped West. With some friends, he worked on survey parties at Peru, Illinois, and shortly afterward joined a survey party on the Illinois Central. Its was at Peru that he met Anne Brown, whom he married on May 28, 1854.

Dodge soon tired of the work on the Illinois Central, so it was a stroke of good fortune when he was introduced to Peter A. Dey in 1852. The next year Dodge was made chief of a survey party. As chief engineer of the Mississippi and Missouri Railroad, Dey was about to begin location surveys across Iowa. The surveys commenced at Rock Island and across the river at Davenport, Iowa, on May 27, 1853, with Sheffield, Farnam, and Dey being the moving spirits. Dodge, who then was only twenty-two years of age, was appointed principal assistant in charge of party under Dey.

The surveyors passed Iowa City and on the 22nd of November reached Council Bluffs, formerly known as Kanesville and at the time a river town of some importance. The Mormons had gathered near there in 1846 and it was from that point in 1847 that Brigham Young led the first party across the plains and mountains to found Salt Lake City. On instruction from Dey, Dodge took his party across the Missouri River and examined the country westward across the rolling hills to the Elkhorn River, where they reached the valley of the Platte.

Unfortunately, financial troubles of the following years put a stop to railroad construction in Iowa, with the result that the M. and M. project failed. Dodge then engaged in various kinds of work, and at one time settled on a farm along the Elkhorn River. However, he continued to gather all information available on the emigrant trails to the Pacific and on the nature of the country, so that he was able to prepare a map that was used by emigrants who crossed the Missouri at Council Bluffs on their way west.

In the spring of 1856 Dodge was again at work on the con-

[183]

struction of the M. and M. Railroad, the promoters again were busy trying to get subsidies from the state and counties, and again the work was stopped, this time by the panic of 1857. After a trip to New York, where he explained the situation to the directors of the M. and M. and of the Rock Island, Dodge moved his home to Council Bluffs, where with a partner he engaged in the business of banking, milling, merchandising, contracting, freighting, and real estate. However, in 1859 he was back again in the valley of the Platte making a railroad reconnaissance for Henry Farnam.

It was in that same summer of 1859 that, in connection with real estate interests, Lincoln visited Council Bluffs, and Dodge was called on to give the future President a detailed description of the projected route to the West. Later, when President, Lincoln remembered the conversation with Dodge and called him to Washington for further information.

Dodge was in Washington when Lincoln was inaugurated, having gone there with Farnam, Durant, and other railroad men. Farnam wanted him to give up business so that he could join the Rock Island, and a few days later Dodge did go to New York to talk with the men of that railroad. However, the Civil War broke out shortly after that, and all thoughts of railroading were forgotten for the time being.

Owing to his military training at Norwich, young Dodge was made colonel of the 4th Iowa regiment. He was at the head of his regiment at the Battle of Pea Ridge, where he was wounded and out of action for two weeks. For his services at Pea Ridge he was made a brigadier general, and in 1862 was sent east of the Mississippi to repair railroads that the Confederates had destroyed. Much of his time in the war was spent in such work. He served under Grant in the western campaigns and was assigned to command a division of the Army of the Tennessee. When Grant went east to command all the armies, Dodge was transferred to Sherman's command, being with that general on his march to the sea. Dodge next commanded the Sixteenth

Corps at the Battle of Atlanta, which proved to be the deciding battle of the campaign. Later, in August, the general was critically wounded in the head by a rifle ball and lay unconscious for two days. In fact, a report reached his home in Danvers that he had been killed. On his partial recovery, he went to New York at the request of Durant to discuss the affairs of the Union Pacific, and from there proceeded to Grant's headquarters. He had been commissioned a major general and wanted to get back into the war, but both Grant and Sherman knew that he was physically unfit. He was ordered to the Army of the Tennessee at Nashville, but before reaching it was diverted to St. Louis, where he was given command of the Department of Missouri and told by Lincoln to pacify that state, which was half Union and half Confederate. Dodge took strong measures, remaining in command two months. The war was drawing to a close, so that when the headquarters of the Department of Missouri were moved to Fort Leavenworth to be combined with the Department of Kansas, Dodge was placed in command on January 30, 1865. When the war ended, Grant asked that Dodge remain in the regular army.

At this time the Indians had become more troublesome than usual, and after Lincoln was assassinated and it was found that the Missouri troubles were not likely to break out again, Dodge was given command of all the United States forces in Kansas, Nebraska, Colorado, and Utah. It was during the military movements of 1865, when General Dodge was returning through the Black Hills from Fort Laramie, that the long sloping ridge from a mountain pass was discovered. It was the key to an entrance through the mountain fastness for which Dodge had been looking, and it was along that ridge that the Union Pacific was later built.

During the war, and afterward in the Indian campaigns, Durant was in constant touch with Dodge and frequently asked him to leave the army to become chief engineer of the railroad, which was then getting started. Durant had tried to handle the engineering with several subordinates but had not succeeded, since in the meantime he had alienated Peter Dey. His associates were suspicious of his actions, with the result that after he had spent a large part of his own fortune he could not raise any more money. It was not until the Indian campaign was completed that Durant prevailed on Dodge to leave the army, and Dodge in turn prevailed on Grant and Sherman to allow him to leave. Dodge met Durant in April, 1866, and on obtaining a leave of absence from the army from General Grant, he entered upon his duties as the Union Pacific's chief engineer at Omaha, May 6, 1866.

At that time the Hoxie contract was under way and the railroad was moving west toward the 100th meridian. From that point on, the story of the Union Pacific was to a great extent the story of its chief engineer. Dodge's attention was directed first to determining the route over the Black Hills and across the Wyoming Basin to Salt Lake. As chief engineer of the railroad he did not have charge of construction and had no control over contractors, but he did occupy a position of trust with the parties in the organization opposed to Durant and they relied upon him to counterbalance Durant's questionable moves. It was Dodge who stood his ground when Durant revised the location of the line to the disadvantage of the railroad at a great increase in cost, most of which went into the treasury of the Credit Mobilier.

Throughout the entire work Dodge had the full confidence of the men who were furnishing the money, and he also had the full confidence of Generals Grant and Sherman. While Durant had the power, and while he made enemies at every turn, the influence of Dodge went a long way in holding Durant in check and in keeping the project moving.

Mrs. Dodge, with money probably furnished by her husband, bought 100 shares of Credit Mobilier stock; and the Wilson Committee, in 1873, endeavored to blacken Dodge's reputation from this circumstance. Fortunately the attempt failed, and

[186]

the honorable reputation of the great engineer increased with the years.

After the Union Pacific was joined with the Central Pacific at Promontory, Dodge spent a good deal of his time in bringing the road up to standard. Durant was gone, and a large part of the internal strife that had marked the construction of the road vanished. Dodge played an important part in constructing the bridge over the Missouri River between Omaha and Council Bluffs, a work that finally completed the original Union Pacific. Although he resigned from the service of the road in 1870, he served afterward on the company's board of directors.

In 1866 Dodge was elected a representative to Congress from the fifth Iowa district and served one term. He declined renomination, but afterward he was often in Washington in the interests of the Union Pacific and other roads.

After completion of the Union Pacific, Dodge resigned to become chief engineer of the Texas Pacific in 1871. That road failed in 1873, whereupon Dodge became identified with the projects of Jay Gould, for whom he worked ten years. Afterward he conducted the surveys that formed the basis for the extension of the Union Pacific to Portland and Puget Sound. Under Gould, Dodge became president of a number of southwestern railroads and was employed in the management of the large system of roads. He found time, however, to examine projects in association with Sir William Van Horne of the Canadian Pacific for railroads in Cuba, and directed the construction of a road across the island.

Increasing age finally compelled Dodge to retire from active participation in railroad affairs after 1912. It was nearly sixty years since he carried his surveys across Iowa to Council Bluffs for the Mississippi and Missouri Railroad, and then had crossed the Missouri on a flatboat for the investigation westward that marked the beginning of the Union Pacific. In length of service and in magnitude of works, General Dodge must be classified as the foremost railroad engineer of his century. In recognition of his services to the profession of engineering, the American Society of Civil Engineers, on March 2, 1915, conferred upon him the degree of Honorary Member, the highest award the Society can bestow.

### PETER A. DEY

The first chief engineer of the Union Pacific was a man of sterling character who enjoyed a long and honorable career. His connection with the railroad was brief and it terminated before much construction work had been done. However, as the predecessor of Grenville Dodge and as the man in direct charge of engineering at the beginning, his work is worth noting.

Peter Anthony Dey was born at Romulus, New York, on July 27, 1825, and he died at the advanced age of eighty-six years, July 12, 1911. His ancestry was Dutch. His early life was spent in New York where after a two-year course at Geneva College, ending in 1840, he studied law for two years and was admitted to practice. From there his inclination led him into railroad engineering, and for two years he worked for the New York and Erie Railroad, after which he was employed for two years on the canals of New York, constructing locks. In 1850 he came into contact with Joseph E. Sheffield and Henry Farnam, the railroad builders, on the La Porte section of the Northern Indiana Railroad, and was with them when the Michigan Southern Railroad entered Chicago in March, 1852.

When the railroad builders were moving westward, Dey was made one of the principal assistant engineers under William Jarvis on the Chicago and Rock Island, in which capacity he hired young Grenville Dodge in 1852. The surveys across Iowa in 1853 led to the reconnaissance of the Platte Valley, and when the intermittent work on the Mississippi and Missouri Railroad was going forward, Dey was with that line as chief engineer of construction.

It was while living in Iowa City that Dey married Catherine

Thompson, on October 23, 1856. In 1860 he was elected mayor of the town.

Three years later, in 1863, Durant ordered Dey to make surveys for a railroad westward from Omaha to the Platte Valley, and also to make a reconnaissance up the Platte Valley across the Rocky and Wasatch mountains to Salt Lake City. Returning from the trip, Dey went to Washington and New York with the report.

Ground for the Union Pacific was broken at the end of 1863, and on January 3, 1864, Dey was appointed chief engineer of the railroad, a position he was to occupy for only a year. It was when construction out of Omaha was started on the line Dey had located that the controversy over the route took place, and this was also the time when the first of the construction contracts, the so-called Hoxie contract, that was later turned over to the Credit Mobilier, was drawn up. Dey strenuously opposed the contract, with the result that he resigned rather than be a party to a form of proceeding that had hindered the construction of the M. and M. line. His resignation and protest to General Dix, president of the railroad, had no effect, and from that time on Dey had no connection with the railroad he had helped to start. However, he testified at the Credit Mobilier investigation in Washington in 1873.

Of Dey, General Dodge said: "Mr. Dey was made chief engineer of the M. and M. and took me to Iowa as assistant, and placed me in charge of the party in the field—certainly a very fine promotion for the limited experience I had had—and it is one of the greatest satisfactions and pleasures of my life to have had his friendship from the time I entered his service until now. Mr. Dey is not only a very distinguished citizen of Iowa, but is one of the most distinguished engineers in the country. He is known for his great ability, his uprightness, and the square deal he gave every one, and he has greatly honored the state in the many public positions he has held. I look back upon my service with him with the greatest pleasure. My practical experience under him and the confidence he placed in me were of incalculable benefit to me, and the example he set us has lasted me through my life, and I shall always honor, respect, and hold him in the highest consideration and friendship."

### SAMUEL BENEDICT REED

By perusing the biographies of the engineers who were connected with the Union Pacific, one can trace the history of American railroad construction all the way from the eastern states in the early part of the nineteenth century to the Far West when the line across the continent was completed in 1869. Take, for example, the life story of Samuel Benedict Reed.

Reed was born at Arlington, Vermont, November 18, 1818, and after a long life mostly taken up with railroad building, he died near Pasadena, California, on Christmas Day, 1891. In 1855 he married Jane Eliza Earl, a Pennsylvania girl, whose letters from her husband show that she was a good and faithful wife.

Reed was educated at Middleport Academy and, like many another young engineer, worked on the Erie Canal in 1841. In 1842 he went west to find employment on the Detroit and Pontiac Railroad. Then he moved to Joliet, Illinois, with his father, and later became locating engineer on the Michigan Central. It was there that he became friends with Sheffield, Farnam, John B. Jervis, and Peter A. Dey. Before the road was completed to Chicago, Reed was engaged on location for the Chicago and Rock Island from Joliet to Chicago. In 1859 he was in Iowa on the Burlington Railroad, and finally in 1864 he began work for the Union Pacific.

Reed was sent to Salt Lake City by Peter A. Dey as chief engineer in charge of one of the three parties on the final surveys before definite location. The only other surveys that had been made in that portion of the country had been made by a son of Brigham Young in the previous year. After extensive surveys, the work closed down for the winter, but by 1865 Reed was again in charge of the job in that region. He also conducted a reconnaissance of the Wasatch Mountains and surveys across the deserts south of Great Salt Lake to the Humboldt River.

Active construction work on the railroad started in 1866, whereupon Reed was taken from the surveys and made superintendent of construction. For the next three and a half years he was at the head of the construction forces and, largely in response to his efforts, the railroad was driven westward at a speed never before equaled. It was a time of trial, hard work and disappointments, due to the high-handed actions of Dr. Durant. At one time Reed wanted to resign, but Dodge supported him, as did other men in the East, with the result that Durant reappointed Reed to his former position. In the end Reed carried the work to a conclusion at Promontory where, together with Strobridge of the Central Pacific, he placed in position the polished laurel tie that held the last spike of gold.

That Mr. Reed was a competent engineer was well recognized during his life time, nor was he forgotten after his death. When a celebration was held on October 10, 1922, at Joliet by the Chicago, Rock Island and Pacific Railway to commemorate its seventieth anniversary of service, a monument supplied by that road and the Union Pacific was dedicated to Samuel B. Reed. It was an eighteen-ton granite boulder from Echo Canyon and was placed in the courthouse yard, that being the spot where Reed began his surveys for the road seventy-two years before. A bronze tablet set in the boulder recites the facts of the first survey, together with the manifold services of the engineer.

### JOHN STEPHEN CASEMENT

General Casement's career is a good example of how an able man of character and determination could reach a position high among those who developed the country when the movement westward was in full tide. His parents came from the Isle of Man, and shortly after they reached America, he was born at

[191]

Geneva, New York, January 19, 1829. As a boy, he found a boy's employment on a railroad. Later, when he was fourteen, the family moved to a farm near Ann Arbor, Michigan, near which he worked as a common laborer on the Michigan Central when he was sixteen. Although of slight stature, young Casement was noted for his strength and ability in railroad work. His father having died at an early age, the young man made a home for his mother and maintained it.

At the age of twenty-one, in the spring of 1850, Casement worked as a laborer on the Cleveland, Columbus and Cincinnati Railroad, later becoming foreman of a track-laying gang. From 1852 to 1853 he ran a freight train on the Cleveland, Painesville and Ashtabula Railroad, now a part of the New York Central System, and in the spring of 1853 he took his first contract for filling ravines crossed by trestles, as well as for laying some sections of double track. At this period Casement married Frances Jennings and made his home at Painesville, Ohio.

His next contract was for laying track and ballasting 300 miles on one road and 150 miles on another line. While he was engaged in this work, the Civil War broke out. Leaving the contracts in charge of his brother Dan, John Casement enlisted in the 7th Ohio Volunteer Infantry, where he was made a major. At the battle of Cross Lanes in West Virginia he performed such good service that he was made a colonel, and mustered the 103rd Ohio Volunteers, which regiment he commanded to the end of the war. For distinguished service at the battle of Franklin, Casement was breveted brigadier general by President Lincoln.

At the close of the war he formed a partnership with his brother Daniel under the firm name of J. S. and D. T. Casement, whereupon they took the contract for laying the track of the Union Pacific, which contract was to include a large part of the grading. On completing that work the firm engaged extensively in railroad construction throughout New York, Pennsylvania, Ohio, Indiana, Kentucky, Nebraska and West

Virginia. In 1897, at the age of sixty-eight, he contracted with the government of Costa Rica for railroad work that required six years for completion. He served a term as delegate to Congress from the territory of Wyoming and he also served a term in the Ohio State Senate. He died in his eightieth year. His work on the Union Pacific was done, in the language of General Dodge, by "the best-organized, best-equipped, and best-disciplined track force I have ever seen."

### SIDNEY DILLON

Of all the men connected with the building of the Union Pacific Railroad, Sidney Dillon had had more railroad experience than anyone else, not even excepting Thomas C. Durant. In 1887 he testified: "I saw the first locomotive run in the United States over the Albany and Schenectady Railroad, the little 'John Bull,' and since that day I have done nothing much but build railroads and manage them."

It was estimated that he built from 2,500 to 3,000 miles of road, costing somewhere between $75,000,000 and $100,000,000, sometimes alone, at other times with associates.

Dillon was born on May 7, 1812, in Northampton, New York, where the family had resided for several generations, his grandfather having served with the American forces during the Revolution. He received such elementary education as the times afforded, but native ability explained his rise to the position of success that he attained in his long life of eighty years.

He first served as errand boy on the Mohawk and Hudson Railroad, and later on the Rensselaer and Saratoga Railroad. Next, as overseer for contractors and later as foreman, he worked on railroads in Connecticut and Massachusetts. He then entered the contracting business on his own account. In this capacity he executed contracts for a predecessor of the Boston and Albany, for the Troy and Schenectady, the Cheshire Railroad of Vermont, the Vermont and Massachusetts Railroad, the Rutland and Burlington in Vermont, the Central Railroad of New Jersey, the Philadelphia and Erie, the Erie and Cleveland, the New Jersey Central, the Morris and Essex, the New Orleans, and the Mobile and Chattanooga. He had a contract for widening the Morris Canal, and even when the Union Pacific was under construction he was associated with John I. Blair in contracting for Iowa railroads as well as executing contracts on the Boston, Hartford and Erie Railroad, the Connecticut Valley, the Chillicothe, Council Bluffs and Omaha, and the Canada Southern, together with additional work on the Morris and Essex line. One of his major contracts was the building of the tunnel for the Grand Central Station in New York, a job that cost $5,000,000.

Dillon first became interested in the Union Pacific project in 1865, when he became a stockholder in the Credit Mobilier. His wide experience in railroad building led him to take an active part in the work, so that when Durant was ousted from control of the company Dillon was made president, a position that he filled until the road was finished. He was a member of the board that had charge of the Oakes Ames and the Davis contracts, and with John B. Alley and Rowland Hazard, formed the executive committee of the trustees. Dillon became a stockholder in the Union Pacific Railroad and at a meeting in New York October 3, 1886, was elected a director, in which capacity he served for nearly twenty-six years. He was president of the Union Pacific for two periods: March 11, 1874, to June 19, 1884; and again, November 26, 1890, to April 23, 1892, for a total of nearly twelve years. For a long time he was a member of the executive committee of the Union Pacific, especially during the construction of the road, and after his retirement from the presidency he remained as chairman of the board of directors until his death.

Wealth came to him from his many contracts, so that after 1870 his time was largely taken up with financial affairs. He was an associate with Jay Gould in the management of the properties controlled by Gould, and later was a director of the

Western Union Telegraph, the Manhattan Elevated Railroad, the Missouri Pacific Railway, the Wabash Railway, the Chicago, Rock Island and Pacific Railway, the Canada Southern Railway, the Wheeling and Lake Erie Railroad, the Pacific Mail Steamship Company, and other smaller organizations.

Dillon was elected a Fellow of the American Society of Civil Engineers on March 20, 1870.

As a typical representative of the Union Pacific men, Sidney Dillon's useful career has been set forth at some length. He was active in the construction of the railroad and was present when the roads were joined at Promontory on that day in May, 1869, receiving the silver spike that was driven after the golden spike. He was highly esteemed by his associates and on his death a resolution was adopted by the Union Pacific's board of directors, from which the following is taken: "The part taken by Mr. Dillon in the construction of the Union Pacific Company's lines and in the administration of its affairs, his steadfast devotion through evil and through good report, and his long and honorable service in its executive departments have more than once been attested by this board. Those of us who have been associated with him know with what pride he contemplated the growth and development of the enterprise, his confidence in its future, and his zeal for its further growth and expansion. His pride was almost paternal, his loyalty to it was strenuous and constant."

### GEORGE FRANCIS TRAIN

While Train was not directly connected with the building of the Union Pacific, he was a factor in its organization, and as such merits our attention. He was born in Boston May 24, 1829, and died in New York, January 19, 1904. The son of a Boston merchant, he was sent to Liverpool at the age of twenty-one to take charge of that branch of his father's business. He became a partner in 1853, and in 1854 he was in Australia. In 1858, on terminating the partnership, he became interested in

English street railways and also was instrumental in floating bonds for the Atlantic and Great Western Railroad. During the Civil War he made speeches in England in favor of the Northern side.

Returning to America, Train plunged into the world of railroading, where he was active in the organization of the Union Pacific, having subscribed for twenty shares of the original list. He was commissioned by Durant to purchase the charter of the Pennsylvania Fiscal Agency, which he did, the name being changed later to the Credit Mobilier. He was also in the Credit Foncier, which was organized to deal in lands along the Union Pacific when towns were laid out by the railroad company and lots sold. One who saw him in 1866 describes him this way:

"He organized and conducted a heavy commission business in Australia and astonished his neighbors in that era of fabulous prices, with Brussels carpets and marble counters and a free champagne luncheon daily in his business office. Afterward he made the circuit of the world, wrote books of travel, fought British prejudice against street railways, occupying his leisure by fiery and audacious American war speeches to our island cousins, until he spent a fortune. and enjoyed the delights of a month in a British prison.

"Thence he returned to America, lectured everywhere; and now he is trying to build a belt of cities across the continent. At least a magnificent project. Curiously combining keen sagacity with wild enthusiasm, a man who might have built the pyramids, or been confined in a straight jacket for eccentricities, according to the age he lived in, he observes dryly that since he began to make money, people no longer pronounce him crazy."

Train was at the breaking of ground at Omaha and helped in the Grand Pacific Excursion, making speeches and trying to please everyone. Such a man could not possibly get along with Durant. Superintendent Reed observed:

"The political fight . . . was terminated so that all were disappointed. George Francis Train, as he says, was sacrificed by

[196]

the railroad men and cursed long and loud. He gave us all notice that none that are now in good places will be there in thirty days from the time of his starting for New York, including T. C. Durant. One stage coach or steamboat could not hold two such men as T. C. Durant and G. F. Train on their way east. George Francis goes from Nebraska disgusted with western politics, and I think with a large flea in his ear."

In 1868 Train was a candidate for the presidency. He made five trips around the world, wrote many books, was in the Paris Commune of 1871, and was finally adjudged insane. His land speculations at Council Bluffs were largely a failure and he claimed title to land in Omaha worth $30,000,000, but nothing ever came of it.

The sketches of the careers of the most prominent men connected with the building of the Union Pacific, as given in the preceding pages, illustrate the type of men that carried the enterprise to completion. It remains to mention others who played a greater or lesser part in the work.

Oliver Ames, the younger brother of Oakes Ames, was president pro tem of the railroad company during the absence of General Dix, and in March, 1868, became president, a position he held until March, 1871. He was also connected with the Credit Mobilier. Other directors either of the railroad or of the Credit Mobilier were John B. Alley, Cornelius S. Bushnell, Rowland G. Hazard, John R. Duff, at one time vice president, Henry S. McComb, and Charles A. Lambard. John J. Cisco was treasurer for a time, and at another time E. H. Rollins was treasurer and secretary of the railroad. Henry V. Poor was secretary when the Union Pacific was organized, the same position being held in 1876 by Charles Tuttle.

Operation of the railroad was under the direction of Webster Snyder, who was an active and efficient railroad man.

Among the engineers were Colonel Silas Seymour, the consulting engineer, B. B. Brayton, F. M. Case, and Samuel B.

Reed. James A. Evans and J. E. House, along with Reed, were division engineers in charge of surveying parties. Chief of the survey parties, designated as assistant engineers, were Percy T. Brown and L. L. Hills, who were killed by Indians, Colonel J. O. Hudnut, M. F. Hurd, Thomas H. Bates, F. C. Hodges, Jacob Blickensderfer, Jr., John O'Neill, James R. Maxwell, Francis E. Appleton, and J. F. McCabe. Reed and Evans became superintendents of construction on completion of the surveys. The first geologist employed was James T. Hodge, who was followed by David Van Lennep.

# CHAPTER 9

# The Union Pacific Railroad Company

THE ELECTION of Abraham Lincoln as the sixteenth President of the United States, together with the commencement of the Civil War, brought the subject of a Pacific Railroad clearly before the public and before Congress. Durant's group had already paid the cost of the surveys and had urged that the road be built. It had also been decided by Congress that the road, if built, should be constructed by a private corporation assisted by the government. Politicians of many degrees of ability had their favorite plans, but it was not until March, 1860, when Samuel L. Curtis, representative from Iowa, was named chairman of the Select Committee of Congress, to which all Pacific railroad bills were referred, that a proper law began to take shape. Earlier, the northern route to Ogden had come to the fore, as had a proposal for two roads, one on the central route, favored by a majority of the committee, and one on the 32nd parallel of latitude, the southern route.

[199]

With the secession of the Confederate States the southern route was, of course, eliminated, but the Northern Pacific supporters still remained active. St. Louis was situated too close to the disputed territory, which fact allowed the Chicago interests to become the most active and influential.

A special session of Congress was called, and it was at this session that Representative Curtis introduced his bill for the creation of the company to build the road. Again the Northern Pacific and the St. Louis interests presented their bills. Notwithstanding, the final bill creating the Union Pacific Railroad and recognizing the Central Pacific Railroad was at last passed in June, 1862. The Senate vote on June 20 was twenty-five to five, and the House vote on June 24 was 104 to twenty-one. The long contest over the project was ended when President Lincoln placed his signature on the bill on July 21.

It has often been said that both the Union Pacific and the Central Pacific influenced Congress unfairly in the proceedings that led to the passage of the Act. The fact is that both parties did use their influence with Congress, but the efforts of the Union Pacific were greater, since the Union Pacific Company was organized by the federal government, while the Central Pacific Company came under the laws of California. It was also supposed at that time that the Union Pacific would build westward to the border of California, there to meet the Central Pacific.

The Act of 1862 bore marks of the politicians' work. The Union Pacific Company was created, to be composed of 158 persons, whose names were duly listed. To this body were added five commissioners representing the national government. These 163 men were from twenty-five states, including California and Oregon. The group, which was called the Board of Commissioners of the Union Pacific Railroad and Telegraph Company, were to open books for subscription for stock. When 2,000 shares had been subscribed and 10 per cent paid in, a meeting of the stockholders was to be called by the commissioners, at which meeting directors were to be elected. After the work of the commissioners had been done, the stockholders were to conduct the affairs of the company.

The stockholders were to meet annually and make the usual by-laws, rules, and regulations to govern the company. There were to be thirteen directors selected by the stockholders, with the government appointing two directors who could not be stockholders. The directors were to appoint the officers of the company. The corporation was "authorized and empowered to lay out, locate, construct, furnish, maintain and enjoy a continuous railroad and telegraph, with appurtenances, from a point on the one hundredth meridian of longitude west from Greenwich, between the south margin of the Republican River, and the north margin of the valley of the Platte River on the territory of Nebraska to the western boundary of Nevada territory." The point was to be selected by the President of the United States after actual surveys had been made. The road was to meet the Central Pacific Railroad of California. Rights of way 400 feet wide over public lands were granted the company, as were necessary grounds for stations, shops, and other buildings.

The land grant consisted of public lands "to the amount of five alternate sections per mile on each side of said railroad, on the line thereof, and within the limits of ten miles on each side of said road not sold, reserved or otherwise disposed of by the United States." All mineral lands were excepted from the grant, but the timber could be used. Patents to the land were to be issued when forty miles of railroad had been completed.

The credit of the government took the form of subsidy bonds given to the company as a loan to be repaid in thirty years. The bonds were to bear 6 per cent interest, which could be "paid in United States Treasury notes, or any other money of currency which the United States have or shall declare lawful money and a legal tender." The bonds were to be of $1,000 denomination, and on completion of forty miles of road and its acceptance by

[201]

the government commissioners, sixteen bonds per mile were to be given to the companies. The bonds were to be a first mortgage on the railroad and telegraph line, and in case of default in repayment by the company, the government could take possession of the property. It also provided, "that for three hundred miles of said road most mountainous and difficult of construction, to wit, one hundred and fifty miles westerly from the eastern base of the Rocky Mountains, and one hundred and fifty miles eastwardly from the western base of the Sierra Nevada Mountains, said points to be fixed by the President of the United States, the bonds to be issued to aid in the contruction thereof shall be treble the number per mile hereinbefore provided, and the same shall be issued, and the lands herein granted to set apart upon the construction of every twenty miles thereof, upon the certificate of the commissioners as aforesaid that twenty consecutive miles of the same are completed; and between the sections last named of one hundred and fifty miles each, the bonds to be issued to aid in the construction thereof shall be double the number per mile first mentioned." It was further provided that "no more than fifty thousand of said bonds be issued under this act."

Other railroads were authorized to share in the grants. The Leavenworth, Pawnee and Western Company of Kansas could construct some line and a connection with the Union Pacific on the 100th meridian. The Hannibal and St. Joseph Railroad and the Pacific Railroad Company of Missouri could unite with the Kansas company. The companies could even enter California if the Central Pacific failed to build to the state line. The Central Pacific Railroad Company of California, "after completing its road across said state is authorized to continue the construction of said railroad and telegraph through the territories of the United States to the Missouri River, including the branch roads specified in this act upon the routes hereinbefore and hereinafter indicated on the terms and conditions provided in this act to the said Union Pacific Railroad Company, until said roads shall meet and connect and the whole line of said railroad and branches and telegraph is completed."

The Act provided for the initial point to be located on the 100th meridian, which in the Platte Valley was about 247 miles west of the western border of Iowa. That point was near Fort Kearney. The Union Pacific was authorized to build to that point on the same terms, and three other roads were given the same privilege. The Union Pacific was obliged to build the line from Sioux City whenever some other line had been built westward across Iowa to that point. The Missouri branch was to be constructed by the Leavenworth, Pawnee and Western Railroad Company. This road afterward became the Union Pacific Railway Company, Eastern Division. From St. Joseph the branch was to be an extension of the Hannibal and St. Joseph.

There were numerous other provisions of the Act, a few of which may be mentioned. The road was to be completed and ready for use by July 1, 1876, or the roads would be forfeited to the United States. The railroad companies could arrange with existing telegraph companies to have the telegraph lines placed along the railway. When net earnings exceeded 10 per cent the government could reduce rates. The companies must keep the lines in repair and transmit dispatches and transport mails, troops, and munitions of war, supplies and public stores, and the compensation for such services must not exceed that charged private parties. The companies must accept the terms of the Act by a given date. The several companies might consolidate after completing the roads. The track should be of a uniform width as fixed by the President, and the grades and curves should not exceed the maximum of the Baltimore and Ohio Railroad. Provision was made for the retention of 15 per cent of the bonds until the road was entirely completed.

After the first act was passed, the President set the gauge of the road at five feet, but Congress decreed, on March 3, 1863, that the gauge should be four feet, eight and a half inches.

[203]

# The First Transcontinental Railroad

In conformity with the Law of 1862, a convention of the commissioners of the Union Pacific Railroad and Telegraph Company was held at Bryan Hall in Chicago on September 2, 1862. Seventy-three delegates from twenty states were present, which number included the five members appointed by the government. From California came three delegates, James T. Ryan, D. O. Mills, the banker, and John R. Robinson. From that state also came O. M. Wozencroft, appointed by the President. Apparently from that time on, however, no California men were interested in the Union Pacific.

The convention organized by selecting Major General Samuel R. Curtis of Iowa as temporary chairman. The permanent officers of the company were William B. Ogden of Chicago, president; Thomas W. Olcott of New York, treasurer; and Henry V. Poor of New York, secretary. The convention passed resolutions having to do with the Civil War, approved the action of Congress in delegating the railroad construction to an incorporated company, passed several other minor resolutions, and arranged to open stock subscription books in thirty-four cities on the first Wednesday of the following November. After this the convention adjourned, *sine die*.

The officers of the company appointed by the convention did indeed open subscription books in thirty-five cities and advertised them in numerous newspapers. Two weeks were allowed for the books to be open, but it was not until September, 1863, after a year had passed, that 2,000 shares had been subscribed and the necessary 10 per cent paid to the treasurer. There obviously was no wild rush to subscribe, since the total of subscribers numbered only 123. Most of the subscriptions were for twenty shares, although there were eight for fifty shares. Brigham Young purchased five shares.

On September 25, 1863, a call for a meeting of the stockholders was issued, and at the meeting held October 29, thirty directors were named, even though the law provided for only thirteen. The list included General Dix and Thomas C. Durant. The next day sixteen directors and the two government directors met to elect Major General John A. Dix as president, Thomas C. Durant as vice president, John J. Cisco as treasurer, and Henry V. Poor as secretary. Because of the scattered residences of the directors, an executive committee of seven was authorized to conduct the affairs of the company. Work on the railroad was to be started as soon as the President of the United States selected an eastern terminus. Dr. Durant submitted a report on the work he had done in sending survey parties into the field and on the instructions given them. The Union Pacific Railroad, after years of talk and over a year spent in organizing, was at last started.

To show that the company meant business, arrangements were made for breaking ground for the new line at Omaha. The misinterpreted decision of President Lincoln was rendered on November 17, and the ceremonies took place December 2, 1863. Hosts of people came and politicians talked. The Governor of Nebraska and the Mayor of Council Bluffs spoke, as did George Francis Train, together with Messrs. Monell, Larimer, and Poppleton. Omaha itself made a general holiday of the great occasion. Numerous telegrams from Washington personages were read, General Dix from New York congratulated Peter Dey, and from New York Durant sent a long telegram of explanation to the committee in charge of the arrangements. Brigham Young was terse in his telegram. The Mayor of Denver pledged the mountains of Colorado gold to the aid of the enterprise, although no one seemed to know how he was going to deliver it. Even Leland Stanford waxed poetic when he stated that "mountain and desert shall soon be overcome." Such things were always said on occasions of that sort. The troubles were to come later.

In the year 1864, following the ground breaking and after some work of grading had been done, Durant decided to change the location of the road out of Omaha. In so doing, the line was lengthened nine miles and the railroad debt increased $450,000. This action stirred up controversy that lasted until late in 1865. In the meantime the Hoxie construction contract of October 3, 1864, was signed, and a course charted that was to be followed by the company until the road was completed.

After the Act of 1862 had created the Union Pacific Railroad Company, efforts to attract capital had failed, owing to a number of causes. The country was involved in the Civil War, which claimed the attention of most of the better men of the country. Then, too, the fact that the government subsidy bonds constituted a first mortgage on the road and since it was not known what the road would cost nor what the future would be, the possibility that the government would foreclose its mortgage and take the property was frightening to private capital. Other important factors were the characters of Durant and of that flamboyant individual, George Francis Train, the men who were in possession of the railroad company and were the active promoters of the project. Cautious men simply would not invest when operators of their type were in control. Something had to be done in order to interest capital in building the road. In California, the men in charge of the Central Pacific were having the same difficulties about money, although their character was different and inspired more confidence.

It was under such conditions that a bill was introduced in Congress to liberalize the existing law in order to rectify the conditions that held the project back. President Lincoln was in favor of a change, and powerful lobbies led by Durant of the Union Pacific and Huntington of the Central Pacific worked for passage of the bill. What arguments they used will never be known, but the result was the Act of 1864, passed in June and signed by the President on July 2, 1864. The most important change from the Act of 1862 related to the status of the subsidy bonds and to the amount of the land grant. The rate of bonds per mile for constructing different sections of the road was not changed, but the two railroad companies were now permitted to issue first-mortgage bonds of their own in an amount not to exceed the government bonds. In this way the government held not a first but a second mortgage on the road. Thus the greatest stumbling block in the way of financing the project was removed. The issuance of government bonds as the road was completed was also liberalized. Two thirds of the bonds could be issued when grading was completed, and the other third was to be available when the rails were laid and equipment was in place. The Act also provided that no bonds were to be retained by the government.

The land grants in the new law were doubled in amount. They consisted of ten alternate sections on each side of the line to a distance of ten miles each way, with permission to issue patents for the lands whenever twenty miles of railroad had been built and accepted. These grants included lands with coal and iron. Under the Law of 1862, whatever the railroads earned for transporting government troops and materials was to be retained and placed to the credit of the roads. The Law of 1864 required that one half the sum earned should be paid directly to the railroads.

The time for completion of the road was extended one year, to July 1, 1877. The right to condemn private lands for right of way was granted. The number of directors was increased to fifteen and the number of government directors was increased to five. In addition, three government commissioners were provided, whose duties were to make periodic examinations. The Central Pacific was limited to an extension into Nevada of 150 miles, in place of the former provision that the road could build eastward until it met the road building westward. It was not until July 3, 1866, that the former permission was restored, under which the Central Pacific built eastward until it met the Union Pacific at Promontory, Utah. As a final evidence of government good faith, it was "further enacted, that Congress may at any time, alter, amend or repeal this act."

# THE FIRST TRANSCONTINENTAL RAILROAD

## THE CONSTRUCTION CONTRACTS

Even though the Law of 1864 permitted a satisfactory form of financing, and though the Civil War ended early in 1865, only forty miles of railroad were completed by the end of 1865. It had been left to Durant and his friends to raise money, some of which was indeed obtained by those promoters. In order to secure to themselves a part of the funds that became available from the sale of bonds, the first of the construction contracts was signed.

The laws that today govern and provide for the limited liability corporation had not been passed in 1864. However, the legislature of Pennsylvania had chartered the Pennsylvania Fiscal Agency with general powers, and it was this charter that Durant bought, changing its name to the Credit Mobilier. This name was the same as that of a French company formed for general financing and construction purposes. The capital stock was set at $2,000,000, later raised to $2,500,000, and again to $3,750,000. It obviated the risk that individual partnerships had for the several partners, as the liability for the debts of the concern was limited by the number of shares held by any one individual. This was the company that financed the Union Pacific, acting as the actual contractor in one case and as the real contractor in the other two contracts.

While Peter Dey was in charge of the first work at Omaha, the work was awarded to small contractors, but such procedure was not satisfactory to Vice President and General Manager Durant. Therefore Durant made an arrangement with an employee of the company, a man of no financial standing, to contract for the first 100 miles of the road. This was Mr. Herbert M. Hoxie, who made an offer to build that much of the line for the uniform amount of $50,000 per mile. On September 23, 1864, the offer was accepted by the railroad company. The contracts required that Hoxie build and equip the 100 miles of line and side tracks. There were several other clauses covering the burnetizing of ties; the cost of any one bridge was limited to

$85,000; and equipment of buildings, tanks, etc., was not to exceed a cost of $5,000 per mile. If railroad iron cost over $130 per ton, the excess was to be paid by the company. Hoxie agreed to take the company's first-mortgage bonds at 80 per cent of their par value and land grant bonds at 70 per cent of par and to subscribe for $500,000 of Union Pacific stock.

On October 4 of the same year the contract was extended to cover 247 miles, which was the distance of the 100th meridian, the initial point of the railroad indicated in the law. The subscription for company stock was increased to $1,000,000. Hoxie then agreed to assign the contract to five men: four directors of the railroad, T. C. Durant, Cornelius Bushnell, C. A. Lambard, and H. S. McComb, and a fifth, H. S. Gray, a stockholder. The five men thus became the contractor. The provision of the law that full price should be paid for the railroad company stock was evaded by the contractor giving a check in full amount for the stock subscribed, which check was then handed back as payment on the contract without going through a bank. It was another illustration of a well-known fact that no law can be passed that is not easy to evade, provided all parties to a transaction desire to do so. The five men formed a partnership and together subscribed $1,600,000, which was used to build the road. Twenty-five per cent was paid in before the partners became afraid their individual risk was too great. Hoxie and the other then assigned everything to the Credit Mobilier, with the $1,600,000 being applied to the purchase of Credit Mobilier stock. The Credit Mobilier thus became the actual contractor for building the railroad.

It was because of the high prices paid for the construction that Dey resigned as chief engineer and notified General Dix that the road was being overcapitalized. General Dix, however, did nothing about it.

The arrangement with the Credit Mobilier provided sufficient funds for the building of the 247 miles west of Omaha, including the excess length of nine miles added by the change

[209]

at that city. On October 5, 1866, the contract was completed. It had taken nearly three years from the date of the ground-breaking ceremonies at Omaha to build 247 miles on the easiest part of the route of the railroad, namely along the Platte River from Elkhorn to a point near Fort Kearney.

It was quite clear, therefore, that this first group of men headed by Durant could not finance the railroad project. Stronger men were needed and were soon found in the Ames brothers, Oakes and Oliver. It was these men who brought to the project large wealth of their own and who were also able to bring in other investors of equal financial standing who would provide the funds. They knew of the Credit Mobilier and what it was doing in 1865, for they were then stockholders. With them were friends and business associates, notably Alley, Hazard, and Dillon, whose names thereafter appeared in the proceedings of both companies. Oliver Ames was elected a director of the Union Pacific in October, 1866, and became president in November of that year when General Dix was appointed Minister to France. Although a stockholder in the Credit Mobilier, he was never an officer of the company. Oakes Ames became connected with the Credit Mobilier in August, 1865, and was also a stockholder in Union Pacific and a director, although he, too, was never an officer of the company. He was, as has been mentioned, a member of the United States House of Representatives for several terms, being there in 1864 when the Act of that year was passed. Practically all the stockholders of the Union Pacific, together with all the officers, were stockholders in the Credit Mobilier. For the most part, the personnel of the two companies was the same.

By the time the Hoxie contract was completed in October, 1866, the friction between Durant and Oakes Ames had developed to the point where it became necessary to oust Durant from his position in the Credit Mobilier. A similar effort to eliminate him from the Union Pacific failed, and Durant remained as vice president and general manager until the road was completed in 1869. Oliver Ames, in his testimony before the Wilson Committee in 1873, said, regarding the $435,000 that had been disbursed by Durant in 1864:

"We examined every bill that is there, in the details to the full amount of $435,000. The charge was that Dr. Durant, instead of spending this money as he alleged he had spent it, for the purpose of getting a charter and for doing all things necessary, had put the money in his own pocket."

Durant's opinion of the others was expressed in his testimony before the Poland Committee, in which he said:

"As I have stated, Mr. Ames, Mr. Alley, and their friends were not original stockholders in the company. They came into it by virtue of their character as contractors and their interests in the Credit Mobilier, and did not come into the direction until after several hundred miles of road had been completed, and nearly five hundred miles had been completed at the time of the execution and assignment of the Oakes Ames contract. The claim of patriotism and of far-seeing, intelligent, and honest policy put forward in their behalf, is ridiculous."

All parties were in agreement that the work should proceed. Durant, in his capacity as vice president, and acting under the authority conferred by a resolution of the executive committee of the railroad, let a contract to L. B. Boomer of Chicago for 150 miles of road west of the 100th meridian, where the Hoxie contract had expired. This contract was never approved by the directors, but the work proceeded. Then the directors of the railroad passed a resolution extending the Hoxie contract fifty-eight miles, to a point where the Boomer contract had built the road. When Durant heard of this he protested and obtained a court injunction that caused the directors to rescind their action. Then the directors arranged a contract on March 24, 1867, with John M. S. Williams, a stockholder, to build 268 miles west of the initial point, the contract to include the part already constructed. The contract was assigned to the Credit Mobilier, but Durant stopped that with another injunction. In

June the directors made yet another effort to sign a contract with Williams, but this, too, was stopped by Durant. Durant assumed great credit for himself in thus preventing contracts at high prices on a stretch of road easy to build and parts of which were already constructed. His efforts would appear more altruistic had he not himself later become a party to the Ames contract that covered line already built.

The gist of the matter was that Durant, having been ousted from the Credit Mobilier, was taking his revenge. It was finally recognized that both parties were necessary to each other. Oakes Ames concluded a contract with the railroad company by which he agreed to construct 667 miles of road, extending from the 100th meridian westward, for the following amounts and in this sequence:

| | | |
|---|---|---|
| 100 miles at $42,000 per mile ............. | $4,200,000 |
| 167 miles at   45,000 per mile ............. | 7,515,000 |
| 100 miles at   96,000 per mile ............. | 9,600,000 |
| 100 miles at   80,000 per mile ............. | 8,000,000 |
| 100 miles at   90,000 per mile ............. | 9,000,000 |
| 100 miles at   96,000 per mile ............. | 9,600,000 |
| 667 miles | Total | $47,915,000 |

Of this length of road, 138 miles were already completed and had been accepted by the government. The engineering expenses were borne by the railroad company. The contract covered the line across the Black Hills and through Wyoming Basin about as far west as the present town of Evanston. Afterward there was considerable talk about the contract being a wild venture, which quite possibly it was, since the route had not been selected across the Black Hills and the cost of course was unknown. The Ames contract was ratified by the railroad directors on October 1, 1867.

It is to be remembered that in 1865 General Dodge had discovered what he believed to be the favorable approach to the summit of the hills by way of Lone Tree Creek. As soon as he became chief engineer in 1866, he ordered surveys to be made at that place and in his report dated at Omaha, November 15, 1866, he said: "The Lodge Pole Creek main line . . . has the best alignment, costs less per mile, has the best grades and less bridging; and when considered with branch to Denver, enters the best coal fields, and has less road to run and build than any of the other lines.

"Considering the lines in a purely engineering point of view, I do not hesitate to give the opinion that the Lodge Pole Creek approach to the base of the mountains is superior to all others and should be adopted."

Maps and profiles, with grades, distances, and other information, were filed with the report. In forwarding the report to the board of directors, Durant said: "It will be found to contain all the information necessary to enable them to determine upon a location as far west as the crossing of the Laramie River." On November 23, 1866, the "Committee on Location and Construction," to whom the report of General Dodge was referred, "unanimously recommend the adoption of the Lodge Pole Creek line crossing the mountains on the Lone Tree and Crow Creek divide line."

The matter was settled and the road was built on that line. It can hardly be maintained that Oakes Ames was ignorant of the character of the mountain crossing and of the decision as to the location when, ten months after the Dodge report, he entered into the contract to build the line over the mountains.

The most inexcusible part of the Ames contract was that it included a section of the road 138 miles long that had already been constructed. When the Hoxie contract was completed to the 100th meridian, construction went on haphazardly while the factions in New York and Boston quarreled. The cost of the 132 miles in the Platte Valley was $27,000 per mile but it was taken into the Ames contract at $42,000 per mile, with a corresponding profit of $15,000 a mile to the contractors. No valid excuse for this procedure was ever made other than that

Oakes Ames, in making his proposal, based it on average costs over the 667 miles covered by the contract. This argument will not hold water, for there is no proof that his costs per mile took this into consideration. The company ultimately paid the Credit Mobilier $1,104,000 on this account.

When the Ames contract was settled in 1867, the opposition of Durant had ceased. The contract contained most, if not all, of the objectionable features that he had protested in the earlier contracts proposed by Ames. Arrangements had obviously been made and a compromise effected. Oakes Ames did not perform the contract himself. Within two weeks the contract was assigned to the following seven trustees, who carried it out: Oliver Ames, Sidney Dillon, Cornelius Bushnell, John B. Alley, Henry S. McComb, Benjamin E. Bates, and last, but not least, Thomas C. Durant. In this manner Durant appeared as one of the contractors. Another agreement between Oakes Ames, the Credit Mobilier, and the trustees provided that the contract was to be administered for the benefit of the stockholders of the Credit Mobilier. Durant had insisted that the written consent of all Union Pacific stockholders should be obtained first, which was done.

After this struggle between the factions, the work of construction proceeded rapidly. When the Ames contract was completed, another was made with James W. Davis, who assigned it to the same trustees and the road was completed to the junction with the Central Pacific.

While the conflict between the two groups was going on, the "Fisk raid" of 1867-1868 took place. It has since been stated that Fisk, who had become notorious in his dealing with the Erie Railroad, tried to blackmail the Union Pacific in an endeavor to have the Credit Mobilier thrown into receivership, all of which would have delayed construction work. Working with the Tweed Ring in New York and with corrupt judges, Fisk made an attempt to secure the papers of the Union Pacific Company. This was prevented by sending them to New Jersey.

After permission was given by Congress, the office of the company was removed to Boston. There was some intimation that Durant was assisting Fisk, but those charges, like many others that were made then and afterward, were never proved.

### FINANCES

As a part of construction of the railroad, interest attaches to the financing of the road, because in the end, without money and the anticipation of profit, the road would not have been built. The data of costs and financing, such as they are, are largely found in the reports of the Wilson Committee of Congress in the investigations of 1872 and 1873. Testimony was given by Henry C. Crane, an officer and assistant treasurer of the Credit Mobilier; by Benjamin F. Ham, a director, assistant secretary, and treasurer of the same company, as well as at times auditor of the Union Pacific; and by E. H. Rollins, treasurer of the Union Pacific after May, 1869.

The total cost of the road, as computed by Mr. Ham was as follows:

### TABLE 1

| | |
|---|---|
| The Hoxie contract | $12,974,416.24 |
| The Ames and Davis contracts | 80,571,871.04 |
| Engineering | 890,865.69 |
| Equipment | 1,460,676.20 |
| Discount and interest on loans | 2,581,180.09 |
| Bond interest during construction | 4,000,000.00 |
| Bond discount (Losses) | 10,740,747.91 |
| Miscellaneous, 16 items | 3,512,591.35 |
| Total | $116,732,348.52 |
| Deduct credit sale to Central Pacific Railroad | 2,698,620.00 |
| Net cost | 114,033,728.52 |

The above sum given by Mr. Ham represented substantially what the road had cost to the end of 1872. Up to the end of 1870, the reported cost was $108,722,134.35. As work went on after the rails were joined in 1869, the difference is explained. The sum given is merely the bookkeeper's summation, which does not represent actual cost. In the sum is included 367,623 shares of comon stock at its face value of $100 per share, or $36,762,300. The sixteen miscellaneous items mentioned in the table are made up of station buildings, shops and tools, snow sheds, roadway and track, bridging, fencing, telegraph, express outfit, the expenses of government commissioners, legal expense, revenue stamps, preliminary expense, and amounts paid to the Cedar Rapids and Missouri River Railroad. Of the total sum, the three contracts amounted to $93,546,287.28, with expenditures or commitments of the railroad company direct of $20,487,441.24. In both these categories, stock appears at its face value of $100 per share.

Money for construction of the road, whether by the company or by the contractors who took securities in payment for their work, was raised principally by the sale of bonds. The record of bond sales is as follows:

TABLE 2

| Class of Bonds | | Face Value | Discount | Net Sum Received |
|---|---|---|---|---|
| First Mortgage | 6% | $27,213,000 | $3,494,991.23 | $23,718,008.77 |
| Government | 6% | 27,236,512 | 91,348.72 | 27,145,163.28 |
| Land Grant | 7% | 10,400,000 | 4,336,007.96 | 6,063,992.04 |
| Income | 10% | 9,355,000 | 2,818,400.00 | 6,536,600.00 |
| Totals | | $74,204,512 | $10,740,747.91 | $63,463,764.09 |

It will be noted that the money realized from the sale of the government subsidy bonds amounted to slightly less than 43 per cent of the total. The statements of the Wilson Committee and of others since that the government furnished practically all of the money for building the road are largely without foundation. In addition, money from other sources was made available by the company.

It can easily be seen that the bonded debt was a heavy burden on the company for many years, especially so when the following statement of the interest is added to the above table. The government paid the interest on its bonds until maturity, which relief was of great assistance during the years while the road was beginning to function. Even so, the accumulation of interest into one sum due in thirty years was one of the reasons for the company's final insolvency. The interest on the three types of company bonds was as follows:

TABLE 3

| Class of Bonds | Face Value | Annual Interest | Net Sum Realized | Actual Interest |
|---|---|---|---|---|
| First mortgage 6% | $27,213,000 | $1,632,780 | $23,718,008.77 | 6.8% |
| Land grant 7% | 10,400,000 | 728,000 | 6,063,992.04 | 12.0% |
| Income 10% | 9,355,000 | 935,500 | 6,536,600.00 | 14.7% |
| Total or average | $46,968,000 | $3,296,280 | $36,318,600.81 | 9.0% |

While the average rate of interest on the total bonds was about 7 per cent, the actual rate of interest on the cash received from the sale of the bonds was 9 per cent. It was evident that the first-mortgage bonds, even with the government bonds placed second to them, were sold only at a considerable discount, about 12.8 per cent, and that the actual interest on the money received was 7 per cent. When it came to issuing land grant and then income bonds in the desperate struggle to obtain cash, great discounts were absolutely necessary and high rates of interest were paid to obtain money, reaching 12 per cent and 14.7 per cent, as shown in the table. The interest rates are mute evidence of the struggle of the railroad builders to complete the project.

In addition to selling bonds, both the railroad companies and the Credit Mobilier sold the common stock of the railroad. No statement, however, is now available as to the amount or the receipts. In general, the stock was held by the contractors as a profit, although Durant and some others sold their holdings in the years immediately following the joining of the rails in 1869. Calculations as to the value of the stock have since been made on a basis of thirty cents on the dollar, but the price in the market varied. Again, the market value of a stock is not necessarily a criterion of its actual value. Only the earnings of the railroad in later years provided a basis of value and such a gauge of value was not available when the road was built.

### REVENUES FROM OPERATION

As soon as the railroad was opened for any distance, the completed sections were placed under the operating department, where they began to earn money, notwithstanding the fact that operating trains interfered with the construction trains passing westward to the end of track. By the second of January, 1867, the government had accepted 305 miles of the completed road, which was operated by the company after April of that year. Statistics of operating receipts and expenses are given as follows:

### TABLE 4

| Year | Receipts | Expenses | Net Earnings |
|---|---|---|---|
| 1867 | $1,015,195.29 | $     658,880.54 | $   356,314.75 |
| 1868 | 4,186,832.09 | 3,213,565.83 | 973,266.26 |
| 1869 | 7,342,271.16 | 5,894,268.63 | 1,448,002.53 |
| 1870 | 8,344,371.08 | 5,649,573.45 | 2,694,797.63 |
| Total | $20,888,669.62 | $15,416,288.45 | $5,472,381.17 |

Thus, during the three active years of construction, the company came into possession of about two and three quarters million dollars that could be applied to construction purposes, and the first year of through line operation, 1870, the profits justified the faith of the builders that the road would be a paying investment.

### CONSTRUCTION COST TO THE RAILROAD

In Table 1, above, the total cost to the company, including the stock then issued at par value, was $114,033,728.52. Included in this sum were the discounts on the several types of bonds, referred to by Mr. Ham as losses, of $10,740,747.91. While this amount would have to be amortized in future years, it was not a part of the construction cost. Deducting that sum leaves $103,292,980.61, which may be considered as the sum directly contributed by the railroad company. However, as stated before, there is included in the sum noted the stock amounting to $36,762,300. estimated at its face value of $100 per share. The stock realized but a small fraction of this amount when sold. From here on, the estimates were made in 1873 on the basis of thirty cents on the dollar, and using that figure the stock represented a real money value of $11,028,690. This represents a reduction from the cost named above $25,733,610.00, leaving the construction cost to the company of $77,559,370.61.

### COST AND PROFITS TO CONTRACTORS

In their testimony before the Wilson Committee, Mr. Ham and Mr. Crane presented statements of the recorded cost of the three contracts, which are embodied in the following table, together with the face value of the contracts:

### TABLE 5

| Contract | Contract Price | Contractors Cost | Apparent Profit |
|---|---|---|---|
| Hoxie | $12,974,416.24 | $ 7,806,183.33 | $ 5,168,232.91 |
| Ames | 57,140,102.94 | 27,285,141.99 | 29,854,960.95 |
| Davis | 23,431,768.10 | 15,629,633.62 | 7,802,134.48 |
| Total | $93,546,287.28 | $50,720,958.94 | $42,825,328.34 |
| Add for payments to Credit Mobilier for 58 miles ......................... | | | 1,104,000.00 |
| | | | $43,929,328.34 |

It is again necessary to call attention to the fact that these are bookkeeper's figures that include stock at its par value and also bonds. Various individuals have tried to determine the actual amount of profit to the contractors, but the data are so meager and lacking in essential parts that only general statements may be made.

In estimating payments by the railroad company to the Ames and Davis trustees, Mr. Ham stated that the trustees subscribed for first-mortgage bonds at 85 per cent of the face value, the land grant bonds at 55 per cent and the income bonds at 60 per cent of the face value. As payment for the two contracts, there were received bonds and stocks, the total stock issued being about $30,000,000, which at thirty cents on the dollar would alone reduce the profit $21,000,000, or from $42,825,328.34 to some $22,000,000. Mr. Ham stated that these securities were sold by the trustees at less than the prices paid for them. They sold one $1,000 first-mortgage bond, one similar land grant bond, and fifty shares of stock for $2,000. This, at the purchase price of the bonds as noted, would make the stock worth $12 a share. They sold one income bond and twenty shares of stock for $800. At the stated price of $600 for the bond, the stock was rated at $10 per share. Mr. Ham also presented his calculated cost of the road, revised to include only the contractors' cost instead of the contract prices given in Table 1, as $71,208,399.18. He also stated that, taking account of the prices that were received by the contractors in disposing of their securities, the profit on the two contracts was not more than $9,000,000. Adding this to the profits on the Hoxie contract, which were not examined, the total profit to the contractors was somewhat over $14,000,000.

Estimates that vary widely were prepared by others who examined the same figures, and may be mentioned briefly.

Mr. Rowland Hazard, one of the executive committee of the seven trustees, in a paper, "The Credit Mobilier of America," stated in 1882: "On (the) basis of (fifty cents on the dollar in 1881 for the Central Pacific stock) the total profit received by the stockholders of the Credit Mobilier was about $15,000,000 and an expenditure of about $70,000,000, or at a little over 20 per cent. This is a high estimate, and is probably more than realized by a great majority of the stockholders. . . . On (the) basis of (the value of the stock as estimated at the time) the total profit would be about $6,000,000, or less than nine per cent on the expenditure." Mr. Hazard apparently considered the contractors' cost to have been over $70,000,000.

The Wilson Committee, after estimating the discount on

securities of $19,548,455.80, reached the conclusion that the profit was $23,366,319.81 on an expenditure of $50,720,958.94. These calculations were based on the cash value of bonds and on the stock at thirty cents on the dollar. The details are as follows:

TABLE 6

Profit on the Ames and Davis contracts:

| | |
|---|---|
| Bonds (cash value) | $11,310,900.00 |
| Twenty-four million of stock | 7,200,000.00 |
| Cash | 2,346,000.00 |
| | $20,856,900.00 |
| On the Hoxie contract: | |
| Bonds | 965,250.00 |
| Stock, $5,147,232.71 at 30 | 1,544,169.81 |
| Total | $23,366,319.81 |

The Wilson Committee also called attention to the relation of the supposed cost of the work of construction to the actual sums of money obtained by the sale of the first-mortgage and of the government subsidy bonds.

| | | |
|---|---|---|
| First-mortgage bonds issued | $27,213,000.00 | |
| Sold at a discount of | 3,494,991.23 | |
| Yielding | | $23,718,008.77 |
| Government bonds issued | $27,236,512.00 | |
| Sold at a discount of | 91,348.72 | |
| Yielding | | $27,145,163.28 |
| Total | | $50,863,172.05 |

The committee reached the conclusion that the cost was $50,720,958.94, the two totals being substantially equal, and that the contractors made a real profit of $23,000,000 on the work. There are several items for which general vouchers only existed as one payment to C. S. Bushnell for $126,000 and one to Thomas C. Durant for $435,754.21, which were unexplained. However, the above does not represent the entire case. The value of the stock included in the preceding calculation estimated at thirty cents on the dollar of face value, amounted to $8,744,169.81 or about 33 per cent of the total assumed profit. Had the railroad proved a failure in its earning capacity, the value of the stock would have been far less, and might even have been rendered completely worthless by foreclosure. In such a case, the profits of the contractors would have shrunk to about $15,000,000. This was just one of the risks that the contractors shouldered when building a road into unknown country and in taking part of their payment in stock. As it turned out, the contrary proved to be the case, but there is no question that it could have been otherwise.

The Wilson Committee felt that the railroad builders had misused their trust and had gained enormous profits out of the contracts made with themselves. The railroad men had no such view. They took the stand that the railroad incorporators and the construction company were really one and the same organization, managed by the same individuals. It is no one's affair how much profit they made as long as the security behind the government bond issue was not impaired. At that time the interest of the general public in the capitalization and profits of railroads was not recognized. The railroad belonged to those who built it, and if they repaid borrowed money that was all that was asked of them. A suit instigated by the Wilson Committe to recover undue profits was lost in the Supreme Court.

It remains to examine the statement of what the profits were. The Wilson Committee rested their case on the testimony of Mr. Ham, the treasurer of the Credit Mobilier. Others differed with him. Oakes Ames stated that the cost of the contracts was $60,000,000, and that on his contract the profit was about 15 per cent. General Dodge believed that the cost as given by Mr. Ames was correct. Where the Wilson Committee erred was in omitting the money obtained from bonds based on land grants and upon earnings. From the $10,400,000 land grant bonds there was obtained $6,063,992.04, and from the $9,355,000 income bonds there was obtained $6,536,600, a total from these two classes of bonds of $12,600,592.04, which, added to the $50,863,172.05 obtained from the sale of first-mortgage and government bonds, makes a total of $63,463,764.09. The records of the railroad show that the company expended directly $9,746,683.33, which, added to the contract costs to the contractors, makes a total of $60,467,641.27. The two sums are in fair agreement, the total expenditures being less than the sum obtained from bonds of $2,993,122.82.

It will be recognized that there are various viewpoints from which to estimate the profits on the construction. That of the Wilson Committee has been stated. Henry Kirke White estimates the total profit was "$16,710,432.82, or slightly above 27½ per cent of the cost of the road . . . which does not seem an immoderate profit."[1]

Mr. J. B. Crawford, using the data, finds that the cash value of the net profits was $8,141,903.70 after deducting from a total the loss of the Credit Mobilier capital of $3,750,000—a total loss. He gives the expenditure as $70,000,000, the profits being about 12½ per cent.[2]

Mr. Nelson Trottman, at a later date, using the same basic data, reaches the conclusion that the actual cost of the railroad from all sources was $60,467,641, and subtracting this amount from the total capitalization of $110,996,812, obtains what he terms "fictitious capital" of $50,529,171. Repeating the statements of the Wilson Committee, he finds the total securities issued in excess of cost as $47,304,513.11. The capital stock is entered at its face value of $100 per share and the land grant bonds at their face value. If the prevailing assumption of thirty cents on the dollar on the stock and the discounted cash realized on the bonds is entered in the table, the contractors' profits amounted to $17,234,895. Mr. Trottman, agreeing with the Wilson Committee, finds the cash profit to have been approximately $23,366,514.81.[3]

[1] Henry Kirke White, *History of the Union Pacific Railway.* 1895.
[2] J. B. Crawford, *The Credit Mobilier, Its Origin and History.* 1880.
[3] Nelson Trottman, *History of the Union Pacific.* 1923.

[223]

Mr. John P. Davis, also using the figures given in the Wilson report and after deducting the capital of the Credit Mobilier, estimates the contractors' profit as $25,771,213.11.[4] He criticizes Mr. Crawford and Mr. Hazard for basing the profits on a percentage of the money spent, and seems to imply that the profits should be a reasonable percentage of the capital of the contracting company, or $3,750,000. This contention is made because the contractor was reimbursed as each section of road completed was paid for.

It would have been more helpful to Mr. Davis and the others had they been better acquainted with contracting and contractors. This writer has had contact with such men and their work for half a century. Contractors do not base their proposals on the amount of their capital, which may be very small. They estimate the cost to them of doing the work on a project and add to that sum their anticipated profit as a percentage of the total estimated cost. The contract is taken and the work performed on that basis. For capital, the average contractor depends upon borrowing whatever he requires above his own resources, from a bank or from other sources of funds. Whenever a project is of such a size that it is beyond the financial resources of one contracting company, several combine to do the work with their united resources. Much of the large work in the West in recent years has been done in this manner. The Hoover Dam, for which a contract of approximately $165,000,000 was awarded, is an example. Here, six contracting firms came together to do the work, with money being borrowed from banks to finance the contract. On the other hand, no work of magnitude is done without the owner making payments as it progresses. The financial costs are thus very much reduced, since it would be the height of folly to require a contractor to furnish capital in any amount, as in the example cited, and rely only upon one payment on completion of the work. In the

---

[4]John P. Davis, A.M., *The Union Pacific Railway*. 1894.

end the owner would pay the cost of this capital, while presumably he would have resources of his own at hand.

The return on capital is fundamental to modern industrial life. Men must make a profit on their ventures, or all industry would stop. What is designated as "costs" in all these discussions refers to direct costs of labor and materials. Contractors' profits are also costs, as legitimate as the wages of the most humble laborer on the work. The contractors' profits, however they may be estimated and whatever they were, are part of the cost of building the railroad. Money does not, of itself, get out and build a railroad. It takes the intense effort of many men—in the present instance, of the Ames brothers and their associates in the East; of Durant, Dodge, Reed, Evans, Casement, and many others in the West, working under discouraging conditions and through long years to bring the enterprise to a successful conclusion. The commentators, casting and recasting the figures of the Wilson Committee Report, fail to appreciate this phase of the subject.

Another element enters into the contractors' profit, and that is the time consumed in doing the work. When the contract extends over a period of years, say four or five, the contractor must assume the risk of rising prices of labor and material. Such a rise may consume his entire profits or, in case of a decline in prices, may augment his profits. A proper contract would take account of such changes, since in the end the owner pays for them.

In the case of the building of the Union Pacific Railroad, the contracting company assumed a number of risks. It had to depend upon selling the securities of the railroad, which it took as payment for work done. The construction period extended over five years and almost anything could happen to the security market in that time. The value of the stock that it took in part payment, was dependent upon the future of the railroad and on the traffic that it would develop. It was quite possible that the stock of the railroad would be valueless. Many railroads, built into the fertile portions of the Mississippi Valley, had become insolvent and the stockholders had lost all of their money. Here was a railroad project into an uninhabited region, much of which was and remains a complete desert. No one could forecast the possible business for such a road. Of the $23,000,000 estimated profits on the contract, as determined by the Wilson Committee, close to $9,000,000 was based upon a valuation of the stock at thirty cents on the dollar. That valuation may have been a reasonable estimate in 1873. In 1867, when Oakes Ames assumed the burden of his contract, the value of the stock was on the knees of the gods. In this case, as in others, it is easy to be wise and critical after the event. In the history of contracting, it is doubtful if a more venturesome contract was ever signed than that of Oakes Ames.

### GOVERNMENT REPRESENTATIVES

During the construction period and afterwards, the five government directors served with ability, although it does not appear that they were ever an important factor in the progress of the work or in solving the many problems that were presented.

The law also provided for three government commissioners whose duty it was to make periodical examinations of the road and to report on its condition. These men gave attention to their work, and the fact that one commissioner was an extortionist should not obscure the work of the other two men. This one commissioner refused to accept a section of the completed road until his demands for $25,000 had been complied with. There may have been other attempts at blackmail of this type, but if so they are not on record. In commenting on the work of the commissioners, mention should be made of the good work done by J. L. Williams, a civil enginer of Fort Wayne, Indiana, whose reports bear evidence of careful study by a man competent to understand and appreciate the work of the railroad builders. Mr. Williams also served as government director of the road.

[226]

After the joining of the tracks at Promontory, a special five-man commission of Congress, appointed by resolution on April 10, 1869, reviewed the entire railroad and in its report, dated October 30, 1869, gave general approval of the work. It also brought in an itemized statement of work remaining to be done and estimated that the cost would be $1,586,100. The list of requirements dealt largely with temporary work on bridges and culverts, filling of trestles, and changes to reduce grades.

The government directors and commissioners, with varying personnel, continued to function in the years that followed the completion of the original line. Their reports are of interest as showing the work of extending the railroad system and the gradual improvement of the line, and as a discussion of the financial relations with the government. They are not properly a part of this history.

### SUBSIDY BONDS

The first section of forty miles was accepted January 24, 1866, and on the 27th, government bonds in the amount of $640,000 were issued to the company. In all, forty sections were approved from time to time, the last issue of bonds being dated July 4, 1870. A total of $27,236,512 face value government bonds were issued to the company.

### LAND GRANT BONDS

An important item in the financing of the railroad was the land grant, upon which bonds were issued and sold by the railroad company. Up to May 26, 1886, the statistics of the land grant were as follows:

| State | Acres Granted | Acres Selected by Company |
|---|---|---|
| Nebraska | 4,853,844 | 2,495,660 |
| Colorado | 590,000 | 640 |
| Wyoming | 5,016,000 | 79,682 |
| Utah | 850,000 | 40,196 |
| | 11,309,844 | 2,616,178 |

The selection of lands was a phrase used to designate lands for which sales had been made, such lands being patented only when sold. In this manner the company avoided taxation on the lands by the states, which point was made the subject of lawsuits that were carried to the Supreme Court of the United States, the Court deciding that unpatented lands were not subject to taxation, as they were legally still in the possession of the government.

The character of the lands varied widely. From the compilation, it may be seen that by far the largest acreage sold by the company was in Nebraska. In the report of the government directors for 1883 it was stated that 8,877,893 acres remained unsold:

| | | |
|---|---:|---|
| Nebraska | 2,580,000 | acres |
| Colorado | 690,000 | " |
| Wyoming | 4,580,000 | " |
| Utah | 1,027,893 | " |
| Total | 8,877,893 | acres |

These lands were classified as: agricultral, 1,000,000 acres; grazing, 7,477,893 acres; and coal, 400,000 acres. A different estimate made by the company listed:

| | | | |
|---|---|---|---:|
| Agricultural | 600,000 acres at $3 per acre | | $1,800,000 |
| Grazing | 7,700,000 acres at $1 per acre | | 7,700,000 |
| Coal | 400,000 acres at $20 per acre | | 8,000,000 |
| Total | 8,700,000 | | 17,500,000 |

The agricultural lands were in Nebraska. The arid plains of Utah and western Wyoming were covered with sagebrush or desert sand. The grazing lands were located in central and eastern Wyoming, northern Colorado, and western Nebraska. At the present time there remain unsold 905,250 acres of the original grant. A final determination of the land grant showed an area of 11,401,296 acres, of which 11,401,176 acres were patented, a difference of only 120 acres.

[228]

The land grant was of value to the railroad company beyond the amounts obtained from direct sales. The lands were used as a basis of a bond issue during the construction of the railroad in order to obtain funds. In all, $10,400,000 worth of land grant bonds were sold at a large discount, the amount of money obtained from the sales being $6,063,992.04, or, roughly, sixty cents on the dollar. In his report to the stockholders for 1880, President Dillon stated that "there has been cancelled of these bonds $4,329,000. The land contracts, cash on hand, accrued and accruing interest, amount to a sufficient sum to retire all of the land grant bonds."

### THE OMAHA BRIDGE

For a number of years the question of a bridge over the Missouri River between Omaha and Council Bluffs was in dispute. The Union Pacific Railroad Company did not want to build the bridge, as it would cost a considerable sum and would add little or no revenue from traffic. It was obvious that the railroads centering in Council Bluffs would not build the bridge for the same reasons. Finally, in 1871, the Union Pacific built the bridge but refused to run its main line trains across the structure. A shuttle train was operated across the bridge, with all passengers being forced to change trains at Omaha and again at Council Bluffs, where tolls were charged for the crossing.

The company claimed that the decision of President Lincoln fixing the initial point "on the western boundary of Iowa, east of and opposite to the east line of section 10, in township 15, of range 13, east of the principal meridian in the Territory of Nebraska," really meant on the western bank of the river. They claimed that the Iowa border was the western bank of the stream and the maps of that time show a point on the shore labeled "The Initial Point."

The subject eventually reached the courts, with the United States Supreme Court ruling that the Union Pacific should operate its trains across the bridge, evidently relying upon the well-established principle that the center of a stream is the boundary line between two jurisdictions. Undoubtedly General Dodge, when he advised President Lincoln to fix the initial point in Iowa, intended that the terminus of the road should be at his home, Council Bluffs. The river has shifted its course since those days of the builders, with the result that the initial point, as claimed by the railroad, is probably now out in the stream.

To finance the building of the bridge, bonds in the face amount of $2,500,000 were issued and sold at a discount, which provided about $1,750,000 in funds to meet the cost.

# CHAPTER 10

# Locating the Union Pacific Railroad

THE PROBLEMS encountered by the engineers in locating the Union Pacific Railroad were, in general, the same kind of problems as those faced by the engineers of the Central Pacific. There was, however, considerable difference in detail.

Once the terminal point on the Missouri River had been fixed near Council Bluffs by President Lincoln, the general route of the road was west toward central California. The east and west valley of the Platte River fixed the route for some 500 miles westward from Omaha. The Rocky Mountains were then encountered where the Wyoming Basin offered the best location for that part of the line. Then the basin of Great Salt Lake had to be reached, and from there on the obvious route was by way of the Humboldt River to the border of California.

There were thus a number of possible solutions to be investigated before the best location could be determined. When the forks of the Platte were reached, should the route follow the

Emigrant Trail up the North Fork and thence by the Sweetwater River, through South Pass to Green River; or should the route take the South Fork of the Platte and by way of Lodgepole Creek or the Cache la Poudre branches, reach the divide of the Black Hills (Laramie Mountains) and there cross the Wyoming Basin to Green River? From Green River, several routes were possible across or around the Wasatch Mountains to the plains of Great Salt Lake. Should the route pass north or south of Great Salt Lake, and what line should be followed to the Humboldt? Once that stream was reached, there were no uncertainties as to where the railroad should be built. To solve these problems many surveys were required, just as the desires of several localities, such as Denver and Salt Lake City, had to be considered.

In commenting upon the location of the Union Pacific Railroad, General Dodge said: "It is a singular fact that in all of these explorations (by the government) the most feasible line in an engineering and commercial point of view, the line with the least obstacles to overcome, of lowest grades and least curvature, was never explored and reported on. Private enterprise explored and developed that line along the forty-second parallel of latitude.

"This route was made by the buffalo, next used by the Indians, then by the fur traders, next by the Mormons, and then by the overland immigration to California and Oregon. It was known as the Great Platte Valley Route. On this trail, or close to it, was built the Union and Central Pacific Railroads to California, and the Oregon Short Line branch of the Union Pacific to Oregon."

The statement is essentially correct, as there were no government surveys for a railroad from Council Bluffs to Fort Bridger, a distance of 942 miles. However, surveys had been made by the government engineers westward from Fort Bridger via Salt Lake City to and along the Humboldt River as far west as Winnemucca. The Weber River, down which the railroad was finally built, had been selected as one of two possible crossings of the Wasatch Mountains, and the route along the Humboldt had been explored. The route along the Platte River needed no surveys, while the line across the Wyoming Basin had been explored but not surveyed by Captain Howard Stansbury, and to some extent by Frémont.

In the summary of the several routes as surveyed by the government in 1853 and 1854, Captain A. A. Humphreys stated:

"The eastern terminus of the route may be either Council Bluffs or Fort Leavenworth. It ascends the Platte and passes through the eastern chain of the Rocky Mountains (the Black Hills), either by the North Fork and its tributary, the Sweet Water, or the South Fork and a tributary called Lodge Pole Creek. By the former it enters upon a great elevated tableland in which the headwaters of the Platte and the Colorado of the West are found, by the South Pass, the ascent having been gradual from the first mountain gorge in the Black Hills, 30 miles above Fort Laramie, to the summit of the so-called pass, a distance of nearly 300 miles, bounded generally on either side by mountains. . . . By the second route, the same difference of elevation is overcome by the Cheyenne Pass, probably in about the distance usual in the Rocky Mountain passes, the route thus entering the Laramie plains, which may be considered to form the eastern part of the Great Plateau first mentioned."

In a later paragraph he adds: "The route along the South Fork of the Platte and Lodge Pole Creek, by the Cheyenne Pass and Bridger's Pass, is not so well known as the other. Lodge Pole Creek has never been continuously explored, and there is no profile of this route."

With regard to the Cheyenne Pass, Captain Stansbury says his "examinations fully demonstrate the existence of a route through the Black Hills, not only practicable, but free from any obstructions involving in their removal great or unusual expenditure." He gives no estimated grades, and had no barometer or other instruments for measuring elevations.

[233]

"From the Cheyenne Pass to Fort Bridger," Stansbury continues, "the country can be crossed in many places, the choice being determined by considerations of fuel and water."

As has been stated before, the route indicated by Captain Stansbury from his exploration in 1850 was substantially that upon which the railroad was built from the head of Lodgepole Creek across the Black Hills and the Wyoming Basin to Green River. The surveys westward from Green River made by Lieutenant E. G. Beckwith, indicated the possibility of using the Weber River as a passage through the Wasatch Mountains to the plain of Great Salt Lake. It can be seen from these abstracts that the general route of the railroad from Council Bluffs to Salt Lake Valley had been outlined before the surveys of the railroad company started.

In June, 1856, Lieutenant F. T. Bryan, of the Topographical Engineers, accompanied by three topographers, a geologist, and thirty men, escorted by a company of infantry, traveled up the Kansas River and passed over to the Platte at Fort Kearney. They then followed the Platte to Lodgepole Creek. The region was explored, the Black Hills were crossed at the head of Lodgepole Creek, and the Wyoming Basin explored as far west as Bridger Pass, the party going south of Medicine Bow Butte. Returning, they passed north of that mountain, and from the Laramie Plains crossed probably by Antelope Pass, to the Cache la Poudre, and by that stream to the south fork of the Platte. A detachment explored the region from Howard Creek to Crow Creek. The Republican River was explored on the return trip. The party had been close to the future line of the Union Pacific along several hundred miles of the trip.

The selection of the general route for the railroad was comparatively simple, because the way was an open one, over a route that had been known for many years. In referring to this subject, General Dodge said:

"There never was any very great question, from an engineering point of view, where the line crossing Iowa and going west

[234]

from the Missouri River, should be placed. The Lord had so constructed the country that any engineer who failed to take advantage of the great open road out of the Platte Valley, and then on to Salt Lake, would have not been fit to belong to the profession."

When Congress passed the first law for building the road, every populated center along the Missouri River started campaigns to have the initial point located at their town. How the point at Council Bluffs was selected was later related by General Dodge:

"I returned to Council Bluffs (1857) and continued my examinations until 1861. I remembered that in 1859, when I returned from a trip on the plains, I met Mr. Lincoln at the Pacific House. Mr. Lincoln came up from St. Joseph on a steamer to look after an interest he had bought in the Riddle tract from N. B. Judd, of Chicago. He also found here and visited some old Springfield (Illinois) friends, W. H. M. Pusey, Thomas Officer and others. Mr. Lincoln sought me out, and was greatly interested in the subject of the Pacific railroad, and I gave him all the information I had, going fully and thoroughly into it. I was very decided that the Great Platte route was, from our explorations and surveys, the best, most feasible, and far superior to any of the routes explored by the Government. . . .

"In 1863, I think about June, while in command at Corinth, Miss., I received an order to report in Washington, and was informed that the President wished to see me. I had no idea what the President could wish to see me about—in fact, was a good deal puzzled at the order. When I reached Washington and called upon the President, I found that he desired to consult me upon the proper place for the initial point of the Union Pacific, and that he had not forgotten his conversation with me in 1859. . . .

"After his interview with me, in which he showed a perfect knowledge of the question, and satisfying himself as to the engineering questions that had been raised, I was satisfied that he would locate the terminus, at or near Council Bluffs."

Lincoln's first order was issued on November 17, 1863, in these words:

"I, Abraham Lincoln, President of the United States, do hereby fix so much of the western boundary of the State of Iowa as lies between the north and south boundaries of the United States township within which the city of Omaha is situated as the point from which the line of railroad and telegraph in that section mentioned shall be constructed."

This description was not considered definite enough by the Union Pacific Railroad Company, and on March 7, 1864, President Lincoln issued the second executive order:

"I, Abraham Lincoln, President of the United States, do, upon the application of said company, designate and establish such first-named point on the western boundary of the State of Iowa east of and opposite to the east line of section 10, in township 15, south of range 13, east of the sixth principal meridian in the Territory of Nebraska."

Formal notification was given to the United States Senate on March 8, 1864, when Lincoln explained the later change. That closed the subject.

The Union Pacific Railroad Company was organized in late 1862 and early 1863. Before completion of the organization, Durant had selected Peter A. Dey to make a complete reconnaissance from the Missouri River to Salt Lake Valley, instructions for which were contained in a letter dated September 6, 1862. He was to examine the passes between the 100th and the 112th degrees of longitude with reference to their practicability for a railroad route.

Dey's preliminary report covered the salient features of the country to Salt Lake City. The rolling prairie between Omaha and the Platte Valley could be crossed without difficulty. The Platte Valley, with its tributaries, as far as the mouth of Lodgepole Creek, was an excellent location for the road. Three possible routes through the Front Range of the Rocky Mountains

[236]

existed, all from the South Fork of the Platte. The first was by way of Lodgepole Creek and Cheyenne Pass, the second via the Cache la Poudre and Antelope Pass into the Laramie Plains, and the third up the South Fork of the Platte to Denver and thence up Clear Creek to Berthoud Pass. Once in the Laramie Plains, the road could use Bridger Pass to reach Green River from Fort Bridger. Two routes from that point were possible, one by Kamas Prairie and the Timpanogas (Provo) River, the other by Weber River to Salt Lake Valley.

While Dey did not settle on any one route, he expressed definite objections to the one by way of Denver and Berthoud Pass, basing his opinion upon the survey made by Francis M. Case and on a report issued by John Evans, the governor of Colorado Territory. The distance from Omaha to Great Salt Lake Valley was estimated as 960 miles. A list of possible products of the country along the route, such as coal and iron, was included in the reconnaissance. The report evidently formed the basis for the surveys of the following year.

While the location of the railroad westward from Omaha to the valley of the Platte River is mentioned in some detail, the first real problem of importance was found in the Laramie Mountains, or, as they were called then, the Black Hills. These mountains are an extension northward of the main mass of the Rocky Mountains, where the elevations range from 11,000 feet up to peaks over 14,000 feet. At the region of the Colorado-Wyoming boundary the mountains break down to elevations of from 8,000 to 10,000 feet in the higher peaks. The northern limits of the range are indicated by the North Platte River, which, rising in the northern slopes of the main ranges, flows across the Wyoming Basin northward and then curving eastward and southward around the north end of the mountains, joins the South Platte to form the main river. The only stream that crosses directly through the mountains is the Laramie River.

The course of the railroad was due west, and in keeping to

[237]

that course it was compelled to cross the range or go around it. Hence a pass to the Laramie Plains and the Wyoming Basin was of prime importance. On the east, the mountains joined the Great Plains at elevations of about 5,500 to 6,000 feet; on the west, the Laramie Plains were at elevations from 7,000 to 7,500 feet.

The summit of the Laramie Range is a tableland or peneplain formed of Pre-Cambrian granite, the width varying from one to three of more miles. From a point at the headwaters of one of the tributaries of the Cache la Poudre, where the tableland joins Boulder Ridge, which is a spur of the southern mountains at an elevation of about 8,000 feet in the highest portion of the tableland, the distance from Laramie east to Cheyenne Pass is about twenty miles. It is in this stretch of the mountains that a concentrated search for a pass was made by the surveyors. The tableland lies generally north and south, but at its southern end it curves westerly to the junction with Boulder Ridge. Northward from Boulder Ridge there is a gradual rise, with the elevation at Cheyenne Pass being about 8,600 feet. On the westerly slope numerous streams descend 1,000 feet or more into the Laramie Basin and the Laramie River. On the easterly slope a number of streams, Lodgepole and Crow creeks and their tributaries, flow easterly out onto the rolling plains. Lone Tree Creek, south of Crow Creek, flows from the summit east to a point near Cheyenne and then turns southward to a junction with the Cache la Poudre, with various tributaries such as Dale and Fish creeks draining the southern portion of the Sherman tableland.

The granite core of the Laramie Mountains is bordered on the east by the upturned strata of the Great Plains, of much older formation. In general, these strata have been eroded below the summit of the tableland, the drop from Cheyenne Pass being over 500 feet in two miles. From the base of the tableland as exposed, the plains run out in ridges between the local streams, so that the problem before the engineers was not so much to find the lowest pass as it was to discover the best approach to the granite tableland where the passage from the sedimentary rocks to the granite tableland would involve the smallest amount of heavy grades between the two. As a matter of fact, the lowest point was at Antelope Summit, elevation about 8,050 feet at the upper end of Dale Creek, but, as will be described later, the line up the South Platte and the Cache la Poudre was thirty-seven miles longer than the adopted line and this difference in length overcame any disadvantage that the lower pass might have had. The adopted location was up the ridge between Crow Creek and Lone Tree Creek, the ridge running directly east and west and leading without a break to the granite formation of the tableland. This location was also best for descending the western slope of the mountains into the Laramie Plains.

Crossing the main range of the southern Rocky Mountains westerly from Denver was also given consideration, but at no time did it offer a line at all comparable to those over the Black Hills. The route up the North Platte had a number of disadvantages, such as the narrow canyons through which it flowed above Fort Laramie, as well as the much longer length. That route was therefore discarded. The Laramie River, passing as it does directly through the mountains, would seem to have offered a favorable route and it was examined with care, but it was rejected because of its narrow, steep, and precipitous canyon. The choice narrowed down to the short length of the Sherman tableland at the head of Lodgepole, Crow, Lone Tree, and Dale creeks, and here the determining factor of the location was the advantageous ridge between Crow and Lodgepole creeks.

Durant, in his report to the directors of the Union Pacific, dated October 30, 1863, gave details of Dey's surveys and refers to the examinations made the previous year by General Dodge and Mr. Dey being of great value. Requests for military escorts and provisions were refused, as there was no authority for such action. A geologist, Professor J. T. Hodge, was sent with the parties to examine the character of the coal fields and iron deposits. As the railroad company was not yet organized, the expense of the surveys had to be born by individuals.

The first survey to the Rocky Mountains was in charge of B. B. Brayton, civil engineer, with instructions to survey the Cheyenne Pass over the Black Hills and the Bridger Pass over the Continental Divide in the Wyoming Basin. Since the party did not reach the mountains until late in the year, the work was made exceedingly difficult, owing to heavy snow conditions. The survey from the summit of Cheyenne Pass eastward down the branch of Lodgepole Creek revealed the tortuous nature of that route where the stream descends from the mountains. Brayton was of the opinion that a route south of that over Cheyenne Pass would be better. In his report he says:

"From a point of rocks some two hundred feet above the general plane of Pass, I, with a field glass, observed a route to the south of the one I examined, which would enable us to reach the summit by a grade apparently easier. The line would leave the plains on the east side of the mountains from one to three miles south of Camp Walbach (on the Lodgepole), and reach the summit east of Willow Spring Station, fifteen miles southeast of the station on Big Laramie. From this summit west, the grade will probably not exceed fifty feet per mile. The line would be over good ground, and the distance would not be increased."

This was practically a description of the summit of the Black Hills over which the railroad was built. Brayton could not examine this suggested route because of lack of provisions and the approach of winter. In the face of driving snowstorms and heavy winds, Brayton went west and made a survey through Bridger Pass, which he found good for a line. Professor Hodge, who accompanied Brayton, found indications of coal and iron, but lack of time and presence of snow prevented him from making a complete geological survey. Brayton's report contains tables of grades over the two passes and some estimates of costs.

[240]

For explorations in the Wasatch Mountains in 1863, Durant communicated with Brigham Young at Salt Lake City, who sent his son, Joseph A. Young, with a party to survey a route up the Timpanogas Canyon as far as Kamas Prairie. This line was run, and at Kamas Prairie information was obtained that there was no pass from the upper reaches of the Timpanogas across the Unita Mountains to the headwaters of Bear River. The Weber River also borders the prairie, and an attempt was made to run line upstream into the mountains, but the party was turned back by a severe snowstorm on November 10, 1863. As a result of the surveys, Young described two routes, one by the Timpanogas across Kamas Prairie and by way of the upper Weber River to a crossing to Bear River. The second route led up Weber Canyon from Great Salt Lake to Chalk Creek and by way of that stream over the divide to Bear River. Young gave a table of grades and advised additional surveys when the season would permit explorations in the mountains. In this work Brigham Young had cooperated willingly in the surveys, even to the extent of paying the expenses of his son's field party.

While a party under Brayton and the one under Young were busy in the autumn of 1863, Dey had been active in making surveys from Omaha westward across the fifteen miles of rolling prairie to the valley of the Platte River. Six survey lines were run, two of which were north of Omaha, the third somewhat westerly, the fourth southerly from Omaha to Papillion Creek, and thence up that stream, across a low divide through the bluffs on the east of Elkhorn River to the Platte Valley. The fifth line ran from Bellevue, a village on the bank of the Missouri about seven miles south of Omaha. It was carried up the valley of the Papillion into the Platte Valley by the same route as number four. The sixth line ran up the Platte Valley from the junction of that stream with the Missouri. It is clear that the entire region was carefully surveyed by Dey and that the information gathered enabled him to make his final location from Omaha to the Platte Valley and westward for 100 miles.

[241]

In his 1863 report, Dey favored the fourth or "South Line," as it was called. Apparently his selection was confirmed by the company, for it was upon this line that construction was started when ground was broken on December 2, 1863.

The surveys of 1864 were devoted to a more accurate determination of the several routes through the Rocky Mountains from the eastern base to the Salt Lake Valley. Silas Seymour had been appointed consulting civil engineer for the company on January 1. 1864. Three survey parties were sent to the mountains and a locating party under Mr. Ogden Edwards was also employed.

Mr. James A. Evans started his survey at the abandoned Camp Walbach on Lodgepole Creek where it is crossed by the Cheyenne Pass. Incidentally, there is some confusion of names here. An open valley at the eastern foot of the Black Hills, extending from Crow Creek northward some thirty miles to Chugwater Creek was known as the Cheyenne Pass because it was the route followed by the Cheyenne Indians in their annual migrations. Camp Walbach was located in this valley. The term Cheyenne is also applied to a pass from the Laramie Plains east of Laramie across the Black Hills to the headwaters of Lodgepole Creek. In 1864 there was a wagon road through this pass, and it was by this route that B. B. Brayton made his survey in the fall of 1863. This pass is the one to which the name Cheyenne is usually applied.

After crossing Cheyenne Pass to the Laramie Plains, Evans went westward across the Laramie to the North Platte River, which at that point runs northward from its source in the Medicine Bow Range. The Medicine Bow Mountains were passed on the north, with the line continuing through Bridger's Pass, thence by way of Muddy and Bitter creeks to Green River. The survey line was 270 miles long. The elevation of Cheyenne Pass was determined to be 8,656 feet and Bridger's Pass to be 7,534 feet, which is close to the correct elevations. On his trip westward, Evans noted that there were no obstacles to a line along the Platte and up Lodgepole Creek that would prevent the construction of a railroad. The line over Cheyenne Pass would require a switchback and maximum grades of 116 feet per mile. At the summit, a tunnel 1,500 feet long would be necessary. In his report Evans describes other features of the passes and streams, and while using the permitted maximum grades, he found nothing to prevent the building of the road. He comments upon the presence of coal and timber and notes that the emigration road by this route was increasing in importance over the longer route by the North Platte and the South Pass.

Evans also mentioned that further examination of the summit of the Black Hills should be made to the north and south, in order to determine where the best crossing should be made. Time and other circumstances did not permit his doing this. However, on his return he made some surveys on the west side of the Black Hills southward but found elevations too great at the crest of the range. He was kept away from the tributaries of Crow Creek on the eastern side nor did he extend his line far enough to the south to discover the pass that was later used. With a few men from his party, Evans went northward to the Laramie River and made a reconnaissance of that stream. He found that it passed through the Black Hills by a canyon not adapted for a railroad and rejected it as a possible route. Instructions had been sent to Evans to make reconnaissance of the South Pass route, but as the Indians were then active and as there was no provision for supplying him with an escort or transportation, he returned with his party to Omaha in the fall of the year. However, he talked with Jim Bridger and learned of the difficulties of the route up the North Platte and the Sweetwater to South Pass, information that was of considerable value.

The second party of 1864 was organized under F. M. Case, who was given the problem of investigating the several passes through the southern Rocky Mountains on the upper reaches of the South Platte. Six passes in all were examined, two of which, the Berthoud Pass due west of Denver, and the Hoosier Pass on the South Platte, were surveyed. All the passes through the Front Range were over 10,000 feet in elevation, they were in a region of heavy snowfall, the mountains were steep, and long tunnels would be necessary for any line of railroad—all in all, no place for the Union Pacific. Case therefore devoted his time to a survey over the Cache la Poudre route and Antelope Pass into the Laramie Plains, where he connected with Evans' surveys. It is significant that Case suggested that a line could pass the Black Hills by a pass at the heads of Crow Creek or Box Elder Creek, the foot of the mountains being much higher than where Evans started his survey, and possibly furnishing a uniform grade to the summit. He referred to the report by Captain Stansbury regarding such a pass and urged a greater study of that region.

Samuel B. Reed was in charge of the third survey part of 1864, which he organized at Salt Lake City with the help of Brigham Young. His first line ran from Salt Lake City northward to the mouth of Weber River Canyon, thence eastward up Weber River to Echo Creek, and up that stream across the mountains to Sulphur Creek, a tributary of Bear River. This line proved much more favorable than had been anticipated. He also made a survey eastward across the range by way of Chalk Creek to Bear River. From Bear River the surveys were extended over the intervening summit eastward via Muddy Creek and Black's Fork to Green River, where practicable connection was made with Evans' surveys. The length of line by way of Weber River and Echo Canyon from Salt Lake City to Green River was found to be 233 miles. The general conditions were more favorable to this line than to the one by way of Chalk Creek.

Reed also ran a line down the Timpanogas River. It started from the line on Weber River, ran southward twenty-six miles up the valley of the Weber to Kamas Prairie, thence down the

Timpanogas River to the valley of Utah Lake. The difficulties of the route are discussed in Reed's report. In addition to the instrumental surveys, Reed also made extensive explorations of the region between Green River and the Salt Lake Valley, especially the crossing of the Wasatch Mountains. He concluded that the Weber River-Echo Creek line was the best, and it was along this line that the railroad was later built. Reed reached Omaha on the 18th of November, where he made his report to Durant in New York.

While the eastern terminus of the road had been fixed by President Lincoln on the Iowa side of the Missouri, near Council Bluffs, the effective starting point was at Omaha, across the Missouri River from Council Bluffs. Both of these cities are located on or near the plateau of rolling hills that rise from 100 to 200 feet or more above the river, which itself is at an elevation of 980 feet above sea level. The development of the city of Council Bluffs was largely on the level ground of the river bottom, but Omaha, where the river washes close to the bluffs, was built upon the undulating plain of the high ground.

Between the two bluffs, the flood plain of the Missouri River is about four miles wide. The present channel of the river, which is adjacent to the Iowa shore above Council Bluffs, swings across the flood plain and runs close to the Nebraska shore below the central part of Omaha. The rolling hills extend southward along the river to the valley of the Platte River, which joins the Missouri about thirteen miles south of Omaha. The hills, which are actually an elevated plain, extend westward some fifteen miles to the valley of the Platte, where the Elkhorn River is reached. A line of bluffs borders the valley, at the base of which the Elkhorn River flows southward on its way to the Platte. A railroad from Omaha to the Platte Valley must cross this elevated plain and descend to the Platte Valley. This was the first location problem to be solved, and to that end the surveys of Peter A. Dey were directed.

The rolling plain is drained by Papillion Creek, a stream

[245]

with several branches that flow in a generally southeasterly direction, and after uniting, discharge into the Missouri. West of Omaha the stream has incised channels into the gravel and loose formation of the region to depths of more than 100 feet below the general surface. To locate the railroad directly west across the several streams was inadvisable; so the first location was bent southward to avoid the principal branches of the stream, and then use the west branch northwestward to the bluff above the Elkhorn River, through which bluff there was a low pass down to the valley of that river.

As Dey first located the line, after climbing about two and a half miles out of the terminal at Omaha on a grade of sixty-six feet per mile, it went down into and climbed out of the two branches of Papillion Creek on grades up to eighty feet per mile until the westerly branch of the creek was reached. The line then ascended the stream valley and proceeded through the bluffs to the Elkhorn River in the Platte Valley. Grades up to eighty feet per mile were used there too, such being well within the limits set by the government. It was claimed by Dey that these grades could be reduced at some later time by deepening the excavations as well as by increasing the height of the fills across the streams.

Silas Seymour, who had been appointed consulting engineer of the company on January 1, 1864, began in the fall of 1864 to question the location made by Dey, and with Williams, a government director of the company, he visited the work then in progress. In a report to the directors, dated December 21, 1864, Seymour advocated a change in location, although the work of construction had been in progress for a year. The change meant relocating the line south of Omaha along the Missouri to Mud Creek, a tributary of Papillion Creek that ran parallel to the Missouri River. Mud Creek was to be followed to a point near the junction with Papillion Creek and to proceed thence up the westerly branch of Papillion Creek to join the Dey location. It increased the length of the line by some thirteen miles, but the grades were reduced to forty feet per mile or less. A number of prominent railroad engineers gave their opinion that the change was to better the road and was therefore advisable.

In accordance with the Law of 1862, President Lincoln had approved the original location, and it was therefore deemed necessary to have the change of location approved by the President. It was approved by the railroad directors in January, 1865, and on May 12 of that year General Dix asked for the presidential approval and urged a speedy decision. However, the President desired the opinion of a disinterested person, whereupon Secretary of the Interior Harlan appointed Colonel J. H. Simpson, U. S. Engineer Corps, to make a full investigation. Colonel Simpson visited Omaha and Council Bluffs in July, 1865, looked over the ground with railroad and government enginers, heard the testimony of committees of citizens, and ordered surveys to be made of the new line. He was bombarded with letters from interested parties, in one of which Durant maligned Dey, stating that he had never been chief engineer of the railroad, questioned his accounts and ability, and generally disparaged him, although Dey had been in the employ of the company for several years on surveys, as well as on actual construction for nearly a year. Citizens of Omaha accused Durant of various crimes, such as desiring to move the railroad terminus to Bellevue and awarding the contract for building the road at sums far exceeding the estimated or actual cost.

Colonel Simpson made his report to the Secretary of the Interior on September 18, 1865, approving the change in location, and on September 23, President Johnson gave his approval. Durant had stopped work on the original location in December of the preceding year, thus allowing ten months to be lost in the controversy. It may seem that here was an engineering problem, but actually there were other matters of more importance involved. The company had spent about $100,000 on the original line and had tried construction with minor contractors, but the procedure had not proved satisfactory, as men were scarce in that remote region and the Civil War was on. It was then that the notorious Hoxie contract, for the first 100 miles, was signed, dated August 6, 1864, and accepted by the company on the 23rd of that month. Hoxie was to receive $50,000 per mile for the work. As has been described elsewhere, Hoxie was nothing more than a subterfuge for the Credit Mobilier. When the contract was seen by Chief Engineer Dey in November of 1864, at about the same time that the change of location was being agitated, he would approve neither the contract nor the change of location, and so resigned. His letter to General Dix was dated December 7, 1864; therefore his resignation was evidently based upon the Hoxie contract, as the location change was not finally adopted until ten months later.

Engineers Office,
Union Pacific Railroad,
Omaha, December 7, 1864.

Dear Sir:—

I hereby tender you my resignation as chief engineer of the Union Pacific Railroad, to take effect December 30, 1864, one year from my appointment. I am induced to delay until that time that I might combine the results of surveys of the present year and present them to the company and to myself in a satisfactory manner. My reasons for this step are simply that I do not approve of the contract made with Mr. Hoxie for building the first hundred miles from Omaha west, and I do not care to have my name so connected with the railroad that I shall appear to indorse this contract.

Wishing for the road success beyond the expectation of its members, I am

Respectfully yours,
Peter A. Dey.

Hon. John A. Dix.

In the same enclosure Dey sent another letter to General Dix, in which he called attention to the disastrous effects of issuing bonds and stock beyond the actual cost and cited the experience of the Mississippi and Missouri Railroad. He concludes his letter in the following words:

"You are doubtless uninformed how disproportionate the amount to be paid is to the work contracted for. I need not expatiate upon the sincerity of my course when you reflect upon the fact that I have resigned the best position in my profession this country has ever offered to any man."

It was another case where an honest engineer would not countenance the method of extracting undue profits in an underhand manner. From that time on, the methods of Dr. Durant became the procedure by which the Union Pacific was constructed. The struggle of Dey is reminiscent of the similar contest that Theodore Judah had with the people building the Central Pacific. One man resigned and the other died.

In defense of his project for the change in location, Silas Seymour assembled estimates of the cost of the line located by Dey with that which he advocated. Such comparisons are not of much value, but it is interesting to note that Seymour's statement of the cost of the proposed line for 30.76 miles was at the rate of $34,141 per mile. However, he did not protest the Hoxie contract at $50,000 per mile, which actually represented an even higher rate, as some seventy miles was over the Platte Valley, where the unit costs were materially less than on that portion of the line across the tableland west of Omaha. It is not in the records that Seymour objected to the Hoxie contract, and it is certain that the government directors approved not only that contract but those of a similar nature that followed.

While the location change near Omaha might be justified on engineering grounds, the additional cost to the company was at least $400,000, which, added to the money expended on the original line that was not used, makes about half a million dollars' extra cost. It should also be noted that when the Union Pacific Railroad was rehabilitated at the turn of the century, the new route west from Omaha followed substantially the route selected by Dey on his first location. On the situation, General Dodge, who should know, had the following to say:

After the location of the road at Council Bluffs, the first serious question threatening Council Bluffs was the change of Mr. Dey's line from Omaha to Elkhorn, adding nine miles in distance, claiming to avoid heavy work and heavy grades. Many saw in this change, advocated by Colonel Seymour, the consulting engineer, and Mr. Durant, the vice president of the Union Pacific, an intention of utilizing Bellevue instead of the Bluffs as the real terminus of the road, and this aroused not only Omaha, but the Bluffs with all the influence of Iowa against such a result.

The main argument for adding nine miles of distance in thirteen miles of road was that it eliminated the eighty and sixty-six foot grades of the direct line. If this had been done there would have been some argument for the change, but they only eliminated the grades from the Omaha summit, which it took three miles of sixty and sixty-six foot grades to reach, and east of the Elkhorn summit, which was an eighty foot grade, so by the change and addition of nine miles they made no reduction in the original grades or in the tonnage hauled in a train on the new line over the old line if it had been built.

The Government provided that the change should only be made if the Omaha and Elkhorn grades were eliminated, the first by a line running south from Omaha two miles in the Missouri valley and cutting through the bluffs to Muddy Creek, giving a thirty-five foot maximum grade, and the Elkhorn, by additional cutting and filling without changing the line; but this was never done. The company paid no attention to the decision, but built on the changed line, letting the grades at Omaha and Elkhorn stand, and the government commissioners accepted the road, ignoring the conditions of the change, and bonds were issued upon it, although it was a direct violation of the government order.

The extensive surveys of 1865 were directed to a final determination of routes through the Rocky Mountains to Great Salt Lake. A survey was also run connecting the surveys from

[250]

the east at the 100th meridian with those at the eastern base of the Black Hills. Seymour outlined a program of work for two parties, in which he arranged the line in two divisions, the Atlantic and the Pacific, meeting at the continental divide in the Wyoming Basin. The work was naturally placed in charge of the men who had carried on the surveys of the previous year.

Mr. James A. Evans was appointed engineer for the Atlantic Division. His work showed that a line up the Platte Valley was a good location; also that a line over the Black Hills by the general route of the Cache la Poudre branch of the South Platte and over the Antelope Pass into the Laramie Plains was feasible under the limitations imposed by the government. Evans also ran a new line from the Lodgepole, where it meets the mountains, by way of Crow Creek over a pass that Durant named Evans Pass. The survey showed that a good line could be obtained by this route. This was near to the pass that was eventually used by the railroad, but the line from the Lodgepole was changed by later surveys. Although longer than the route by Cheyenne Pass by about twenty miles it was shorter than the one over Antelope Pass by nearly thirty-five miles. Under instructions from Evans, Case made a partial examination of the Laramie River as affording a possible route up the North Platte into the Laramie Plains. Evans also made surveys showing the possibility of connecting the line with the valley of the Republican River to the south, as a part of the plans of the company. He found the valley of the Republican narrow and crooked when compared with that of the Platte.

The work of the Pacific Division was placed in charge of Samuel B. Reed, who had conducted the surveys of the previous year. His party was organized at Salt Lake City and in general continued the surveys of 1864. He made a survey for a possible route from Black's Fork of Green River across the country to South Pass and a short distance down the Sweetwater River toward the North Fork of the Platte. Reed considered the route inadvisable on account of snow and the greater length of line

[251]

over the more southern route. Additional surveys were made along the line of his 1864 surveys and some work was done on Weber and Echo canyons. Reed also made a complete survey of a line westward from Salt Lake City by a route south of Great Salt Lake and across the deserts of the former Lake Bonneville. The line was extended across the intervening valleys and mountains to the Humboldt River. Lack of supplies prevented the extension of the survey to the California line. Reed considered this a good line. Another problem that was also considered on instructions from Durant was a reconnaissance across the Wasatch Mountains to Green River south of the Uinta Mountains. The result of this trip was to condemn the plan of a road through the central part of the southern Rocky Mountains.

The surveys of 1865 amounted to 1,254 miles of continuous instrumental line and gave sufficient information upon which to base the main location of the railroad. The work was completed in the following year.

The surveys of 1866 brought to a close the final determination of the route of the railroad as far west as the valley of Great Salt Lake. After the resignation of Dey there was no chief engineer, as Durant took upon himself the direction of the field parties during 1865. When the Civil War ended in 1865, the officers of the Union Pacific requested General G. M. Dodge to take the position, which he did finally on May 1, 1866. In a letter to Dodge, General Sherman expressed the hope that his going on leave of absence from the army would "be the real beginning of the work" of the railroad. Dodge went to the mountains, and additional surveys were made by several parties, the results of which, along with those of preceding years, were assembled by Dodge in a comprehensive report made to Vice President Durant at Omaha, dated November 15, 1866. The report sets forth the various routes that had been investigated by reconnaissance and by instrumental surveys, all of which Dodge had examined. It closed with a definite recommendation for the location.

During the progress of the surveys in the mountains, the people of Denver, then an active mining town, wanted the railroad to be built through their community. A number of passes through the Rocky Mountains had already been suggested, which led to their examination by the Union Pacific. Some of these have been mentioned. In 1866, additional surveys were made by way of Clear Creek and Berthoud Pass. Other passes were either examined or surveyed as the situation indicated, the important ones being Boulder Pass, elevation 11,700 feet; Argentine Pass, at the head of Leavenworth Creek; Quail Creek Pass; Jones Pass; Vasquez Pass; a pass at the head of Fall River; and another at the head of North Boulder Creek. All of the later passes were higher than Berthoud Pass, where the elevation was 11,304 feet above sea level (1866 measurements). A tunnel 3.1 miles in length would have been required, as well as many miles of maximum grades through a difficult mountain canyon. To these obstacles were added the troublesome country west of the Front Range through the Yampa, White, and Uinta valleys and over the Wasatch Mountains. It would also have necessitated a crossing of the Colorado River; all of which united to cause rejection of this and any other route across the mountains westward from Denver.

When the routes mentioned had been turned down, General Dodge considered the possible lines through the Black Hills.

Examination of the route by the North Platte, Sweetwater, and South Pass, including the line to Green River, had caused its rejection for many reasons, among which were the greater length, greater snowfall, and difficult construction, when compared to the southern route across the Wyoming Basin. After several reconnaissances of the Laramie River, it was finally surveyed by Evans and rejected on account of the difficult construction in a winding canyon with mountains walls up to 1,500 feet in height. The location of the line thus narrowed down to the region between Cheyenne Pass on the north and Antelope Pass on the south. While there was a possibility of a route being found anywhere in a distance of sixty miles along the eastern base of the mountains, the descent on the west was limited to a length of about ten miles between the passes named.

Because streams in that area have an excessive fall at their heads, it was necessary to seek an approach to the pass by a rising ridge between two streams. It was a problem similar to that faced by Judah when locating the Central Pacific over the Sierra Nevada, but on a smaller scale. Final surveys were made by Evans of the lines up the Cache la Poudre, up Crow Creek, by Cheyenne Pass, and also up Lone Tree and Crow Creek divide. Other surveys were made on the sloping plain leading up to Crow Creek. The Cache la Poudre route was found to be thirty-seven miles longer than by Evans Pass. In summing up the advantages of the line up Lodgepole and Crow Creeks and to the summit of the ridge between Crow and Lone Tree, Dodge emphasized the remarkable condition that the ridge led by an uninterrupted rise to the pass. He said:

"This line commences ascending the mountains in the valley of Crow Creek. . . . The divide line between Lone Tree and Crow Creek is reached with easy grades and light work. It crosses the junction of the sedimentary and granite rocks at a point where they come together at nearly the same level; and it is the only point, so far discovered, where this occurs in these mountains. At this point an elevation of 1,169 feet is reached in 18.1 miles, being the same meridian on which all other lines have to commence their ascent.

"The mountains, at this point, run out into the plains in a succession of ridges, some twenty miles in length, while at all other points the mountains end abruptly, falling in one mile at the base from 500 to 1,500 feet.

"The line follows the ridge between Lone Tree and Crow Creeks, making the summit at Evans Pass, with an elevation of 8,242 feet above the sea."

After crossing the pass, the line led down the west side of the mountains to the Laramie plains. The problems of grading and bridging were simpler and of less cost than by any other route, and Dodge thought they could cross the mountains with the track in 1867.

Along with the search for a pass over the Black Hills, there was the problem of reaching Denver by a branch line. A number of routes were considered, the total length of line being one basis for reaching a conclusion. In the end a branch line from the future city of Cheyenne, 112 miles southward to Denver, proved to be the best. Dodge strongly urged the route with the branch to Denver and on November 23, 1866, it was adopted by the board of directors of the railroad. Thus ended the long investigation to obtain the best route over the greatest obstacle on the way west, the Black Hills of Wyoming. Dodge states that to achieve that goal more than twice the amount of survey work had to be done in 1866 than in any previous year.

The discovery and location of the pass over the Black Hills was a development of many years. In 1850, Captain Howard Stansbury passed that way and camped for the night. He was within two or three miles of the pass through which the railroad was built eighteen years later. It has been recorded on a preceding page how Engineer B. B. Brayton saw the pass in the distance but did not have time to examine it. From an engineering point of view it was not the pass that was most important in that particular location, but rather the long sloping ridge approach from the plains up to the summit. This was the key to the problem, and the ridge up to the pass between Crow and Lone Tree creeks was discovered by General Dodge, while still in command of the troops in the Indian campaign of 1865. He tells the story in these words:

> In 1865, as I was returning from the Yellowstone country, after finishing the Indian campaigns, I took my command along the east base of the Black Hills, following up the Chug Water, and so on south, leaving my train every day and going to the summit of the Black Hills with a view of trying to discover some approach from the east that was feasible. When we got down to the crossing of the Lodge

Pole, I knew the Indians were following us, but I left the command with a few cavalrymen and guides, with a view of following the country from the Cheyenne Pass south, leaving strict orders with the command if they saw smoke signals they were to come to us immediately. We worked south from the Cheyenne Pass and around the head of Crow Creek, when I looked down into the valley there was a band of Indians who had worked themselves in between our party and the trains. I knew it meant trouble for us; they were either after us or our stock. I therefore immediately dismounted, and giving our horses to a couple of men with instructions to keep on the west side of the ridge out of sight and gunshot as much as possible, we took the ridge between Crow Creek and Lone Tree Creek, keeping it and holding the Indians away from us, as our arms were so far-reaching that when they came too near our best shots would reach them . . .

We made signals for our cavalry, but they did not seem to see them. It was getting along in the afternoon, as we worked down this ridge, that I began to discover we were on an apparently very fine approach to the Black Hills, and one of the guides has stated that I said, "If we saved our scalps I believed we had found a railroad line over the mountains."

About four o'clock the Indians were preparing to take the ridge in our front. The cavalry now saw our signals and soon came to our rescue, and when we reached the valley I was satisfied that the ridge we had followed was one which we could climb with a maximum grade within our charter and with comparatively light work.

As soon as I took charge of the Union Pacific I immediately wired to Mr. James A. Evans, who had charge of that division and who had been working on this mountain range for nearly a year, describing this ridge to him, as I had thoroughly marked it by a lone tree on Lone Tree Creek, and by a steep-cut butte on Crow Creek, and a deep depression in the ridge where the granite and sedimentary formations joined. He immediately made an examination and discovered a remarkably direct line of only a ninety-foot grade reaching from the summit to the valley of Crow Creek where Cheyenne now stands, and this summit I immediately named for my old commander, General Sherman. The Union Pacific is constructed over this line and it is one of the two eighty-foot grades left on the Union Pacific that they were unable to reduce during the construction of the road.

As the years went by, the decision of General Dodge to avoid the crossing of the Rocky Mountains directly west of Denver was proved correct when other railroads were built therein. Comparison of lengths in east and west directions may be made between Cheyenne and Ogden on one hand and Denver and Salt Lake City on the other, since Cheyenne and Denver are substantially on the same degree of longitude, and the same is true of Ogden and Salt Lake City. The distance from Cheyenne to Ogden by the Union Pacific as now operated is 483 miles.

In 1883, fourteen years after completion of the Union Pacific, the Denver and Rio Grande Western Railroad was completed to Salt Lake City. It was a narrow-gauge road, and by using 4 per cent grades it surmounted Marshall Pass at an elevation of 10,856 feet, the distance between the two cities being 719 miles. It exceeds the Union Pacific in distance by 50 per cent. This writer recalls a trip over the Rio Grande in the winter of 1885 when four locomotives were required to haul five passenger cars over the summit where the snow depth was higher than the car windows. Later, when the road was converted to standard gauge, the mountains were crossed at Tennessee Pass at an elevation of 10,240 feet. The line was lengthened to 745 miles to Salt Lake City, thus exceeding the Union Pacific by 54 per cent.

In the intervening years the Denver and Salt Lake Railroad, the "Moffat Road," was built westward from Denver, up South Boulder Creek to a crossing of the continental divide at Corona, elevation of 11,660 feet. In 1923 the Moffat Tunnel through the divide, six and two tenths miles long, was started by the railroad and completed in 1928 by a state improvement district. The tunnel reaches an elevation of 9,239 feet; and a connection

[257]

with the Denver and Rio Grande Western, the "Dotsero Cutoff," was built at a later date. The maximum grades are 2 per cent. The cost of the tunnel was about $18,000,000. The distance to Salt Lake City by this route is 570 miles, which is eighty-seven miles longer than the Union Pacific from Cheyenne to Ogden.

These comparisons are not made to disparage the work of the able railroad engineers who have built railroads through the southern Rocky Mountains in the most difficult situations, but rather are made to show that the engineers of the Union Pacific made no mistake in locating that line through the Wyoming Basin.

When the passage of the Black Hills had been fixed at Evans' or Sherman Pass in the winter of 1866, the problem of crossing the Wyoming Basin was in front of the engineers. The eastern end at Sherman Pass became a fixed point, but the passage through the Wasatch Mountains into Salt Lake Valley was still uncertain. In 1867 and 1868 the several routes were explored at great length, and the final route narrowed down to a definite line as more information became available.

In one sense, the location across the Wyoming Basin was a difficult one to solve. While the country appears as a rolling plain bordered by mountains, it is actually cut by streams, and so the question of keeping close to a straight line was combined with the requirement of keeping the grades as light as possible. Once the Sherman Summit had been fixed, the descent into the Laramie Plains presented no difficulty and the same applied to the line northwestward around the Medicine Bow Range. From there, several alternate routes were examined, with Dodge making a long reconnaissance late in 1867 northward from Salt Lake City up Bear River, then eastward across several ranges of mountains to Green River and South Pass, thence across the basin to the lines being surveyed on the south. At that time he also had in view the possible construction of a railroad to Oregon. A survey line had been run up Bear River from its mouth at Great Salt Lake to the bend around the north end of

the Wasatch Mountains and thence south up the river to a connection with the lines across the divide to Weber River. Similar
surveys had been made by the Central Pacific.

The results of all the surveys was the location substantially
where the railroad now runs. The North Platte was crossed at
Fort Steele, after the line had been found through the Rattle-
snake Hills by way of a small stream called Mary's Creek. From
the North Platte, the summit of the continental divide was
reached by way of Rawlins Springs, Separation Creek, and
Dodge's Pass, thus passing about twenty miles to the north of
Bridger's Pass, through which the first surveys were made. From
the divide, the line passed across the southern rim of Red Desert
to the headwaters of Bitter Creek and down that stream some
seventy-five miles to Green River. The divide to the west was
reached by way of Black's Fork and Muddy Creek Valley, thence
down to Bear River, and then across the second divide into Echo
Creek a tributary of Weber River. The line followed down
Echo Creek and Weber River to what is now Ogden, at the edge
of the Salt Lake Valley. The tracks of the railroad had reached
Cheyenne in the fall of 1867, when construction work was suspended for the winter. The surveys were continued into 1868,
extending across the mountains and down the Humboldt River,
since it was expected that the Union Pacific would be built to
the border of California. The surveys and examinations made
of a possible route south of Great Salt Lake, when compared
with those on a line north of the lake and across the low mountains to Humboldt Wells, had forced the Union Pacific to the
conclusion reached by the Central Pacific engineers that the
best route lay north of the lake. Brigham Young wanted very
much to have the line pass through Salt Lake City and was
greatly disappointed when the final decision was reached. At
first a survey was made across Bear River Bay to the southern
end of Promontory Point; and General Dodge, who was in favor
of the route, said in his report of January 1, 1868:

"I may say that a careful examination convinced me that our

true line west is north of Salt Lake and that if the Bear River arm could be crossed in three miles distance, in shallow water, it is better to do so rather to overcome the high grades and elevation of Promontory Point, with the heavy work involved." Evidently later investigations caused Dodge to change his opinions. His statement that the width was three miles indicates that the investigations were for a line across the northern portion of Bear River Bay. The location of the Central Pacific Railroad, made a third of a century later, is across the bay directly from the extreme southern point of the Promontory Mountains, where the crossing is eight miles in length. The plan considered by Dodge was to cross the bay and then continue around the shore of the lake at lake level. However, in making the survey the party in a sounding boat nearly drowned. The lake had risen fourteen feet since the time of Stansbury's survey in 1849-1850, and there was no certainty that it would not go higher. The crossing of the western arm of the lake had water twice as deep as on the east arm of the lake. Even to build to Promontory Point was beyond the means of the railroad, and the line was forced to the route north and over the Promontory Ridge, where the two railroads met in 1869.

The work of the surveyors who explored the country was one of exceeding difficulty. The region was uninhabited; it was at a high elevation; and much of the Wyoming Basin was desert, where the parties suffered from winter storms, lack of good water, and the terrible alkali dusts of the plains. The work had to be done under the constant protection of companies of the regular army, as the Indian menace grew worse the further west the line went. It was especially bad from the Black Hills to Salt Lake. Two of the best chiefs of parties, Percy T. Brown and L. L. Hills, were killed by Indians and their parties dispersed. General Dodge describes their deaths in the following words:

In the spring of 1867 there was a party in the field under L. L. Hills, running a line east from the base of the Rocky

Mountains. The first word I received of it was through the commanding officer at Camp Collins, who had served under me when I commanded the department. He informed me that a young man named J. M. Eddy had brought the party into that post, its chief having been killed in a fight with the Indians. I enquired who Eddy was and was informed that he was an axman in the party, and had served under me in the Civil War. . . . The fight in which Mr. Hills, the chief, was killed occurred some six miles east of Cheyenne, and after the leader was lost young Eddy rallied the party and by force of his own character took it into Camp Collins. Of course I immediately promoted him.

In July, 1867, Mr. Percy T. Brown, whose division extended from the North Platte to Green River, was running a line across the Laramie Plains. His party was camped on Rock Creek, where they were attacked by Sioux. Brown was out on the line with most of the party, but those in camp were able to hold the Indians off; but a small party out after wood, under a promising young fellow named Clark, a nephew of Thurlow Weed of New York, was killed with one of his escort, and several of the escort were wounded.

The Indians on the plains this year were very aggressive and were not satisfied with stealing. Brown, on reaching the divide of the continent found it an open prairie, extending some 150 miles northeast and southwest and seventy miles east and west. The Rocky Mountains had from an elevation of 13,000 feet dropped to one of 7,000 feet into an open plain, and the divide of the continent is really a great basin some 500 feet lower than the general level of the country.

Brown, in reconnoitering the country, expected to find a stream leading to the waters of the Pacific, dropped into this basin and in exploring it near its southern rim he struck thirty Sioux Indians who were on the war path. He had with him eight men of his escort and he immediately took possession of an elevation in the basin, and there, from 12 o'clock until nearly dark, fought off those Indians.

Just before dark, a shot from one of the Indians hit Brown in the abdomen. He begged the men to leave him and save themselves but the soldiers refused to do so. They had to give up their horses, and as soon as the Indians obtained them they fled, and those eight soldiers made a litter of their carbines and through the tall sagebrush for fifteen miles they packed Brown to La Clede Stage Station, thinking to save him, but he died soon after reaching the station."

It is hardly to be wondered that the hand of the white man was turned against all Indians. The outrage described above was but one of hundreds of useless attacks on parties. The emigrants, being without escorts, suffered the most, and everyone was in constant danger from the savages.

The work of locating the railroad over the Wyoming Basin and the bordering mountains was delayed by constant friction in the company, together with the efforts of Durant to foment strife among the men in charge of the location and construction. Here again appears Colonel Silas Seymour, the so-called consulting engineer. A man of some experience, he seems to have been a pedant who tried to apply eastern railroad practice to this new road. Apparently he followed Durant in whatever action that gentleman desired to take. Samuel B. Reed describes him in these words:

"Col. Seymour was outfitted after the following style. First the horse which he selected and paid a good round price for was, or ought to have been twin brother to old 'Knockumstiff.' On the horse he would have placed the saddle, attached to which was his carbine in its case securely strapped and buckled to be convenient in case of a sudden Indian attack; also his poncho, bed, etc., in bulk about a barrel, leaving very little room for the Colonel. When mounted he would hoist his umbrella and leisurely follow in the wake of the escort or perhaps leading them a few paces. The Pawnee made fun of him from beginning to end."

It would be of little point to mention Seymour were it not that Dr. Durant apparently used him for his own ends. Changes were made in the line that Seymour seemed to have initiated. Reed was of the opinion that "Seymour seems to be determined to delay the work as much as possible. The object apparently is to injure somebody's reputation. General Dodge appears to be the scapegoat."

Two of the important changes are thus described by Dodge:

Two changes were made by the contractors [the Ames trustees] in the line so as to cheapen the work, and this was at the expense of the commercial property. This was always opposed by the division engineer [Evans] who located the line, and he was supported by the chief engineer [Dodge]. The changes were always made when the chief engineer was absent. The company would agree to a change, and the work on the changes would be so far advanced that it was too late to rectify the matter when the chief engineer returned. The first change was of Mr. James A. Evans' location on the eastern slope of the Black Hills from Cheyenne to Sherman. Evans had a ninety-foot equated grade with a six degree maximum curvature. It was a very fine location and the amount of curvature was remarkably small for a mountain line. It rose ninety feet to the mile in a steady climb. Col. Silas Seymour, the consulting engineer, undertook to reduce this grade to eighty feet, but increased the curvature so much that an engine would haul more cars over Evans' ninety-foot grade than on Seymour's eighty-foot grade, but Seymour was obliged when he reached the foot of the mountains, to put in a ninety-foot grade to save work as he dropped off the foothills to the plains, and a portion of this grade remains today. When Evans took up the change in his report and compared it with his line, he made it so plain that the change was wrong that the government directors adopted it for their report.

The next change was from the Laramie River to Rattle-snake Hills, or Carbon Summit. The original line ran north of Cooper Lake, and O'Neil, who had instructions to locate on that line, changed it by order of Col. Silas Seymour, consulting engineer, to a line dropping into the valleys of Rock Creek and Medicine Bow River to save work. This increased the length of the line twenty miles and caused the report that we were making the line crooked to gain mileage and secure $48,000 per mile of the bonded

[263]

subsidy. The amount of grading on this line was about half that of the original line. During 1903 and 1904, in bringing the Union Pacific line down to a maximum grade of forty-seven feet to the mile, except over the Wasatch Range and the Black Hills, the company abandoned this principal change made by the consulting engineer, and built on or near my original location, saving twenty-miles in the distance.

It may appear at first thought that it was strange that the contractor should desire to lengthen the line by twenty miles, but the object is clear when it is recalled that the work was being done under Oakes Ames' contract, which at that place was being paid for by the Union Pacific Railroad Company at the rate of $96,000 per mile. By increasing the length of the line at or near that point by twenty miles, the contractor, under the Oakes Ames contract, received from the railroad company $1,920,000 additional pay for building unnecessary railroad at a smaller cost than by the shorter line located by Dodge and his engineers. The government bonds for that extra length were at the rate of $48,000 per mile, or a total of $960,000. The line was probably built for less than that amount, as the construction was relatively light, so that the change undoubtedly netted the contractor over a million dollars. The railroad had twenty miles of extra and unnecessary railroad to maintain and operate and an additional amount added to its debt. It is small wonder that Durant relied upon a consulting engineer who would countenance such a procedure. As Dodge said, when the railroad was rebuilt, in 1903 and 1904, the changed route was abandoned and the railroad rebuilt along the original location of thirty-five years before.

The changes made by Durant and Seymour in the line led to emphatic protests on the part of Dodge, as shown by his report of January 1, 1868. The matter was carried to Washington, as the Ames interests were opposed to Durant and, in general, supported Dodge. Finally, a notable delegation of army men (no less than eleven general officers) and government directors came to Fort Sanders. The party included Generals Grant, Sherman, William S. Harney, Phil Sheridan, Dodge, August Kautz, Frederick Dent, John Gibbon, Adam Slemmer, Joseph Potter, and Louis C. Hunt, Dr. T. C. Durant, and Colonel Silas Seymour. The whole subject of Durant's interference with the work of the chief engineer and his locating parties, together with the conduct of the work, was thrashed out. Dodge told the meeting that the interference with his work had to be stopped immediately or he would resign. No engineer could work under the conditions that prevailed. The result was that General Grant ruled that Dodge was to continue as chief engineer and Durant should stop his methods of interference. As General Grant was soon to become President of the United States, Durant accepted the situation, because he needed the help of the government. From that time on, no further changes were made in the line selected by Dodge.

During the location and construction of the road, the location was subject to the review of the government directors, and late in 1868, when all important problems had been solved and the road nearly completed, O. H. Browning, Secretary of the Interior, appointed a special commission to examine and report

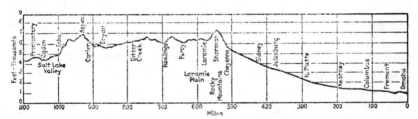

Route of the Union Pacific Railroad in profile

upon the Union Pacific and other railroads that came under the laws of 1862 and 1864. After an examination, the commission made an exhaustive report, in which there is the following comment upon the location:

"Taken as a whole the Union Pacific Railroad has been well

[265]

constructed. The general route for the line is exceedingly well selected crossing the Rocky Mountain ranges at some of the most favorable passes on the continent, and possessing capabilities for easy grades and favorable alignment unsurpassed by any other railway line on similarly elevated grounds."

Progress of the final location is apparent from the following data: First 100 miles, October 19, 1864; second 100 miles, June 20, 1866; from the 200th to 380th mile post, November 23, 1866; from 380th to near the 700th, from April to November 15, 1867; from that point to Ogden, May 1 to July 3, 1868. The map showing the general route from 100 miles west of Omaha to Salt Lake City was filed June 28, 1865.

During the years from 1899 to 1902, after the road had been in service for nearly a third of a century, it was almost completely rebuilt. During that period rolling stock had greatly increased in weight, and the country traversed had been so developed that revenue from traffic was upon a definite basis. Ample funds were therefore provided with which the road was largely rebuilt. Grades were reduced, sharp curves eliminated, and permanent structures built to replace temporary ones. Relocations of the line were made for short distances and elevations over summits reduced by excavating long tunnels.

Two relocations were made that corrected the obvious mistakes of Durant and Seymour. Out of Omaha across the rolling plain to Elkhorn, a new line, the Lane Cutoff, was built close to the original location made by Dey at the beginning of the work in 1864. The saving in distance was nearly nine miles. The other relocation of importance was made between Laramie and Rawlins, where, as has been mentioned, the road was rebuilt close to the location originally selected by General Dodge.

By digging an 1,800-foot tunnel at the Sherman Summit, thirty-one miles west of Cheyenne, the elevation was reduced 236 feet, but about half a mile was added in distance. A fill of 475,000 cubic yards of material was made over Dale Creek, replacing the trestle of the old line.

The other important relocation was made near the western border of Wyoming, at the Aspen Ridge dividing the drainage of Green River from that of Bear River. A section of the old line over thirty miles long was abandoned, and a new line, 21.61 miles long, substituted, effecting a saving of 9.56 miles, together with the use of curves of longer radius and the reduction in curvature from 2,017 degrees to 646 degrees. To accomplish this, some heavy railroad work was done, which included digging a tunnel 5,900 feet long, with a 2,200-foot cut on the east end and a half-mile cut on the west. This operation necessitated the excavation of 420,000 cubic yards of earth and solid rock.

The relocation and reconstruction of the railroad was in charge of J. B. Berry, chief engineer. With two exceptions, the ruling grade of the new line was 0.82 per cent, or 43.3 feet per mile, a material reduction from the former ruling grade of 82 to 97.7 feet per mile. One of the two exceptions was directly west of Cheyenne, the other being in Weber and Echo canyons. The length of line in Wyoming was reduced from 438.89 miles to 408.13 miles, a saving of 30.76 miles. The decrease in curvature was 7,168 degrees and in rise and fall, 632 feet.

At first it would seem that these changes were a censure to the men who made the original location. Actually, the contrary is true. Mr. Berry in his report made the following statement:

> It may appear to those unfamiliar with the character of the country that the great saving in distance and the reduction of grades would stand as a criticism of the pioneer engineers who made the original location of the railroad. Such is not the case. The changes have been expensive and could be warranted only by the volume of traffic handled at the present day. Too much credit cannot be given Gen. G. M. Dodge and his assistants. They studied their task thoroughly and performed it well. Limited by law to a maximum gradient of 116 feet to the mile, not compensated for curvature, they held it down to about 90 feet per mile. Taking into consideration the existing conditions thirty-five years ago, the lack of maps of the country, hostility of

[267]

the Indians, which made United States troops necessary for protection of surveying parties, difficult transportation, excessive cost of labor, uncertainty of probable volume of of traffic, limited amount of money and necessity to get the road built as soon as possible, it can be said with our present knowledge of the topography of the country that the line was located with very great skill.

These conclusions of Mr. Berry only restate the opinions of the members of the engineering profession who are familiar with railroad location. From the Missouri River to the Pacific Coast, the Pacific Railroad was located with uncanny precision. The changes made in later years were of minor amount compared with the overall job of constructing the original railroad. The route selected remains today a magnificent steel pathway across the continent and justifies the faith of those who carried out the great work.

# CHAPTER 11

# Constructing the Union Pacific Railroad

GROUND WAS broken for the Union Pacific on the Nebraska side of the Missouri River some four years before any other railroad reached Council Bluffs on the Iowa east shore. This made it necessary to depend on river transportation for carrying construction materials until the time when the Cedar Rapids and Missouri Railroad, later the Chicago and North Western Railroad, reached Council Bluffs, on Sunday, January 17, 1867, long after active construction had been under way on the Union Pacific Railroad.

Prior to 1867, the nearest railroad was the Hannibal and St. Joseph, which reached the Missouri at St. Joseph, Missouri, 175 miles down the winding Missouri River from Omaha. At best, the river was navigable by steamboats for only three or four months during the spring rise. Steamers threaded the stream for over 1,000 miles above St. Louis, and traffic into the northern Rocky Mountains was also mainly by river. In those

[269]

times, navigation of the stream was most uncertain, due to sand bars and also to innumerable snags of sunken trees. During the winter the river was completely closed by floating or solid ice.

The only other means of obtaining the necessary supplies was to haul them by wagon over dirt roads from the end of the track of the Iowa railroads that were slowly making their way across that state toward Council Bluffs.

The only materials locally available were ties, stone for culverts and bridge piers, and material for making brick for buildings. The greatest item of weight was iron rail, with the necessary chairs, fish plates, spikes, and bolts. All rolling stock, including locomotives, freight and passenger cars, and similar equipment, with the exception of some cars that were built at the Omaha shops of the company, were brought up the river from St. Joseph. The company employed steamers for this purpose and also used barges that were towed up the river. Equipment for the shops came by the same route, although some was sent by rail and team across Iowa.

When the North Western Railroad reached Council Bluffs early in 1867, a spur track was built across the river bottoms to the channel of the Missouri River, from which point the Union Pacific operated steamers as a ferry across the river to a point on the Nebraska shore where the first depot and railroad shops were later located, somewhere near the foot of Dodge Street. At that place the river at low water varies in width from 750 feet to about 1,000 feet, and the rise during floods is about ten feet. During the winter of 1867-1868, when river traffic was suspended, the Union Pacific built a temporary pile bridge across the stream, which cost about $10,000. It is probable that this bridge was renewed during the winter of 1868-1869, as it furnished direct connection with the railroad systems of the East at a time when construction was most active. However, the ferries were kept in use at other times, and as the permanent bridge across the Missouri between Omaha and Council Bluffs was not opened for traffic until 1872, the ferries were generally used for transfer across the river.

The uncertainties of river traffic compelled the company to buy and transport to the yards at Omaha a large amount of material that was stored, pending the demand that was sure to come as the track pushed westward. The storage yards were located on the flat lands below the bluffs where the shops were built, but in some cases material was placed along the track leading out of Omaha.

### MATERIALS

The iron rails for the road were of American make, in accordance with the law creating the road, and were manufactured chiefly at Johnstown, Scranton, Danville, and Allentown, Pennsylvania. For the first section of the road, 440 miles in length, the rails weighed fifty pounds per yard and were supported and connected by a wrought-iron chair, an inferior method of construction, deficient in strength and liable to work loose. For the remaining portion of the road, the rails, usually about twenty-eight feet in length, weighed fifty-six pounds per yard and were connected by fish plates, a device that is still used today. Fishplates, one on each side of the rail, are bolted to rails through slotted holes that permit variations of rail lengths with changes of temperature. The rail joint is today supported by two ties instead of by one, where the old type chair was used. Wrought-iron rails did not last a great length of time, and they had to be rerolled when they wore out. The weight of rolling stock in 1869 had about reached the limit that iron rails would support and it was only later, after steel rails had been introduced, that heavier rolling stock became possible. All original rail on the Union Pacific was of wrought iron.

The use of wooden crossties had become standard before the construction of the Pacific Railroad. The problem of securing crossties was one of the most difficult that the builders of the railroad had to solve. Approximatly 3,000,000 ties were required, the number varying from 2,300 to 2,640 per mile. The trouble was that timber on the bottoms of the Missouri and Platte rivers was mostly cottonwood, subject to easy decay and too soft to hold effectively the spikes that fastened the rails. Some oak and other hardwood timber was available along the bluffs bordering the rivers, while on the sides of the Platte Valley there was some cedar. However, it was not until the summit of the Black Hills was reached that good timber for ties and bridges became available from the pine forests of the Rocky Mountains south of the line. The defects of cottonwood were well know, and as a partial remedy they were burnetized, a method of preservation originated by Burnet in England. At Omaha a treatment plant was erected consisting of a steel cylinder five feet in diameter and seventy-five feet long, into which the load of 250 ties was run. After the door was closed, the air was exhausted by a steam-driven pump, which process opened the pores of the wood, allowing the moisture to escape. The cylinder was then filled with a solution of chloride of zinc, which under pressure entered the pores of the wood. Two batches of ties, amounting to 500, were treated each day. The process was costly and only partially successful, since the wood's holding power was not materially increased.

In August, 1866, it was reported that ties were being floated down the Missouri River in the proportion of about three hardwood ties to ten of cottonwood. The hardwood ties were placed at the rail joints and in the center of the rail, cottonwood being employed elsewhere under the rail. Cedar ties were obtained in the canyons on the north and south sides of the river, and were hauled across the river over a pontoon bridge 400 feet in length. Beyond the Sherman Summit of the Black Hills, ties were cut in the pine, spruce, and hemlock forests of the Medicine Bow and Elk mountains, and were floated down the Laramie, Medicine Bow, and North Platte rivers northward to the railroad. Farther west there were no streams until Green River was reached, after which Henry's Fork, Black's Fork, Bear and Weber rivers were used for the same purpose. In this manner good ties were made available for the western half of the road, and soon after the road was opened cottonwood ties on the eastern section were replaced with hardwood.

All important parts of the Union Pacific's bridges were imported from the eastern states, the timbers for the Dale Creek bridge coming mostly from Chicago. For fuel, cottonwood from Missouri and Platte River groves was used. Several geologists were employed to investigate possible locations of coal and had reported on the coal fields of the Wyoming Basin. These coal fields have since proved to be extensive and have supplied the railroad with fuel right up to the present time.

Stone for culverts and bridge piers, as well as for foundations for buildings, was found in limestone beds along the Missouri and also on Papillion Creek along the line of the railroad near Omaha. For several hundred miles beyond Omaha, the alluvial valley of the Platte afforded very little stone, although occasionally some limestone was found on the bluffs overlooking the valley. When the Black Hills were reached, the road passed out of the fluvial formation of the plains and at the Sherman Summit it reached the granite core of the mountains. This granite furnished good building stone as well as material for ballast. While stone was not abundant along the western half of the road, there was always enough for the railroad's purpose. The practice was followed of crossing small water courses with wooden trestles, which were later replaced by stone culverts or, in the case of larger streams, with truss bridges resting upon stone piers.

## CONSTRUCTION

Except for some twenty miles at the summit of the Black Hills, and for a lesser distance in Echo and Weber canyons, there were no special construction difficulties. One third of the line up the Platte Valley was built on a flat plain of imperceptible rise to the mountains. The open country up the mountains and through the Wyoming Basin offered little obstruction to rapid work since streams were few and not very large. Between Omaha and Granite Canyon, a distance of 535 miles, there was no rock excavation at all. The twenty miles of granite work at the summit of the Black Hills was not especially difficult and with the exception of about three miles in Weber Canyon there was little heavy rock work. Fortunately, the sandstones and the sedimentary rocks of the Wyoming Basin has disintegrated long before into a debris that filled the flat valley through which the small streams wandered. In all the great length of line there were but four short tunnels, three of them being on the line through the Wasatch Mountains.

Many of the good construction features of the line were due to the great amount of surveying that had been done earlier. In general, the construction work was considerably less than eastern roads had encountered in crossing the Appalachian Mountains. What difficulties there were lay rather in the remoteness of the location, the great distances over which supplies had to be transported, the Civil War that engulfed the country during the formative years of the project, and, what was of major importance, the never-ending troubles with the Indians of the plains and mountains. To all of these had to be added the barrenness of the country, over which blizzards swept in winter and on which the sun burned and alkali dust drifted in summer.

It was in the vicinity of the Sherman Summit in the Black Hills that the only heavy work was encountered that required any great amount of blasting. Here the new explosive agent, nitroglycerine, was used in some large blasts. There was also some arduous work in Weber Canyon for a few miles, but in general the grading progressed rapidly. In the higher regions, where snow was abundant in winter, it was necessary to keep the grade line on fills in order to avoid cuts where the snow would drift, and this involved a considerable amount of earth work. There is some mention in reports of the time of a grading machine, but information is not available today regarding its construction nor the amount of work it did. The usual tools of that day consisted of wheelbarrows drawn by men, scrapers drawn by animals, and one-horse two-wheeled dump carts, the latter used where it was necessary to convey earth any distance.

There were four tunnels on the road, with a total length of 1,792 feet. The cross-section clearances for one timbered tunnel were nineteen feet in width at the springing line of the semi-circular arch and seventeen feet in width at the base. The clear height was twenty feet four inches above base of rail. In the hard-rock tunnels the clear width was sixteen feet, with the vertical clearance twenty feet four inches above base of rail. Modern rolling stock demands much greater clearances.

Tunnel 1 was on Mary's Creek in the Rattlesnake Hills, 680 miles from Omaha, and here a sharp turn of the stream required a short tunnel through the spur of the hills. The tunnel, which was 215 feet long, was located on a straight line and was excavated in brown sandstone that had to be timbered. The tunnel was projected to be longer, but it was found expedient to extend the open cut on one end. In order to make progress with the track laying while the tunnel work was being done in May and June, 1868, a temporary track on a sharp curve was built around a spur of the hills.

Tunnel 2 was at the head of Echo Canyon in Utah, 972 miles from Omaha. Its length was 772 feet, making it the longest tunnel on the line. Deep approach cuts were necessary before reaching a weak clay rock, which crumbled on exposure. When work was begun on this tunnel, the track was 300 miles to the east, where all available transportation was needed to haul tools, materials, and provisions over the gap. There was no possibility of obtaining cement nor was there any suitable stone; for this reason the tunnel was lined with timber. Work on the tunnel was started in July, 1868, but the difficult nature of the ground prevented rapid progress. The headings met in January, 1869, so that the tunnel was not finished until May, 1869, shortly after the tracks had met the Central Pacific at Promontory. In order to make progress, a temporary track eight miles in length was built around the tunnel.

Tunnels 3 and 4 were in Weber Canyon, three quarters of

a mile apart, 1,005 miles from Omaha and about twenty-five miles from Ogden. Tunnel 3, which was 508 feet long, was on a three-and-one-half-degree curve. It was excavated through a sharp spur of black limestone and dark blue quartzite. To facilitate progress, another temporary track was laid in a sharp curve around the spur. The work extended from September, 1868, to April 4, 1869. Tunnel 4, located on a four-degree curve, had a length of 297 feet. The work commenced in September, 1868, with the tunnel being finished in January, 1869. Nitroglycerine was used in all these tunnels, with the result that the work was greatly expedited. As the long race with the Central Pacific was then approaching its climax, it is easy to see how imperative it was to complete the tunnels without delay.

The impression should not be given that the grading and tunnel work on the Union Pacific was a minor item in the building of the road. On the contrary, while the nature of the soil and the location of the line made the grading easy, the length of the line made the item of grading one of the major works of its kind.

### BRIDGES, TRESTLES, AND CULVERTS

While the Union Pacific did not encounter any large rivers, its bridges were important in their relation to the progress of the work. Here again, the remote location of the road made it difficult to secure construction material for bridges. It was not until the main line had been built that the one large bridge of the road was erected over the Missouri River between Omaha and Council Bluffs.

When the road was constructed, bridges had been well developed in America. The favorite truss bridge on new roads where economy was an object was, as has been said, the Howe truss, a bridge built with main members of timber and main vertical members of iron rods. Such bridges were put up by contractors, the members being fabricated of selected timbers and shipped to the place of use. Timber trestles were also made in standard forms.

Culverts were constructed of stone masonry, but in the hurry to extend the track, small water courses were crossed by pile trestles, the intention being to substitute the stone structure later when stone could be brought to the location by trains. In the work near Omaha, when the speed of construction was moderate, culverts and drains were built of masonry, but from there on, they were mostly of timber trestles. This temporary work, where cottonwood was used, required replacement within a short time.

Near Omaha, the two bridges over the branches of Papillion Creek were built of 100-foot Howe trusses on masonry piers and with trestle approaches. The next bridge, which was over the Elkhorn, was of a similar type, but with a span of 150 feet resting on masonry piers, followed by about 800 feet of wooden trestle. Shell Creek, Silver Creek, and Prairie Creek were crossed by pile trestles. The first important bridge was at Loup Fork of the Platte River, eighty-four miles from Omaha. This stream was one of the largest crossed and consequently was more exposed to destructive ice floods. The bridge was made up of ten 150-foot Howe truss spans resting on masonry piers, the total length being 1,500 feet. Shortly afterward it was found necessary to add two more 100-foot spans on the bottom lands. The Loup Fork bridge, under construction during a good part of 1866, was completed late that year. As the track had reached the bridge early in the year, a temporary pile trestle was constructed over the stream and early in May it was ready for track laying.

Wood River, a little east of Kearney, was crossed by a 100-foot iron truss structure resting on masonry abutments.

By the time the North Platte was reached, 291 miles from Omaha, the track was so close behind the graders that it was decided to cross the river on a pile trestle bridge 2,300 feet long, built with cedar piles. The river was not subject to heavy ice floods and there was little or no driftwood.

Lodgepole Creek was crossed three times on pile trestles, and at Cheyenne on Crow Creek a 100-foot Howe truss on masonry piers was built.

On the mountain section of the road, the bridge over Dale Creek was the most important. This small stream, a short distance west of the Sherman Summit, flowed in a gorge 130 feet deep and about 713 feet wide. A timber bridge of thirteen forty-foot spans and a fill was erected at this point. The foundations were of granite masonry, upon which rested double-framed trestles rising to the required height. The bents were spaced forty feet apart, with the track being placed on timber trusses supported on the trestle bents. As the road was then close to the pine regions, some mountain pine was used, but the major part of the bridge was made of timber sent west from Chicago. The cost was about $200,000. As there was always the possibility of fire, this bridge was later replaced by a steel trestle of thirteen forty-foot spans and a fill. At the time of the rebuilding of the road, the relocation of the line left Dale Creek bridge as a part of the abandoned line.

West of the Black Hills most of the bridges on the original line were constructed of timber trestles. In order to make progress, many of the streams west of the Sherman Summit were crossed by temporary pile trestles that were later replaced by permanent Howe truss spans resting on stone piers. There were two crossings of the Laramie River, of a total length of 300 feet; one over Rock Creek; one over Medicine Bow River, 200 feet long; one over the North Fork of the Platte, 600 feet long; twenty Bitter Creek crossings of a total length of 2,450 feet; the Green River crossing of 600 feet; one 150-foot bridge over Ham's Fork; and four over Black's Fork of a total length of 1,800 feet, making for all these Howe truss bridges a total length of 6,200 feet.

The several crossings of Weber River were made with trestles, as was the crossing of Bear River west of Ogden. On the way up to Promontory there were several framed trestles, one being about 250 feet long and about eighty feet high. The use

[278]

of the temporary structures on the rapid advance westward was fully justified by the desire to get the road into operation, since they served the purpose for which they were erected. Permanent stone and masonry work could be added later. The reports of government directors for the years that followed the opening of the line contain references to such work. For instance, in the report for 1874 it is stated that eight trestles of a total length of 3,096 feet had been supplied with stone culverts and a fill made in place of the trestle at a cost of $227,155. The procedure that was followed by the Union Pacific in its original construction was entirely proper for a railroad building into a new territory.

## TRACK LAYING

Track laying on the Union Pacific followed methods that had been developed on earlier roads, but it was better systematized, owing to the great length of the line. A keen contest was always going on between the grading and bridging forces on one hand, and the track-laying force on the other. The graders and bridgers were striving to keep ahead of the track, while the track gang hustled to keep up with the graders, partly out of a spirit of rivalry, but also because it was desirable to have end of track as far out ahead as possible so that supplies could be forwarded. Track laying was always a spectacular sight, and it is not surprising that visiting correspondents have left exciting accounts of what they saw.

The Union Pacific's first attempts at track laying in 1864 and 1865 did not produce much in the way of results, as only forty miles of track were set down by the end of 1865. By 1866, however, the project was in better shape and Durant awarded a contract to S. and D. T. Casement to lay the track. Casement Brothers made a written proposal to undertake the job at a given rate per mile, with conditions set forth, which was accepted by Durant in the following terms:

N. Y., Feb. 8, 1866.

"S. & D. T. Casement,
Painesville, Ohio.

Gentlemen:

Your proposition to the Union Pacific Railroad Company under date of Feb. 6, 1866, in relation to track-laying is received and has been considered.

The Company decides to regard your proposition and this acceptance as the agreement upon the subject.

The Company reserves the right to terminate this arrangement in case you do not perform the agreement on your part.

Yours truly,

Thomas C. Durant, V. P."

It will be noticed that Durant referred to the railroad company as making the contract, although the entire contract for building 247 miles was then in the hands of the Credit Mobilier. Under this contract Casement Brothers laid the track on about 1,000 miles of line and also took subcontracts for a considerable amount of grading. A correspondent of the Chicago *Tribune* describes the track laying in the following words:

(It was) under the exclusive control of General Casement, who, with his two brothers, has the contract for laying down the rails. Before he undertook this work it had progressed very slowly on the old system, but he, bringing to bear on it all his ability for organization and the discipline inculcated by military life, quickly revolutionized affairs. He first built four large boarding cars, two for sleeping in, one for eating in, and the fourth for cooking in. These he placed on the track and ran out to its extremity, enabling himself in this way to keep always on hand, close to their work, his force hands, numbering from two hundred to two hundred and fifty men. One of his brothers then undertook the supervision of the lading, on constructions, of the material brought upon boats from St. Joseph by Mr. Hoxie, Master of Transportation. In this lading of the construction trains, Gen. Casement's system was first made apparent. Each car was laden with a certain number of rails, all of the same length, and the exact number of chairs and spikes required to lay them. These were sent out to the work, and the boarding cars having pushed as far as possible to the end of the track, the materials were thrown off behind them, then the boarding cars shoved back and the small cars used in laying the rails could come up to the piles of new material. Horse power being used to draw the small cars to and fro, the mere length of the boarding train was no obstacle. A small car having been loaded in the same manner and with the same precision as the large ones had been, was run forward to the end of the track by horse power. A couple of feet from the rails already down, checks were placed under the wheels, stopping the car at once. Before it was well stopped a dozen men grasped a rail and ran it behind the car, laid it down in its chairs, gauged it, and ere its clang in falling had ceased to reverberate, the car was running over it and another pair of rails run out. The process was continuing as rapidly as a man could walk. Behind the car followed a man dropping spikes, another setting the ties well under the ends of the rails, and thirty or forty others driving in the spikes and stamping the earth under the ties. The moment that one car was emptied of its iron, a number of men seized it and threw it off the track and into the ditch and the second followed on with its load. The work was all done with excessive rapidity, simply because each man had but a certain thing to do, was accustomed to doing it, and had not to wait on the action of anyone else.

General Dodge, who evidently thought well of Casement Brothers, has this to say regarding their work:

> The entire track and a large part of the grading on the Union Pacific was done by Casement Brothers—General Casement and Dan Casement. General Casement had been a prominent brigade and division commander in the western army. Their force consisted of 100 teams and 1,000 men, living at the end of track in boarding cars and tents, and moved forward with it every few days. It was the best-

organized, best-equipped, and best-disciplined track force
I have ever seen. I think every chief of the different units
of the force had been an officer in the army, and entered on
this work the moment they were mustered out. They could
lay from one to three miles of track per day, as they had
material, and one laid 8½ miles. Their rapidity in track
laying, as far as I know, has never been excelled. I used it
several times as a fighting force, and it took no longer to
put it into fighting line than it did to form it for its daily
work. They not only had to lay and surface the track, but
had to bring forward to the front from base all the material
and supplies for the track and for all the workmen in advance of the track. Bases were organized for the delivery
of material generally from 100 to 200 miles apart, according to the facilities for operation. These bases were as follows: first, Fremont; second, Fort Kearney; third, North
Platte; fourth, Julesburg; fifth, Sidney; sixth, Cheyenne;
seventh, Laramie; eighth, Benton (the last crossing of the
North Platte); ninth, Green River; tenth, Evanston;
eleventh, Ogden; and finally, Promontory.

At these bases large towns were established, which moved
forward with the bases, and many miles of sidings were put
in for switching purposes, unloading tracks, etc. At these
prominent points I have seen as many as a thousand teams
waiting for their loads to haul forward to the front for the
railway force, the Government, and for the limited population then living in the country. I have seen these terminal
towns starting first with a few hundred people until at
Cheyenne, at the base of the mountains, where we wintered
in 1867-68, there were 10,000 people. From that point they
decreased until at Green River there were not over 1,000.
After we crossed the first range of mountains we moved our
bases so rapidly they could not afford to move with us.

The passing tracks, or sidings, ranged from 2,000 feet to
3,000 feet in length and in addition, spur tracks were built at
stations as circumstances required. On the first 710 miles of line
there were fifty-one stations, provided with station buildings
and water tanks, the latter operated by windmills in many cases.
The average distance between stations was fourteen miles. Coal

houses were built at points where fuel was taken by the locomotives. At North Platte, Cheyenne, Laramie, and Rawlins, hotels were erected by the company.

One of the obstacles to be overcome was the snowdrifts that accumulated in cuts in the mountain section of the line. The practice of building snow fences to intercept the drifting snow was adopted and has been continued up to the present time. Up to 1873 there were about twenty-five miles of snow fences on the line, in addition to four miles of snow sheds built of timber. Also, about forty miles of track had been raised from one to six feet in order to prevent snow blockades. The snow sheds at that time were regarded as temporary structures. General Dodge describes the experience of the winter of 1869-1870, when six trains were caught in a blizzard at Laramie that lasted several weeks. The trains were brought together by Hoxie, but "the blizzards were so many and so fierce that it was impossible for men to work out in the open, and even when they cleared the cuts ahead they would fill up before they could get the trains through them."

The later efforts to control the snow were eventually so successful that the government directors reported in 1875:

"The protection of the road now against obstruction by snow has been carried to such a degree of perfection that impediments to the operation of the line from that cause will be no greater in the future than may be expected on any of the lines between Chicago and New York. The problem of the practicability of the road for winter operation may be considered as solved."

The agreement with the government had provided that the railroad company should build a telegraph line along the road, a necessity for service during construction and for operation of the railroad later. The telegraph line was usually extended beyond the end of track, and was finished to Great Salt Lake early in 1869. It was a standard two-wire line on wooden poles. Maintenance of the telegraph line was often made difficult by

[283]

the vast herds of buffalo, which had a way of using the poles as scratching posts.

Some fences were built along the right of way in eastern Nebraska as a part of the original construction, but the major part of the line was not fenced, it then being unnecessary.

As in the case of many railroads before and since that time, the builders of the Union Pacfic had to contend with washouts and floods, unexpected because of lack of knowledge about the country through which the line was built. In the severe winter of 1866-1867 much damage was done to the railroad by a storm, Superintendent of Construction Samuel B. Reed describes the results in these terse paragraphs:

> March 25, 1867. Omaha. I arrived here as I expected, without delay. Only one train came in after. The day of my arrival a severe storm commenced at North Platte blockading the road as the storm progressed eastward. Twenty-four hours after its commencement at North Platte, the storm had traversed the entire length of our road and progressed eastward, blocking the C. & N. W. R. R. as far east as Marshalltown. The Missouri River is still fast frozen. I have six locomotives on the east side of the river and would not hesitate to cross them on the ice if we needed their services on this side immediately.
>
> April 18, 1867. I have just returned from the west where I have been trying to put our road in order. Fifty-thousand dollars will not repair the damage done by the flood. The ice broke first at Loup Fork. The bridge sustained the immense pressure and caused the ice to flow out on both sides cutting away the embankment about one mile on each side and depositing the ice in immense quantities along the line of the road for four miles.
>
> At North Platte our bridge stands well, but little damage done. Between North Platte and Kearney the water flowed from the Platte in a stream about half a mile wide, cutting the road its entire width and sweeping with irresistible fury over the country for twenty miles, then recrossing the track near Lone Tree, taking off iron, ties, and embankment. At Prairie Creek the bridge was carried down stream. East of

Shell Creek there are from four to six miles with nothing but ties and iron left. At Elkhorn River, about half a mile of track is gone. The above enumerates all the more serious breaks in the road. It will be ten or twelve days before I can get a train over the road.

Hereafter I shall have no faith in the saying of the oldest inhabitant. The water has risen in all streams emptying into the Platte beyond precedent.

The description of that storm damage will have a familiar sound to many a railroad man who has had to contend with similar difficulties. In the report of General Dodge of January 1, 1868, he states that:

"The track has been raised, new bridges constructed, larger waterways built, and the old structures enlarged, as shown by the floods of April, the highest and most extensive ever known in the country, and it can now be safely said that a repetition of these floods will not materially injure the road or delay the running of trains."

A railroad has more to it than the track upon which the trains run, or the trains themselves. There must be full equipment of repair and manufacturing shops erected at proper intervals, roundhouses, station buildings, provision for water supply, and similar facilities. As it was required by the government, the Union Pacific was provided with such construction by its builders.

Owing to the location of the Union Pacific, it was necessary that shops be built first at Omaha. By the time the line was completed, there were two machine shops at Omaha, as well as a boiler shop, blacksmith shop, tin shop, stationary engine room, storehouse, oil house, sand house, fire engine house, foundry, roundhouse with twenty stalls, and a storehouse for waste. With the exception of the foundry, all of these buildings were made of brick on masonry foundations, with roofs covered with tin. Similar equipment for repairs and for roundhouses was built at Grand Island, North Platte, Sidney, Cheyenne, Sherman, Laramie, Medicine Bow, Rawlins, Bitter Creek, Green

River, Evanston, and Ogden. Seventy-five water stations had to be built about thirteen and one half miles apart. Seven were supplied by artesian wells, seven by gravity sources, twenty-eight by windmills, thirty-eight used steam pumps, while one was worked by hand.

Equally important with other elements that make up a complete railroad is the rolling stock. Beginning with a small number of locomotives and cars, the Union Pacific steadily added to its rolling stock until the road was completed. On July 20, 1865, Springer Harbaugh, government commissioner, reported that there was one locomotive at Omaha that was received July 8, 1865. There was another at St. Joseph awaiting transportation up the river and three more were in use on railroads, moving cars and material belonging to the Union Pacific. There were fifty platform cars at various locations transporting iron for the road. Some twenty cars had been purchased and were on their way west in sections, to be assembled later at Omaha. Two days after that one lone locomotive arrived at Omaha, track laying commenced.

When the road was completed to its connection with the Central Pacific, it had on hand 147 locomotives, 25 first-class coaches, 26 second-class coaches, 9 mail cars, 12 baggage cars, 9 express cars, 2 pay cars, 2 officers' cars, 1 private car named the Lincoln, 1,150 box cars, 1,500 flat cars, 48 dump cars, 50 hand cars, and 3 wrecking cars. There was also under construction at the Omaha shops a number of freight cars. The value of all this equipment was over $3,600,000. The locomotives ranged in weight from twenty-five to thirty-five tons, a standard size for the time.

While the wrought-iron rail used on the road was of standard size, the traffic during construction, especially on the eastern section, was so heavy that rail wear became one of the problems that definitely required solution. In the case of the Union Pacific, rerolling of worn rails was a costly process, owing to large freight bills for the long haul to eastern mills. A rerolling mill was therefore established at Laramie, where it functioned for a time. The introduction of steel rail soon after the road was completed of course made the mill unnecessary.

### THE OMAHA BRIDGE

The bridge across the Missouri River at Council Bluffs was the most difficult engineering problem that the builders of the Union Pacific had to solve. The river at that point is one of the widest in the country, and up to the time that the Omaha Bridge was completed the Missouri had been crossed by but two other bridges—the railroad and highway bridge at Kansas City and the highway bridge at Fort Leavenworth.

The original Omaha Bridge and its two successors have been located 634 miles above the point where the great Missouri joins the Mississippi River near St. Louis. The drainage area above the bridge is 323,000 square miles. The two following paragraphs quote the Corps of Engineers, Omaha District of the United States:

"Measurements of discharge at Omaha, Nebraska, were initiated in September, 1928, and have continued to date. During this period the average discharge has been 25,900 cubic feet per second and the peak discharge was 200,000 cubic feet per second and occurred during the 1943 flood.

"Stage records without benefit of actual discharge measurements are available for Omaha from 1872 to date. These records and also stage records at other points on the Missouri River have served as a basis for estimating discharges by this office of the major floods occurring during that period. We estimate the maximum peak discharge during that period to be 370,000 cubic feet per second occurring during the flood of 1881. We also estimate that the average flow for the past 50 years to be approximately 35,500 cubic feet per second."

The river meanders in a flood plain, being between Omaha and Council Bluffs, four miles wide. While the channel is well defined at low stages of the river, the adjacent flood plain is sometimes covered with water, which rises about ten feet when

[287]

in flood. The bed of the Missouri is the usual alluvial soil brought down from distant mountains, and at Omaha bed rock is found from seventy-five to eighty feet below the low water level of the river. The rock is overlaid by the sand, gravel, and silt of the river deposit. At the location opposite Omaha where the bridge was built, the river was about 750 feet in width at low water, but this width varied from time to time. The depth of the water reached as much as twenty-five feet.

As early as the latter half of 1866, investigations had been made with the object of locating a bridge. The surveys and tests were summarized by General Dodge in a report to President Ames dated December 3, 1866, and in a supplemental report of January 15, 1867. Using the data furnished by Dodge, Seymour also filed a report with President Ames, giving his discursive opinion on the subject and leaving the matter to be decided by the directors. J. L. Williams, government director, also made a report to President Ames near the end of 1867, in which he summarized the investigations to date.

The problem of where to build the bridge was complicated by the fact that the railroad had already been located and partially built out of Omaha and also by the question whether it should be a low-level bridge with a draw span or a high-level bridge under which steamboats could pass without being delayed. As a result of the investigations three main locations were considered. The first, the one most favored by Dodge on account of costs and physical considerations, was at Child's Mill, five miles downstream from the present bridge and eight miles from the railroad shops and depot at Omaha. The second spot, where Dodge had actually located a bridge in the earlier surveys that had been made for the Mississippi and Missouri Railroad years before, was referred to as the South Omaha location. The third was upstream about two miles at a point known as Telegraph Pole Crossing, where bed rock was exposed on the west side of the river.

The Child's Mill location was rejected, because, although it would cost less than the others, it would have left Omaha on a stub track eight miles long and would have made Council Bluffs the main terminus, which was just what the company did not want to happen. The Telegraph Pole location had a number of objectionable features for a high bridge, and a low bridge with a draw span required protection in order to keep the shifting river channel running under the draw span. The bluffs on the Omaha side of the South Omaha site were favorable for erecting a high bridge, with the added advantage that the site could also be reached by a track from the line already built. The final decision therefore was made for a high bridge at the South Omaha, or M. and M. crossing, as Dodge called it, and it was there that the bridge was built. That, in fact, is the location of the present bridge, the third to occupy the site.

The controversy that arose regarding the building of the bridge was concerned basically with the question of which railroad or railroads should stand the cost of the structure. As a number of rail lines were being projected westward across Iowa, it was natural that these roads should desire to connect with the Union Pacific as a source of traffic. The Union Pacific, in its turn, was actuated by the same motive. While the Union Pacific was under construction, the energies of the builders were concentrated on their great problem of building the railroad to the West, one major element of which was finances. For this reason the expensive building of a bridge was deferred and a ferry was used to cross the river. The North Western Railroad was the first to reach Council Bluffs, and others entered the town shortly afterward.

The Union Pacific directors, led by Durant, always maintained that the original order of President Lincoln, which had been lost, provided in fact that the road should start from Omaha. However, his second order clearly stated that the starting point of the road should be on "the western border of Iowa." There was much controversy over the subject, which was settled only after a bitterly contested lawsuit reached the

[289]

Supreme Court. There it was decided that the Union Pacific should extend into Iowa. The decision was handed down after the bridge was built and after the railroad company had been charging tolls on passengers and freight. Thereafter the bridge was an integral part of the Union Pacific Railroad, which established a union depot at Council Bluffs, where the other roads came in from the East.

Work was commenced on the bridge in the spring of 1868, when a contract for $1,089,500 was awarded to the Boomer Bridge Company of Chicago. However, lack of funds prevented any material progress, and on July 26, 1869, the work was suspended. The project lay idle until April 10, 1870, when a new contract was let to the American Bridge Company of Chicago, which completed the job on March 14, 1872. The direct cost was $1,750,000.

The bridge was built with a clearance of sixty feet above medium low water, so that all boats navigating the river could pass under it. As originally constructed, the bridge began at the line of bluffs on the Omaha side with a pile trestle 729 feet long, followed by eleven spans of 250 feet each, center to center of piers, or a total length of 2,750 feet. A two-mile trestle on the eastern end led down a descending grade to the flat lands of Council Bluffs. At a later date, this trestle was filled with earth to make a permanent embankment. The bridge carried a single track and the roadway was not floored so as to accommodate wagon traffic, although this was contemplated in the charter. The spans were constructed of iron in a design known as the Post system, Post being the originator of the construction method. It was a triple intersection truss, in which the posts, inclined from the vertical, were in compression and the diagonals were in tension. What will seem odd to a modern engineer is that there was no intermediate sway bracing between the vertical posts throughout the spans and practically no bracing at the portals. The two trusses forming one span were almost independent of each other.

[290]

The piers of the bridge were made by sinking iron cylinders down to bedrock, which was anywhere from seventy-five to eighty feet below low water, and filling them with concrete. The details of the sub pier are to some extent uncertain. On top of the sub pier, iron cylinders were erected in pairs, braced between to form a pier upon which the spans rested. Considering the time at which the bridge was built, the use of an all-iron structure on a deep-water foundation was a remarkable achievement. It was opened for traffic March 22, 1872.

In common with most railroad bridges of that day, the Omaha Bridge became obsolete within a few years after its completion, owing to the great increase in train and engine loads made possible by the introduction of steel rail. The removal of the Omaha Bridge was primarily due to that cause, but it was also hurried to destruction by a tornado that tore two of the bridge spans from their piers on August 4, 1877. It might be inferred that the failure was due to the lack of proper wind bracing in the trusses. Repairs were made and traffic resumed on September 18, 1877. A large amount of bank revetment was also added to protect the fill at the eastern end of the crossing. In 1886 the original bridge, with the two repaired eastern spans, was removed and a new double-track steel bridge was erected on new masonry piers. The new bridge was shorter than the first one, having four channel spans of 250 feet each, with three approach spans at each end, making a total length of 1,750 feet, the fill on the eastern end having been extended.

The original bridge had served for nearly fifteen years. The second bridge, in its turn, became too light for the increased loads of the trains and was replaced by a still heavier bridge in 1916. The second bridge had a weight of 1,950 tons on the four channel spans. The third bridge had a weight of 3,580 tons, which indicates the increase in strength made necessary by rolling-stock changes over a period of thirty years. Although built after the railroad met the Central Pacific at Promontory, the bridge was, in every respect, a part of the original railroad across the continent and should be dealt with as such.

## INDIAN DIFFICULTIES

When the construction of the Union Pacific was well under way during the latter part of the sixties, Indian trouble on the plains and in the Rocky Mountains was not uncommon. The day of the fur trader had long since passed, and pioneer emigration to the West—to Oregon, the Salt Lake region and California—had reached and passed its zenith. The overland stage route had been in existence for over a decade, and the constant stream of wagons, travelers, and express riders, together with the telegraph line, made clear to the Indians that their land was to be taken from them. Their resistance, at first spasmodic, had in the later days become more systematic.

As a result of hostile Indian activity in the West, the national government was called upon to protect both lines of travel and settlements, and a variable policy of dealing with the Indians was followed. It was necessary to set up army posts and forts along the central route. Fort Leavenworth was established in 1827, Fort Kearney on the Platte River in 1848, Fort Laramie at the junction of the North Platte and Laramie rivers in 1849, Fort Russell at Cheyenne in 1867, Fort Sanders near Laramie in 1868, Cantonment Loring near Fort Hall on the Snake River in 1849, and Fort or Camp Douglas near Salt Lake City in 1858. Farther along the line, in Nevada, Camp Halleck on the Humboldt River and Fort Churchill on the Carson River were military posts where garrisons were kept. During the many Indian campaigns expeditions went forth from these posts, as well as from others of a more temporary nature.

The stories of western travels abound with accounts of depradations by Indians. In 1864, along the Big Sandy valley for three hundred miles west every house and barn was burned, eighty settlers were murdered, and all the stock was stolen. This statement is taken from *Beyond the Mississippi*, by Albert D. Richardson, who, in his description of his western travels says:

"A hundred miles beyond [Virginia Dale Station], the savages

[292]

had driven off the horses and mules from three stations. Two emigrants were found dead upon the road—one scalped, the other with throat cut from ear to ear, and thirteen arrows in his body."

On another page he states:

"While our mules were changed that evening, at a station fifteen miles beyond, we chatted ten minutes with guards and hostlers. Twelve hours afterward the Indians swept down, killing every occupant except two soldiers, who, wounded, made their escape."

Another description reads:

"The most serious of their outrages was the capture of an emigrant train, about thirty miles from Fort Kearney, on Plum Creek, killing and scalping eleven men, taking captive two women and burning the wagons. They burned a large number of cabins, stole the cattle and the settlers fled to Columbus in terror. They made a raid on Julesburg and, the garrison fleeing, one man was killed, and the station burned, and all the stock driven off. The loss fell heavily on Ben Holliday, and the Western Union Telegraph Company, whose line was destroyed, and kept down for several months."

Engineer S. B. Reed, writing from Denver in 1865, said:

"We arrived here this morning after a long tedious ride of seven days from Omaha, escorted nearly all the distance from Fort Kearney. With few exceptions, all the buildings along the road have been burned by the Indians and the whole country looks desolate and deserted. There is quite a large military force at various points along the line."

It is unnecessary to enter into the campaigns of the army against the Indians, except to mention the part played by General Dodge's force and its bearing upon the work of the railroad. In 1865, near the close of the Civil War, when Dodge was placed in command of the Department of the Missouri with headquarters at Fort Leavenworth, the Indians were on the warpath, possibly because of the action of the army against tribes in Colorado, Indians who were supposed to be friendly to the whites. In the winter of 1864-1865 Dodge led a campaign against the savages in which he was assisted by friendly Pawnees. In the summer of 1865, while Dodge was about to carry out a final movement against Indians in the Powder River country north of the Platte, who were attempting to destroy all telegraph stations along the Platte, the government at Washington stopped active operations.

The event that stirred the country to the seriousness of the situation as much as anything could was the slaughter of General Custer and all of his command, over 200 men, on the Little Big Horn in Montana, June 25, 1876. However, the wars in the Northwest were not concluded until the great chief, Sitting Bull, was killed in 1890 and the Indians massacred at the battle of Wounded Knee shortly afterward.

Such were conditions when the railroad was built. Constant appeals were made by the Union Pacific for troops to protect the men on the road. Far in advance of the construction forces, possibly 500 miles ahead, the surveying crews were examining the country and it was obvious that they needed that protection badly. The murder by Indians of L. L. Hills, chief of party, in 1867, at a point some six miles east of the site of Cheyenne, and of Percy T. Brown, another chief of party, in July of the same year when surveying on Rock Creek west of Laramie, was related in the chapter dealing with the location of the road. Dodge thereupon called on General Sherman to provide at least 5,000 troops to cover the railroad forces, with the result that such help as Sherman could give, was furnished.

General Dodge, writing of the troubles with the Indians directly on the road, said:

> When operating in a hostile Indian country they [the field parties] were regularly drilled, though after the Civil War this was unnecessary, as most of them had been in the army. Each party entering a country occupied by hostile Indians was generally furnished with a military escort of

from ten men to a company under a competent officer. The duty of this escort was to protect the party when in camp. In the field the escort usually occupied prominent hills commanding the territory in which the work was to be done, so as to head off sudden attacks by the Indians. Notwithstanding this protection, the parties were often attacked, their chief or some of their men killed or wounded, and their stock run off.

Our Indian troubles commenced in 1864 and lasted until the tracks joined at Promontory. We lost most of our men and stock while building from Fort Kearney to Bitter Creek. At that time every mile of road had to be surveyed, graded, tied, and bridged under military protection. The order to every surveying corps, grading, bridging, and tie outfit was never to run when attacked. All were required to be armed, and I do not know that the order was disobeyed in a single instance, nor did I ever hear that the Indians had driven a party permanently from its work. I remember one occasion when they swooped down on a grading outfit in sight of the temporary fort of the military, some five miles away, and right in sight of the end of track. The government commission to examine that section of the completed road had just arrived, and the commissioners witnessed the fight. The graders had their arms stacked on the cut. The Indians leaped from the ravines, and springing on the workmen before they could reach their arms, cut loose the stock and caused a panic. General Frank P. Blair, General Simpson, and Doctor White were the commissioners, and they showed their grit by running to my car for arms to aid in the fight. They did not fail to benefit from this experience for, on returning to the East, the commission dwelt earnestly on the necessity of our being protected.

From the beginning to the completion of the road our success depended in a great measure on the cordial and active support of the army, especially its commander in chief, General Grant, and the commander of the Military Division of the West, General Sherman. ... We also had the cordial support of the district commanders of the country through which we operated—General Augur, General Cook, General Gibbon, and General Stevenson, and their subordinates. General Grant had given full and positive instructions that every support should be given to me, and General Sherman, in the detailed instructions, practically left it to my own judgment as to what support should be given by the troops on the plains. They were also instructed to furnish my surveying parties with provisions from the posts whenever our provisions should give out, and the subordinate officers, following the example of their chiefs, responded to every demand made, no matter at what time of day or night, what time of year or in what weather, and took as much interest in the matter as we did. . . .

The operating department also had the Indians to contend with. An illustration of this came to me after our track had passed Plum Creek, 200 miles west of the Missouri River. The Indians had captured a freight train and were in possession of it and its crews. It so happened that I was coming from the front in my car, which was a traveling arsenal. At Plum Creek station word came of this capture and stopped us. On my train were perhaps 20 men, some a portion of the crew, some who had been discharged and sought passage to the rear. Nearly all were strangers to me. The excitement of the capture and the reports coming by telegraph of the burning of the train brought all men to the platform, and when I called on them to fall in, to go forward and to retake the train, every man on the train went into line, and by his position, showed that he was a soldier. We ran down slowly until we came in sight of the train. I gave the order to deploy as skirmishers, and at the command they went forward as steadily and in as good order as we had seen the old soldiers climb the face of Kenesaw under fire.

The Indians also learned to wreck trains, and there were a number of instances when the train crew was either killed in the wreck or butchered afterward by the Indians.

Some appreciation of the magnitude of the Indian problem during the period up to 1869 may be found in the speech of Senator W. M. Stewart in the debate on a bill to aid the Northern Pacific and other railroads, February 19, 1869:

"And what is the cost of our Indian wars as compared with the cost of the Pacific railways, which will speedily end the

Indian wars? A compilation from the official records of the government shows that these wars for the last thirty-seven years have cost the nation 20,000 lives and more than $750,000,000. In the years of the quartermaster's department there has been spent $28,374,228 for military service against the Indians infesting the country upon the proposed northern and southern roads to the Pacific, money spent in handling and hauling supplies. The Chairman of the House Committee on Indian Affairs estimated recently that the present current expenses of our warfare with the Indians have been $1,000,000 a week—$144,000 a day."

### RAILROAD BASE TOWNS

The names of the base towns have been given in preceding pages. A number of these places became important cities after the road was completed; others disappeared when their purpose had been served. They marked the points where end of track was established for a short period, where supplies were accumulated before winter, preparatory to an advance in the coming spring, and points where the railroad was turned over to the operating department. Wherever a large number of men are employed in work of this kind, a swarm of men and women will be found who serve the needs of the men doing the hard work. Many of these persons perform a legitimate service in providing the men with clothing and other supplies that are needed. A majority, however, are parasites, such as saloonkeepers, gamblers, and prostitutes, who prey upon the men in various ways and generally succeed in taking most if not all of their money away from them.

The Union Pacific Company, or one of its auxiliary organizations owning the land, laid it off in town lots and streets, and sold the lots. It was a highly profitable procedure. However, in the rugged country of the West there was little stable government, either state or territorial, with the result that where there was an organized town government it was often in the hands of the disorderly element.

[297]

The desperadoes, along with the traders, engaged in cattle rustling, stage robbing, trading with and supplying liquor to the Indians, and creating trouble generally. The upshot was that vigilance committees, made up of respectable citizens, were formed to eliminate the obnoxious characters either by hanging them or by driving them out of town. San Francisco had two such committees, as did Virginia City in Nevada. At Virginia City, Montana, the committee at one time hung twenty-four leading desperadoes and banished many others. General Dodge states that he once received word that a crowd of gamblers had taken possession of Julesburg, and so he wired General Casement to clean up the place. When Dodge arrived at Julesburg, Casement showed him a small graveyard and remarked, "They all died in their boots, but brought peace."

A summary of the conditions that existed in the towns was once given by Superintendent of Construction Reed. Writing from Julesburg, he primly described a trip that he had made through the town. It is easy to see that Reed was impressed.

General Augur and staff returned here last Friday evening and nothing would do but they must see the town by the gas light. I sent for Dan Casement to pilot us. The first place we visited was a dance house, where a fresh importation of strumpets had been received. The hall was crowded with bad men and lewd women. Such profanity, vulgarity and indecency as was heard and seen there would disgust a more hardened person than I. The next place visited was a gambling hell where all games of chance were being played. Men excited with drink and play were recklessly staking their last dollar on the turn of a card or the throw of a dice. Women were cajoling and coaxing the tipsy men to stake their money on various games; the pockets were shrewdly picked by the fallen women of the more sober of the crowd. We soon tired of this place and started forth for new dens of vice and crime and visited several similar to those already described. At last, about 10 P.M. we visited the theatre and were asked behind the curtain to see the girls. From here I left the party and retired to my tent fully satisfied with my first visit to such places.

Still, it must be conceded that the gambling houses and saloons perhaps served a kind of useful purpose, notwithstanding the trouble that they caused. The work of the railroad was done by young, vigorous men who were not content to labor for months in primitive surroundings without some sort of excitement. The big tents with their bars and gambling tables, where there was music and girls with whom the men could consort, were places where the construction worker could blow off steam after long hours of work in winter storms or under summer heat. The kind of men who did the work on the Union Pacific rarely were able to hold onto much money after months of hard toil. They usually spent their pay fast and then wandered off to some other job.

### CONSTRUCTION FORCES

Although the Union Pacific ground had been broken at Omaha on December 2, 1863, only eleven miles of grading were completed by the end of September, 1865, owing to the controversy over the route. By the end of 1865, forty miles had been graded, and track laying had begun on July 10 of that year. It was not until 1866, however, that real construction started. The Civil War had ended, the Hoxie contract had been signed, and finances generally were in better shape. What was of equal importance, Dodge had been made chief engineer and had taken charge of the location work with characteristic energy. By the end of 1866, 305 miles of line had received the track and had been placed in operation, with grading in progress beyond. In 1867, 235 more miles of road were completed, which brought the end of track close to the top of the Black Hills at Sherman Summit. Work was then closed down for the winter and supplies were accumulated at Cheyenne.

In 1868, as soon as the weather would permit, construction was started again and the race with the Central Pacific was on.

About 400 miles were completed that year, with construction being continued on through the winter so far as the builders were able. The remaining 146 miles to Promontory were completed in the first four months and ten days of 1869. Records as to the actual amount of road completed each year are somewhat indefinite because the grading was always far in advance of the track, which was usually considered the point of completion.

In the year 1868 and in four months of 1869, the grading of the line west of Promontory was practically completed as far as Monument Point and a small amount of work was actually done at Humboldt Wells, 220 miles beyond. A total of 600 miles of grading was thus accomplished in about thirteen months. In fact, construction was so rapid that the engineers in charge of surveys had difficulty in keeping ahead of the grading and bridge-building crews.

One of the objectives of the builders of both the Union Pacific and Central Pacific was to complete the road as soon as possible in order to obtain the approval of the government commissioners and thereby secure acceptance by the President, together with the resulting subsidy bonds. This acceptance did not seem difficult to obtain, as the road was well built from the start. The first 40 miles was accepted January 24, 1866; and three and a half years later the final acceptance of 86 miles was made on July 15, 1869. The length of line accepted in 1866 was 105 miles; in 1867, 240 miles; in 1868, 275 miles; in 1869, 380 miles; and in the fiscal years 1869-1870, 86 miles.

One source of controversy was the fixing of a point to mark the eastern base of the Rocky Mountains, where the subsidy rate per mile changed from $16,000 to $48,000 per mile. The point was finally set at 525.78 miles from Omaha, or a short distance west of Cheyenne.

Operation of the Union Pacific was extended in 1867, first to North Platte in April; to Julesburg, 377 miles from Omaha, in June; to Hillsdale, 495 miles from Omaha, by November; and in the same month to Cheyenne, 516 miles from Omaha. In the next year the operating forces took charge as rapidly as the line was completed. It was the function of the operating department to forward supplies from Omaha to the end of the track, the job being in charge of Webster Snyder, with Hoxie as assistant. It was they who fought the Indians along the line and met such other difficulties as washouts and failure to receive supplies from the East at Omaha. Forwarding supplies was one of the most important functions of the railroad organization and much credit is due that part of the company for the work it performed.

Since the actual building of the Union Pacific was under the direction of Samuel B. Reed and James A. Evans, they had charge of awarding work to various subcontractors as well as supervising grading, bridge building, driving of tunnels, forwarding of supplies, cutting and delivering of ties—in fact, everything that pertained to the work. Both men had been on the surveys for the road and had joined the construction department when active work began.

While the building of the Union Pacific was nominally handled by several different organizations, as has been said they were all a part of the Credit Mobilier. There apparently was no clear dividing line between contractors and the railroad company itself. Much work, however, was done by subcontractors. The man in charge of everything was, of course, Dr. Durant, who in his dual capacity of vice president and general manager of the railroad company and as one of the trustees who administered the Ames and Davis contracts, had supreme control. On the other hand, Chief Engineer Dodge, who was employed by the railroad company, also had a large amount of control and assumed more whenever it was necessary. It was clearly a case of wherever McGregor sits is the head of the table. Dodge was a man of such strong personality that he readily accepted responsibility for much of the road's progress. Clashes in authority took place between Durant and Dodge, and it is difficult to determine today just who was the force that drove the construction along. It is obvious that the controlling group was not harmonious, but at the same time there is no gainsaying the fact that they built the railroad.

A great deal of temporary construction was installed on the Union Pacific, notably in bridges and culverts. Poor ties were used in some cases and banks were not always up to standard. After an examination of the road, a special commission of the government rendered a favorable report on the railroad on October 30, 1869, but stated that deficiencies of various kinds between Omaha and Ogden remained to be corrected, the cost of which was estimated to be $1,586,100. The commission also reported that there was a surplus of rolling stock used in construction over that required for operation, amounting in value to $1,800,000. They said the line was "fully prepared to carry passengers and freight with safety and dispatch, comparing in this respect favorably with a majority of the first-class roads in the United States."

At the time of maximum effort, some 12,000 men were directly employed on the Union Pacific. Many more were employed in the iron mines as well as in the mills where track material was manufactured. Engine and car shops were building the rolling stock and, as we know, eastern railroads were transporting material and supplies by several routes toward Omaha. Steamboats were navigating the difficult Missouri River, also bringing supplies to the same point. Farms east of the Missouri and in the Platte Valley were raising food and forage for thousands of men and animals out on the prairies, mountains, and deserts along the line. Sawmills were busy cutting timbers that were to be framed in the East and shipped to the work. In camps throughout the country lumbermen were getting out ties and rafting them down the rivers or hauling them by team to rail and river shipping points. The operating department was managing the ferries at Omaha and moving trains to the front with all kinds of track and bridge supplies.

Far out in advance of everyone, the surveyors were hard at work locating the line and keeping ahead of the construction forces that were moving up at top speed. The grading forces were strung out over the line, in some cases as much as 300 miles ahead of the tracks, while stone masons built culverts, piers, and abutments of bridges to receive the framed timbers from the East. Following close came the track-laying trains of General Casement, always driving ahead to put down the main track and the sidings. At intervals, men erected masonry and brick buildings for shops, water supply, and stations. In the eastern states, the promoters were doing their best to find the money for the work, while in Washington other officers of the company were investigating and allotting the subsidy allowed by law. So for three and a half years this teeming activity was held at maximum effort by those in charge: the Ames brothers and their associates in the East; Durant, Dodge, Reed, Evans, and Casement, in the West. Their work came to an end when the Union Pacific and Central Pacific were joined at Promontory on that historic day of May 10, 1869. After more than a decade of heartbreaking effort, the Pacific Railroad had been built.

# BIBLIOGRAPHY

BOOKS

ACWORTH, W. M., *The Railways of England*. John Murray, London, 1889.

BANCROFT, HUBERT HOWE, *Chronicles of the Builders of the Commonwealth, History of California*. The History Company, San Francisco, 1888.

BEEBE, LUCIUS M., *High Iron*. D. Appleton-Century Company, New York, 1940.

BRADLEY, GLENN D., *The Story of the Santa Fe*. The Gorham Press, Boston, 1920.

BROOKS, NOAH, *First across the Continent*. Chas. Scribner's Sons, New York, 1901.

CARR, SARAH PRATT, *The Iron Way*. Chicago, 1907.

CARTER, CHAS. F., *When Railroads Were New*. Henry Holt & Co., New York, 1908.

CHITTENDEN, GEN. HIRAM MARTIN, *The American Fur Trade of the Far West*. Rufus Rockwell Wilson, Inc., 1936.

CLARK, DAN ELBERT, *The West in American History*. Thomas Y. Crowell Company, New York, 1937.

CLARK, GEORGE T., *Leland Stanford*. Stanford University Press, 1931.

CLARK, THOMAS C., *The American Railway—Its Construction, Development, Management and Appliances*, by Thomas C. Clark, John Bogart, M. N. Forney, E. P. Alexander, H. G. Prout, Horace Porter, Theodore Voorhees, Benjamin Norton, Arthur T. Hadley, Thomas L. James, Charles Francis Adams, B. B. Adams, Jr. Charles Scribner's Sons, New York, 1893.

COPLEY, JOSIAH, *Kansas and the Country Beyond on the Line of the Union Pacific Railway, Eastern Division*. J. B. Lippincott & Co., 1867.

CRAWFORD, J. B., *The Credit Mobilier of America*. C. W. Calkins & Co., 1880.

DAGGETT, STUART, *Chapters on the History of the Southern Pacific*. Ronald Press Company, New York, 1922.

DALE, HARRISON C., *The Ashley-Smith Explorations and the Discovery of a Central Route to the Pacific, 1822-1829*. Arthur H. Clark Company, Cleveland, 1918.

[305]

# BIBLIOGRAPHY

DAVIS, JOHN P., *The Union Pacific Railway*. S. C. Griggs & Company, Chicago, 1894.

DODGE, MAJOR GENERAL GRENVILLE M., *How We Built the Union Pacific Railway*. Senate Document No. 447. Washington, 1910.

ELLIOTT, T. C., *Peter Skene Ogden—Fur Trader*. Oregon Historical Society Vol. IV, No. 3. Sept., 1925.

FREMONT, JOHN C., *Memoirs of My Life*. Belford, Clarke & Company, Chicago & New York, 1887.

FULTON, ROBERT L., *Epic of the Overland*. A. M. Robertson, Publisher, San Francisco, 1924.

GHENT, W. J., *The Early Far West*. Tudor Publishing Company, New York, 1936.

HAFEN, LEROY R., *The Overland Mail*, 1849-1869. Arthur H. Clark Company, Cleveland, 1926.

HAFEN, LEROY R. AND RISTER, CARL COKE, *Western America*. Prentice-Hall, Inc., New York, 1941.

HAYMOND, CREED, *The Central Pacific Railroad Company—Its Relations to the Government*. H. S. Crocker Press, San Francisco.

HENRY, ROBERT SELPH, *Trains*. Bobbs-Merrill Company, Indianapolis, 1934.

HUNGERFORD, EDWARD, *The Story of the Baltimore & Ohio Railroad, 1827-1927*. G. P. Putnam's Sons, New York, 1928.

JOHNSON, JACK T., *Peter Anthony Dey*. State Historical Society of Iowa, 1939.

JOHNSON, JACK T. AND LEONARD, LEVI O., *A Railroad to the Sea*. Midland House, Publishers, Iowa City, Iowa, 1939.

KNEISS, GILBERT H., *Bonanza Railroads*. Stanford University Press, 1941.

LANE, WHEATON J., *From Indian Trail to Iron Horse*. Princeton University Press, 1939.

LEWIS, OSCAR, *The Big Four*. Alfred A. Knopf, New York, 1938.

MACK, EFFIE MONA, *Nevada*. Arthur H. Clark Company, Cleveland, 1939.

MACKAY, DOUGLASS, *The Honorable Company: A History of the Hudson's Bay Co*. Bobbs-Merrill Company, Indianapolis.

MOODY, JOHN, *The Railroad Builders: A Chronicle of the Welding of the States*. Yale University Press, 1919.

PERKINS, JACOB R., *Trails, Rails and War—The Life of General Dodge*. Bobbs-Merrill Company, Indianapolis, 1929.

POOR, HENRY V., *Manual of Railroads in the United States*. H. V. & H. W. Poor Company, New York.

[306]

# BIBLIOGRAPHY

RAE, W. F., *Westward by Rail*. D. Appleton & Company, New York.

RIPLEY, W. Z., *Railroads—Rates & Regulations*. Longmans, Green & Company, New York, 1913.

ROGERS, MAJOR FRED B., *Soldiers of the Overland*. Grabhorn Press, San Francisco, 1938.

RICHARDSON, ALBERT D., *Beyond the Mississippi*. American Publishing Company.

ROOT, FRANK A. AND CONNELLY, WM. E., *The Overland Stage to California*. Crane & Company, Topeka, Kansas, 1901.

RUSSELL, CHAS. E., *Stories of the Great Railroads*. Chas. H. Kerr & Company, Chicago, 1912.

SABIN, EDWIN L., *Kit Carson Days*. The Press of the Pioneers, Inc., New York, 1935.

SABIN, EDWIN L., *Building the Pacific Railway*. J. B. Lippincott Co., Philadelphia & London, 1919.

SMALLEY, EUGENE V., *History of the Northern Pacific Railway*. G. P. Putnam's Sons, New York, 1883.

SPEARMAN, FRANK H., *The Strategy of the Great Railroads*. Chas. Scribner's Sons, New York, 1904.

STANSBURY, CAPT. HOWARD, *An Expedition to the Valley of the Great Salt Lake of Utah*. Sampson Low, Son & Co., London, 1852.

STROBRIDGE, J. H., *An Account of the Central Pacific Railroad*. Pony Express Courier, Placerville, Calif., 1938.

SULLIVAN, MAURICE S., *The Travels of Jedediah Smith*. Fine Arts Press, Santa Ana, Calif., 1934.

TALLOCK, WM., *The California Overland Express*. Introduction by Carl I. Wheat. Historical Society of Southern California, 1935.

THOMPSON, SLASON, *A Short History of American Railways*. Bureau of Railway News & Statistics, Chicago, 1925.

TROTTMAN, NELSON, *History of the Union Pacific*. Ronald Press Company, New York, 1923.

VAN METRE, T. W., *Trains, Tracks and Travel*. Simmons-Boardman Publishing Corp., New York, 1939.

WHITE, HENRY KIRKE, *History of the Union Pacific Railway*. University of Chicago Press, 1895.

## RAILROAD REPORTS

American Railway Engineering Association—Construction of the Pacific Railroad. Vol. 23, No. 237. July, 1921.

# BIBLIOGRAPHY

List of Bridges over the Navigable Waters of the United States—Compiled in the Office of the Chief of Engineers, United States Army and Revised to January 1, 1935. U. S. Printing Office, Washington, 1936.

"The Great Union Pacific Railroad Excursion to the 100th Meridian". The Republican Company, Chicago, 1867.

History of the Union Pacific Railroad—Issued by the U.P.R.R. on the Occasion of the Celebration at Ogden, Utah, May 10, 1919, in Commemoration of the Fiftieth Anniversary of the Driving of the Golden Spike.

Pioneers of Western Progress—Southern Pacific Company. Published by Strassburger & Co., San Francisco, 1929.

Central Pacific Railroad Company—Report of the Chief Engineer (Judah), 1862.

Central Pacific Railroad Company—Report of the President (Stanford), 1863.

Central Pacific Railroad Company—Report of the Chief Engineer (Montague), 1864.

Central Pacific Railroad Company—Report of the Chief Engineer (Montague), 1867.

Union Pacific Railroad Company—Report of Government Directors, 1865-1885.

Union Pacific Railroad Company—Reports of the Director, 1864-1886.

Articles of Union and Consolidation of the Union Pacific Railroad Company, the Kansas Pacific Railway Company, and Denver Pacific Railway and Telegraph Company into the Union Pacific Railway Company. Dated January 24, 1880, and the By-Laws of the Union Pacific Railway Company. Printed for the Company, Boston.

Union Pacific Railroad Reports—Report of the Secretary of the Interior, 1867, 1868.

Union Pacific Railroad Reports—Report of Thomas C. Durant, Vice-President and General Manager to the Board of Directors, in Relation to Surveys made up to the Close of the Year 1864. Wm. C. Bryant & Company, Printers, New York, 1866.

Union Pacific Railroad—Supplemental Report of the Consulting Engineer on Bridging the Missouri River at the Eastern Terminus of the Road. D. Van Nostrand, Printer, New York, 1868.

Pacific Railroads in Congress—Reports to the 39th, 40th, 43rd, 44th, 45th and 48th Congress.

Pacific Railroad Legislation—1862-1874. Congressional Proceedings in the 37th, 38th and 41st Congresses. F. S. Hiskman, Publisher, West Chester, Pa., 1875.

# BIBLIOGRAPHY

Report of the Auditor of Railroad Accounts—Made to the Secretary of the Interior for the Year Ending June 30, 1880.

Report of the Commissioner of Railroads—1884.

Special Session of the Senate—March 6, 1885—Letter from the Honorable Charles F. Adams, Jr.

Report of the U. S. Pacific Railway Commission—1888.

Acts and Joint Resolutions of Congress and Decisions of the Supreme Court of the United States Relating to the Union Pacific, Central Pacific and Western Pacific Railroads. 1897.

## PAMPHLETS AND MAGAZINES

Crothers, George E., Outline of the History of the Founding of the Leland Stanford Junior University. Reprint from the Fortieth Anniversary number of the Stanford Illustrated Review. Published by the Stanford Alumni Association. Vol. XXXIII, No. 1.

Elliott, T. C., "Peter Skene Ogden, Fur Trader." Quarterly of the Oregon Historical Society, Vol. XI, No. 3. Sept., 1910.

Gilliss, John R., "Tunnels of the Pacific Railroad"—A paper read before the Society, January 5, 1870. Transactions, American Society of Civil Engineers.

Guidebook of the Western United States, Part B—The Overland Route. United States Geological Survey, Washington, 1916.

Hazard, Rowland, "Credit Mobilier of America"—A paper read before the Rhode Island Historical Society, February 22, 1881.

Leland, Chas. Godfrey, "Three Thousand Miles in a Railway Car." Ringwalt and Brown, Philadelphia, 1867.

Maguire, Hon. James G., "Pacific Railroads—Claims and Debts." Speech in the House of Representatives, August 15, 16, 1894.

Perry, John D., President of the Union Pacific Railway (Eastern Division) "Economy to the Government." Gibson Brothers, Printers, Washington, 1868.

Reed, Samuel B., Compilation of letters written to his wife and family covering the period of organization of the Union Pacific Company's Construction Department, 1864-1869.

Wheat, Carl I., "A Sketch of the Life of Theodore D. Judah." Quarterly of the California Historical Society, Vol. IV, No. 3. Sept., 1925.

# INDEX

# INDEX